The Economics of Leisure and Recreation

STUDIES IN PLANNING AND CONTROL
General Editors B. T. Bayliss, B.Sc.(Econ.), Ph.D.
Director, Centre for European Industrial Studies
University of Bath
and G. M. Heal, M.A., Ph.D.
Professor of Economics
University of Sussex

Further titles in preparation

THE ECONOMICS OF LEISURE AND RECREATION

R. W. Vickerman

Lecturer in Economics
The University of Hull

© R. W. Vickerman 1975

First published 1975 by
THE MACMILLAN PRESS LTD
London and Basingstoke
Associated companies in New York
Dublin Melbourne Johannesburg and Madras

SBN 333 18300 2

Printed in Great Britain by
UNWIN BROTHERS LIMITED
Old Woking, Surrey

*This book is sold subject to the standard conditions of the Net Book
Agreement.*

*To My Mother
and the Memory of My Father*

Contents

vii

List of Tables

Preface

Leisure and recreation are important subjects of study for all social scientists. For the economist they raise a large number of interesting questions of both a theoretical and practical, policy-oriented, nature. This book is an attempt to draw together the relevant economic considerations in a comprehensive study of all aspects of leisure and recreation viewed as a sector of the economy. It is both theoretical and empirical. The empirical evidence has been drawn from a variety of sources, including some specifically collected from a survey for this study, to test the various hypothesis posed; it is in no sense a specific case study, however, the aim has been towards generality of application.

As well as being a study of the application of economics to an area which is being increasingly investigated by economists, I hope the book will be intelligible to planners and those of other social science disciplines interested in the problems posed by leisure and recreation. I have particularly tried to draw out the implications of the study for planning decisions and to identify the main interferences with the other disciplines. The mathematical and statistical content has been kept to a minimum except where it eases the presentation of ideas; I hope that these parts will not prove too naive for the specialist nor too complex for the general reader.

Since this is a relatively new area of study, I have detailed a large number of other sources throughout the text which are collected together for easy reference at the end of the book. These should help both the non-economist who wishes to trace the economic concepts used further and the economist who wishes to seek a spectrum of the work done so far on leisure and recreation as well as the reader new to both subjects.

This book has its origins in some research into the demand for passenger transport which I started whilst a research student at the University of Sussex in 1969. I became increasingly dissatisfied with the treatment of the growing sector of leisure travel, particularly in the development of modelling and forecasting techniques. Understanding movement implies understanding of the factors which make people want to move and my interest naturally spread backwards to consider the whole nature of the demand for recreational activities.

In research which has extended over the best part of six years one is bound to incur a large number of debts. I have indicated in the text specific acknowledgements for data and assistance but it is appropriate to mention some general debts of gratitude here. The Department of the Environment (then the Ministry of Transport) took an interest in this work from the start, in providing access to data, some funds for data collection and fruitful discussions with many individual officers. I would particularly like to acknowledge the great help I had in the early stages from the late Neil Mansfield of the Department; it was through his good offices that much of the work became possible and he was a persistent but friendly critic of my ideas. I am also grateful for the assistance given by the City Engineer and Surveyor of the City of Oxford following the selection of that city for closer study. Needless to say neither of these organisations is in any way implicated by the use made of material provided by them or the views expressed but I am deeply grateful for their interest in the research and their valuable assistance and comments.

Numerous individuals have discussed various parts of the work with me. I would particularly like to mention Ray Robinson and Julia Hebden of the University of Sussex, John Collings, now of the Department of the Environment, David Hitchin of the Centre for Social Research at the University of Sussex for his help with computing and above all Brian Bayliss who served as supervisor for the original research and suggested that this book might be a logical extension of my doctoral thesis presented to the University of Sussex in 1972. My colleagues at Hull have also patiently listened to and commented upon various ill-formed ideas over the last few years. For their comments on earlier drafts of various sections of the present study I am grateful to Professors Ken Gwilliam and Alan Wilson of the University of Leeds and Michael Beesley of the London Graduate School of Business Studies, all of whom have helped me improve my ideas. I can only apologise to all these people for my stubborn refusal to accept many of their suggestions.

My greatest debt is to my wife, Chris, who has not only sustained and encouraged my interest in the work but also typed the entire manuscript under a tight timetable from a very motley collection of drafts I placed before her. She has had to sacrifice a great deal of leisure in the interests of a husband for whom leisure has meant work.

ROGER VICKERMAN

University of Hull

1. Introduction

Leisure is a growth industry. People are enjoying more leisure time and indulging in more leisure expenditure whilst others are more and more concerned with telling them how to consume it. Household gadgetry produces more time free for recreational pursuits, faster travel makes more destinations accessible and gives more time free for spending at the destination, television expands to fill the gap but produces programmes which encourage new leisure interests and advertisements with a dominant leisure theme. Better recreational facilities in schools also encourage more of the population to maintain their interests in later years. Increases in real incomes bring sports like sailing and skiing within the reach of many more people.

Despite the preoccupation with leisure which is a feature of modern industrial societies in the West, attempts by social scientists to understand the phenomenon have been largely piecemeal responses to specific problems. The economist's interest in leisure as an economic problem has been largely developed from the need to place valuations on it when public money is to be spent on a new recreational site or on a transport improvement which shortens journey times to a National Park or the coast. The approach adopted has usually been to observe people at the destination and compute their costs of access to the site as a function of the distance travelled. Imputing a value of time from exogenous information on people's apparent rate of trading off time for money, this distance decay function can be translated into a monetary demand curve and planning can proceed from there by making the appropriate adjustments to the 'price' of the facility implied by the charge involved. Thus the rate of distance decay is taken as a measure of the valuation placed on the activity itself.

This is an improvement on earlier views which saw leisure essentially as the residual of work, valued simply as opportunity cost of lost income. Only in the last ten years since the seminal article of Becker (1965) have economists started to realise that consideration of leisure opens up a whole new sphere of economics, with the consumer as producer, trading off inputs of time and travel against the satisfaction of indulging in a given activity and the need to work to produce income to pay for it.

1

Realisation of the complexity of the choices and decisions facing the consumer at leisure leads to a need for a very different approach to the evaluation problem. The final demand curve for a given recreation site, the ultimate objective of any cost–benefit appraisal, can only be derived from a complex modelling exercise which attempts to reproduce this choice situation.

This is a subject which has again been tackled in a piecemeal manner, specific problems being investigated in isolation. In this book we attempt to take stock of this situation and provide an integrated basis for the development of the economic analysis of an important sector of the economy. Essentially we shall be providing a framework for recreation planning, but a rather broader view than just the planning of sites for recreation has been taken. The argument which is developed in the course of the subsequent chapters is the need for a sectoral approach both to the understanding of recreation behaviour and to the planning of an adequate supply of recreational opportunities.

The first part of the book, Chapters 2 and 3, is concerned with establishing the existing position. In Chapter 2 the objective is estimating the size of the problem with which we are concerned. As with any subject which has evolved slowly over the years, and with differing emphasis in different disciplines, terminology can lead to much confusion. The first section is therefore devoted to a discussion of the main concepts involved. Thereafter the main indicators of the size and nature of the leisure sector have been drawn together and, where possible, in a time series so that some indication of trends can be seen.

Chapter 3 discusses the main requirement of any model of the recreation sector in terms of the necessary inputs to a final economic appraisal, and the sort of problems of evaluation which are to be faced. This is basically a review of the *status quo* in economic thought concerning recreation but also poses the questions which require an answer in the subsequent analysis.

The second part, which runs from Chapter 4 to Chapter 7, is concerned with consumer behaviour with regard to leisure and recreation. We start with a theoretical economic model in Chapter 4 which introduces time and travel dimensions into a basic model of consumer behaviour. This involves an activities model and derived from this is an economic model of travel demand since the main concern of much leisure planning will be for the associated movement. The theoretical model has two roles to play. Firstly it provides the foundation for an empirical model and secondly it permits interpretation of the parameters of such an empirical model in the context of evaluation exercises. Previous models of recreation behaviour are critically examined in the light of this analysis.

The data requirements of a complete activities model would be prohibitively large but Chapter 5 discusses some smaller-scale empirical testing based on specifically collected data, which confirms the importance of particular aspects of the model. It concentrates on the relative impact of conventional socio-economic indices and variations in time availability on the level of recreational activity, and on the important question of the degree of substitution or complementarity between different activities.

The travel demand model is seen as the key feature of this approach, both because of the importance of the spatial aspect in leisure activities and because of the greater ease of collection of travel data. A basic modelling exercise is outlined in Chapter 6. The contrasts between this model and the conventional transport model are noted and there is a detailed discussion of the specification of the spatial supply price variables, attraction and accessibility.

Estimation of a basic empirical model of leisure mobility is presented in Chapter 7. This uses data from the 1965 National Travel Survey which provides the most comprehensive source available. Particular emphasis is placed on an analysis of the influence of the main determinants of variations in leisure mobility in a selection of different planning regions. Specifically the difference is emphasised between socio-economic determinants of variations in the potential demand for recreation, income, age, and so forth; and variations in the revealed demand occasioned by effective price factors.

The third part of the book is a development of the analysis of these price factors and the implications for planning. Chapter 8 considers the working of part of the recreation sector in a specific urban area. A model of the location of recreational sites is developed and tested. From this more specific indices of attraction and accessibility are developed and related to recreational mobility in the area. The conclusion is reached that the market is not in a stable spatial equilibrium and that planning should be able to result in improvements in both efficiency and overall economic welfare. A planning model is developed in Chapter 9 on the basis of these findings from a particular market. The main problems identified are the difficulty of defining capacity, and consumer benefit in terms of willingness to pay. The importance of planning recreation as a system rather than on a project by project basis is stressed and the implications for a pricing policy and financing recreation are drawn out.

The main conclusions are drawn together in Chapter 10 in the form of an imaginary planning exercise. The basic implications for planning and modelling are summarised and the chapter concludes with an outline of the main subjects for future research.

The relevance of such an exercise can be illustrated on a number of grounds. Recreation is becoming more costly to supply. Rising land values in urban areas squeezes those activities which are land-intensive and do not generate high incomes per acre. Consequently new developments in urban areas are increasingly capital-intensive; new urban sports centres are good examples of this, and therefore involve a much higher initial construction cost. The alternative is a movement away from urban areas but this raises further problems of resource costs. Pressure on rural land for urban recreation will again force up land costs, particularly if a true opportunity cost of lost resources, incorporating conservation and environmental costs, is taken. Of greater importance, however, will be the access costs, both of consumer's time and of fuel. Optimal planning for an energy-scarce economy suggests minimising travel costs wherever possible.

Accurate assessment of the costs and benefits of any project implies detailed knowledge of the working market; it is the economist's job to provide such analysis. The ultimate objective of such economic analysis is essentially to produce guidelines for future planning. Any such implications are bound to invade the provinces of other social scientists, geographers, planners, sociologists, etc. who–within the frameworks of their own disciplines–strive to this common end. The interfaces between the disciplines are noted where these are relevant through the study and it is shown that many of the implications of these alternative approaches can be incorporated in the framework of this study. No attempt is made to do this here but the final analysis of any planning decision is bound to involve many different disciplines; it is hoped that such interchanges will be a feature of the future of leisure analysis as well. The remainder of this study is an attempt to state the economist's case.

2. Concepts and Trends in Leisure

Leisure-An Introduction and Some Definitions

This book is concerned with leisure and leisure travel. It examines trends in leisure and the factors influencing variations in the amount of leisure and it examines ways of estimating the demand for leisure activities. A crucial problem to be overcome right at the start is the more precise definition of all these terms. This is particularly so in that writers about these subjects to date have tended to use differing definitions, attaching greater or lesser precision to the various terms, leisure, free time, recreation, etc. The most noticeable differences are those between writers from different disciplines.

Leisure to the early Marxist writers was symbolic of the bourgeoisie. The leisure class comprised those who were not slaves to the capitalist industrial system, who had time to relax, enjoy life, and be creative.[1] Above all, from the economist's point of view, the leisure class was that group about whom the neoclassical economics of Marshall was largely concerned. Not only did it provide the entrepreneurs, but also the consumers, as only these people were in a position to exercise the sort of choices Marshallian economics required of them. That a distinct leisure class of this type has now largely disappeared, at least in terms of its influence on the economy, is unquestionable. On its decline, perhaps the most graphic comment is that of Bertrand Russell (1960): 'There was formerly a capacity for light-heartedness and play which has been to some extent inhibited by the cult of efficiency. The modern man thinks that everything ought to be done for the sake of something else, and never for its own sake.'

This complaint of Russell has been echoed, and placed in the context of economics by Staffan Linder (1970). Linder has developed an amusing and fascinating theory around the theme that the more leisure people have, the less time they appear to have to enjoy it.

Implicit in these three examples are three differing definitions of leisure: leisure as the distinguishing feature of those classes whose lives are not dominated by the alienating influence of work; leisure as idleness, a time in which to be creative; and leisure as consumption time in an affluent society. These are far from being the only three uses

5

of the term. Leisure is increasingly quoted as a 'problem' or a 'challenge', with reference to the assumed need to educate people for all the leisure they are about to experience, but will not know how to use.[2]

Let us start from some basic assumptions. The economist, in studying the demand for any normal commodity, thinks in terms of allocation— in its simplest terms, the allocation of a given, limited budget amongst alternative ends according to certain aspects of behaviour. Time is usually ignored in this analysis, implicitly the assumption is made that the consumer has instantaneous access to all markets (or at least that the costs of the purchasing activity are equal and sufficiently small as not to influence consumption behaviour), and that the act of consumption is independent of the time taken to consume.

There are activities where these access and consumption time aspects become so great relative to the actual consumption of goods or services that they cannot realistically be analysed within the same framework. A car ride into the country, or a walk, involve outlays of money and/or time, and yet need have no 'price' in the conventional sense. Inter- mediate cases, such as cinema visits, sporting activities, do have a price, but the essential associated outlays are still dominant. It is activities of this type with which this study is concerned. We shall call all these activities 'leisure activities' because they take place in leisure time.

Leisure time is that time which is not spent at work. This is equivalent to the definitions in the economics of work–leisure choice, and the supply of labour.[3] This definition of leisure time does not measure accurately the time spent on leisure pursuits, but has certain advantages. It does reflect the total amount of time available for leisure pursuits, although it is unrealistic to expect that all of it will be so occupied; but probably of greater importance is the relative ease of measuring time so defined for comparison between data sources.

Leisure time can now be divided into more precise periods. A con- siderable part of this time is committed to what may be termed non- active leisure, essential sleep and rest. And we may add to this other essentially committed time spent in the production of personal services, washing, eating, etc.

Many other activities involve a high degree of commitment of time, travel to and from work, essential shopping, and a complete spectrum of other activities of progressively less committed time.[4] The relevance of this commitment is the ease with which substitution of one activity for another can occur in the short run.

The final category is the residual, free time. The crucial feature of free time is that it can be allocated on an *ad hoc* basis in the short run, with a high degree of flexibility. This is the purest form of leisure, often referred to as idleness,[5] although some of the activities may not be thought of as conventionally idle.

The term 'leisure' as used in this study covers activities which can occur in any of these categories. A leisure activity is one occurring in leisure time, and thus may include journey to work, shopping, or any more conventional leisure activity. In practice, however, the journey to work is excluded because the total activity does not take place in leisure time, and, because of its special nature, shopping will be excluded from detailed consideration, except where comparisons are illustratively useful. For convenience, we shall also exclude non-active leisure and personal activities. Beyond these, all other activities are relevant – although it has not been possible to give adequate coverage to internal activities, those taking place within the home.

We refer to these as leisure activities, regardless of the time category into which they fall. A further three-way subdivision will prove to be useful when examining the supply of the relevant external activities, this is into recreation, social, and pleasure activities. The terms are somewhat arbitrary, but convey most readily the essential differences. Recreation is used to denote essentially organised activities, entertainment, sport, eating out, etc. This itself may be of two different forms, market and non-market recreation. Market recreation is where the primary activity is commercially marketed, in saleable units, cinema, professional sport, etc.[6] Non-market recreation is not so sold, although it may nevertheless have to be paid for in terms of club subscriptions, etc. Pleasure denotes those activities which are not organised in this way except on a family basis; trips into the country, walks in the park, and also including holidays, whether these are strictly commercially organised or not.[7] Social activities are essentially those involving people and not places, i.e. the primary purpose of the activity is to visit friends, relations, etc., and not the location where the activity takes place. This is a fundamental difference in the nature of the activity, hence the separate identification.

It should be noted that these definitions are rather different from those used by, for example, Clawson and Knetsch (1966, p. 27) who define recreation as the 'activity or activities (including inactivity ...) engaged in during leisure time. Leisure is time, recreation is activity'. Owen (1969, pp. 20–21) has also preserved this distinction in exploring the 'relationship between leisure time and market recreation', and in particular the complementary nature of the demands for both. However, the crucial distinction is noted by Owen in his references to Becker's activity model of behaviour.[8] In such a model an activity is seen as the product of inputs of time and goods, 'when the goods are recreational, the resulting activity may be regarded as a "leisure activity"' (Owen, p. 21). As was stressed above, many very relevant activities may involve no goods input, but still be a leisure activity; we reserve the term 'recreation' for those with such an input. It must be reiterated, however, that leisure time and leisure activities are not synonymous, leisure time is simply a budget of time available for expenditure on leisure activities. The demand for leisure activities is a primary demand, subject to this budget constraint.

In the long run, pressure on this constraint from the increasing demand for leisure activities may lead to a derived demand for increased leisure time, that is a change in the relative valuations of work and leisure time leading to pressure for a reallocation of time between these two primary categories. It is not, however, proposed to concentrate on this problem of work–leisure relationships in this study; our main concern is the allocation within the set of activities, under the assumption of an institutionally determined work–leisure balance, except where the pressure on resources is such as to cause a direct feedback demand pressure for a change in those institutions.

Leisure and Leisure Travel

A crucial aspect of this study is the impact of changing leisure activity patterns on planning in general, and particularly the effects of the growth of leisure on the appraisal of transport projects. It is now necessary to pay closer attention to what is meant by travel in relation to leisure activities. Just as time as an input is of dominating importance in many leisure activities, so is travel, especially if we separate time into activity time and travel time.[9] In fact, at the limit, many leisure activities are totally travel, particularly those in the pleasure category. There is a further reason why an adequate definition of travel is essential; the most comprehensive data on overall activity patterns outside the home is travel data. Although it is a derived demand from that activity, when the activity is placed in a spatial context the demand for it is essentially measured by the demand for travel to it. To regard it strictly as a derived demand is inadequate, it is more correctly a joint demand. Placed on this more equal footing, we can justify considering the demand for leisure travel as an approach to the overall problem.

The application of conventional demand analysis to the demand for travel poses two interesting problems which arise because of the nature of travel itself. Firstly, there is the question of time periods–travel is a commodity which is highly time-specific, it cannot be stored and must be consumed over a greater period of time. Secondly, demand analysis usually assumes that we are dealing with a homogeneous commodity, whereas with travel we must consider what is essentially almost perfectly heterogeneous. Strictly, in order to obtain a meaningful demand relationship, we should disaggregate as far as is necessary to obtain an acceptable level of homogeneity.

Of these two problems the second is the more relevant to the discussion here. The former is more relevant to the equating of demand and supply, for it shows that these two must be in balance in the market period, there can be no storage or spreading of the demand without affecting the consumers' benefits. It is the level of aggregation necessary which must be considered. There are four dimensions to any particular journey: its purpose, its origin and destination, the mode of travel used and the time at which the journey is made. Only disaggregation by all of these dimensions will yield a reasonably homogeneous 'product'. However, working at such a level of disaggregation is normally very inconvenient, and also the higher the level of aggregation that can be achieved, the more useful the measure is likely to be in practice. It is the degree of substitution between any two journeys which is, in the last resort, the best criterion for disaggregation. This would suggest that disaggregating by the broad categories of leisure activity is essential, recreation, social and pleasure journeys are not such near substitutes as, on the other hand, are trips to the cinema and those to a football match, which may well be competing interests. Disaggregation by journey purpose probably also covers the need to consider separate time periods, the main distinction between peak and off-peak being contained in a split of commuting and non-commuting journeys, and the other main splits reflecting to some extent the times of day at which such activities normally take place. It is also reasonable not to disaggregate by destination as different destinations may be highly substitutable. The remaining difficulty is the decision whether to dis-aggregate by means of transport. To the extent that a decision is made first to make a particular trip for a particular purpose from A to B at a particular time, and only then is a decision taken as to how to travel, such disaggregation is unnecessary. However, if the avail-ability or certain features of a particular means of transport enter into the decision to travel, and given that all means of transport are not always available to all potential travellers, then this disaggregation is probably also essential.[10] Disaggregation by means of transport may require not just a split into rail, car and bus, but a more discriminating distinction between, say, first and second-class rail, stage-carriage bus and express coach, urban and inter-urban bus, car driver and car passenger, since these are all effectively different modes, each with its own characteristics. Unfortunately, many of the distinctions required, particularly with regard to journey purposes, are not available in the published statistics of transport, or, because of sample sizes, not feasible to analyse from survey data.

We have discussed above the level of aggregation which can meaning-fully be achieved. There is a further problem of resolving the units of measurement to be used. Demand studies normally distinguish between physical and value units. In transport there are two possible physical units, the passenger journey and the passenger mile. Whilst the latter tends to be the most usual in official publications and for comparative studies, most transport demand studies use the journey as the basic unit of trip generation and modal split models.[11] The choice of units is another aspect of the homogeneity problem. The passenger mile is a more homogeneous unit than the journey and is thus more meaningful in aggregate forms. If a particular demand can be disaggregated right down to the basic form in all four dimensions, then the journey becomes the basic unit; whenever aggregation over origins or destinations occurs, then passenger mileage becomes the more meaningful unit. We are still left with the problem of whether there is an equal consumption of transport by one person making a journey of ten miles, or ten people making the same one-mile journeys, or ten people making ten separate journeys over ten different one-mile routes.

The passenger mile is a measure of the output of transport services which is consumed. The demand is more correctly the desire of the passenger to move from A to B. The consumed output which is measured, can be argued to be more akin to an input than a true output.

Consider the case of a passenger wishing to travel from A to B. If he travels by car he will presumably take the most direct route resulting in the consumption of x passenger miles. If he travels by service bus this may involve travel by a slightly less direct route to serve all the intermediate centres of population, resulting in the consumption of rather more than x passenger miles. If the third alternative is to travel by train, this may involve travelling via the nearest large centre and changing trains because rail routes tend to converge on such centres and not take cross-country routes – the passenger mileage consumed here may thus be even larger. Strictly the output of each of these journeys is the same, a passenger is moved from A to B, but the actual measure will depend entirely on the means of transport used. To overcome this distortion of the true output the use of standardised passenger miles has been suggested so that output is measured in terms of the shortest distance between two points, regardless of the mode actually used. Passenger mileage as normally used would then stand as a pure input measure which, in conjunction with the standardised-mile output measure, will reflect the relative efficiency of each mode.[12]

The difficulty in using the standardised-mile concept is in the need to create the standardised mileages; this is something which is not possible with existing data, but is another potential product of transport studies. A possible modification of greater potential use in passenger transport would be a time-based measure – a standardised hour – reflecting the shortest possible time between two centres. This would obviously be related to distance but would better reflect quality differences between modes which arise from speed differences when assessing their relative performances. Some use of this concept has been made in econometric approaches to a demand model. The Quand–Baumol abstract mode model uses elements of best time and best cost as well as relative time and cost as explanatory variables so that the traffic by a particular mode between two points depends not only on the time and cost characteristics of that mode but also those of competing modes and particularly the best mode on any single criterion.[13] Although this is not an explicit use of the standardised hour, it is very close to that concept.

The usual way of achieving a higher level of aggregation than is otherwise possible with physical units is to weight each homogeneous unit by some value measure. To the extent that this value weight is a reflection of differing resource usage, it allows output to be measured in a more highly aggregated form, whilst still being a meaningful index. Certainly the higher resource consumption involved in short journeys is often reflected in higher fare rates per mile, the difference in comfort by first and second-class rail fares, to some extent the differences between peak and off-peak journeys by reduced rates for the latter, and even spatial differences in separate central and outer-zone fare scales for London.[14] However, only if prices were a true reflection of marginal costs would expenditure be a reasonable measure of the use of resources in the transport sector. To the extent that cross-subsidies are a continuing feature of transport pricing in both road and rail public sectors, and that the costs of private motoring are subject rather more to political and financial constraints than to true economic criteria, the use of expenditure cannot be regarded as a useful advance on the passenger mile as a unit.

Expenditure figures can, to some extent, show up quality changes in the product which physical units do not; these quality changes can, as in the case of the London-Midland railway electrification, involve the effective introduction of a new mode, and thus cause further difficulties in achieving reasonable output measures.[15]

The conclusion to be drawn from this discussion is that the best and most meaningful way to measure the demand for transport is by the passenger mile, but that this should not be aggregated over different modes. Little space has been devoted to a discussion of the use of the passenger hour. Whilst this does have the advantage over the mileage measure that it does refer to the same passenger regardless of the mode used and hence, particularly if standardised in the way discussed, lends itself to aggregation by mode, there are still severe problems in aggregating by journey purpose in that this implies a valuation being placed on time. Whilst research into such values has been proceeding rapidly,[16] at the present time reliable estimates are limited largely to work and commuting trips, or for income earners only, and it is unlikely that any less biased results could be obtained from a time rather than a distance measure.

Trends in Leisure and Leisure Travel
One of the major problems in coming to terms with the modelling of leisure demand, and more particularly the forecasting of leisure demands into the future, is the difficulty of building up an adequate picture of past trends. Work on these topics, especially the collection of data, has been primarily conducted on an *ad hoc* basis, so that whilst cross-sectional studies of the behaviour of residents of particular areas, or visitors to particular facilities, are available, these are not based on sufficiently common ground to permit any indication of time trends to be deduced. Burton, who has probably contributed most towards the development of a unity of purpose in work in this area, has demonstrated how, even on the question of the basic profile data of samples, six major inquiries of the past ten years in Britain could only provide, out of a total of 41 items, four items on which they could all be compared.[17]

But even adequate counts of heads do not provide a sufficient basis for a real understanding of underlying changes. Any attempt to provide even the most sketchy data on trends in consumer behaviour, those points of interaction between supply and demand, soon runs into the problem recognised by Burton, that 'recreation planning in Britain has not really advanced beyond the stage of making inventories of supplies and surveys of demands'.

What light can be shed on this question? In order that the scene might be set for the later analysis, data on three aspects can be examined. Firstly, on trends in the time budget constraint, what sort of changes in the amount of time available for leisure have been forthcoming? Secondly, on the supply side, what changes in the availability of leisure and recreation facilities have occurred, and what information is available on the use made of these? Finally, what trends are apparent in travel patterns causing, or resulting from these changes?

Trends in the Potential Demand for Leisure
Much has been made of the 'challenge of leisure', a problem resulting from the average person having 'increased leisure time, with more income at his disposal and ... greatly enhanced mobility'.[18] In an historical context Dower (1965) put it even more forcefully as being the fourth 'great wave' of development in Britain since 1800. Following the growth of individual towns, the spread of railways, and the development of suburbs based on the use of the private car, comes 'the surge of a fourth wave which could be more powerful than all the others'. Whilst leisure, or at least the opportunity to enjoy leisure, is more widespread

in the community than ever before, so that the concept of identifying the bourgeoisie as the leisure class is no longer valid in the same terms, this is more the product of improving absolute economic standards than of a great reduction in time spent working.[19]

Detailed comparable expenditure figures on which some initial idea of the changing importance of leisure expenditures can be based only date back to the start of the Department of Employment's annual *Family Expenditure Surveys* in 1957 (Table 2.1). The expenditure on the

TABLE 2.1   Expenditure on leisure-related items, 1957–72

		Expenditure (£s)					
	Item	*1957*	*1960*	*1965*	*1968*	*1970*	*1972*
43	Meals bought away from home	0.45	0.49	0.66	0.80	1.00	1.26
	% Total Expenditure	3.15	2.97	3.10	3.21	3.49	3.59
63	Radio, television and musical instruments	0.22	0.17	0.17	0.21	0.28	0.40
68	Leather, travel and sports goods, jewellery, fancy goods	0.10	0.12	0.17	0.23	0.29	0.32
84	Cinemas	0.10	0.07	0.07	0.06	0.06	0.06
85	Theatres, sporting events and other entertainments	0.10	0.10	0.13	0.17	0.17	0.23
86	Radio, television, licences and rentals	0.07	0.15	0.23	0.28	0.33	0.47
93	Subscriptions, hotel and holiday expenses, miscellaneous other services	0.39	0.46	0.66	0.85	0.97	1.46
	Total above groups	0.97	1.08	1.43	1.79	2.11	2.94
	% Total Expenditure	6.80	6.54	6.73	7.18	7.40	8.39
	Total transport and vehicles	1.16	2.01	2.63	3.27	3.91	4.97
	% Total Expenditure	8.13	12.18	12.37	13.12	13.68	14.18
	Grand Total Expenditure	14.27	16.51	21.25	24.93	28.57	35.06

NOTE   Figures from the surveys for 1957 to 1970 have been converted to new pence and rounded to the nearest whole penny.
SOURCES *Family Expenditure Surveys*, 1957, 1960, 1965, 1968, 1970, 1972.

main identifiable leisure activities in F.E.S. – cinema, theatre, radio and television, and miscellaneous services (including subscriptions, hotels, holidays, etc.) – rose from about £0.66 in 1957 to £2.22 by 1972, at current prices. As a proportion of total expenditure, this represented a small increase from 4.6 to 6.3 per cent. This is a severe underestimate of total leisure expenditure as it excludes all expenditure on leisure goods, foodstuffs, travel, etc. Two items of goods which are primarily leisure-related are identified in Table 2.1 – expenditure on the purchase and repair of radio, television and musical instruments; and leather, travel and sports goods, etc. Expenditure on meals taken out of the home is an overestimate of leisure eating since it includes all such expenditure. The trend in expenditure on transport is also shown as more than quadrupling over the period in question and rising to nearly 15 per cent of total expenditure. It is expected that a substantial share of this increase is attributable to leisure activities. However, these figures do not show any substantial change in expenditure patterns related to leisure activities.

On trends in the amount of leisure time which people have available, Table 2.2 gives data on hours worked in manufacturing and certain

TABLE 2.2   Average weekly hours worked (Manufacturing and certain other industries), 1947–73

Year	Men	Youths	Women		Girls
			Full-time	Part-time	
1947	45.0	46.3	43.7	41.5	42.0
1951	46.3	47.9	44.5	42.0	42.7
1956	46.6	48.5	44.9	41.5	42.5
1961	47.4	43.6	39.7	21.8	40.6
1966	46.0	42.2	38.1	21.5	38.7
1971	44.7	41.1	37.7	21.3	38.2
1973	45.6	41.7	37.7	21.4	38.1

NOTE   Figures for 1947 and 1951 are for April, for other years October.
SOURCES   *Monthly Digest of Statistics* (various).

other industries in Britain in the post-war period, and demonstrates the great stability these have shown. Unions tend to use negotiated reductions in standard hours of work as a means of raising earnings through getting more of the normal working day classified at overtime rates. This is not necessarily unconstrained greed on the part of the unions, but often is the result of historical conditions in particular industries where overtime is regarded as normal, and standard rates of pay become depressed as a reflection of this. There is evidence that many workers have a target earnings level and will work as long as is necessary to achieve that, for example, during the period of adjustment to a new target after a wage increase there may be an increase in absenteeism, until new target horizons are developed.[20]

A further aspect of possible changes in actual hours worked as a result of agreements to lower standard weekly hours is the phenomenon of double job holding. Little research has yet been done on the situation in Britain. The 1966 Census revealed that just over 500,000 male workers (3.3 per cent of the male labour force) and 145,000 females (1.7 per cent) had two jobs.[21] This is much lower than the figure for the United States where the annual survey of 'moonlighting' showed that as early as 1963, 5.7 per cent of the labour force were dual job holders.[22]

In the United States studies, the median total hours worked on both jobs was some 52 hours a week, of which 12 hours were spent, on average, on the second job. Altogether, three-quarters of the multiple job holders worked 41 hours or more, compared to only a third of single job holders. Some 32 per cent did their second job mainly at night and 24 per cent at weekends. The figures from the detailed survey of Scottish dual job holders reported by Alden show a similar pattern, but slightly lower hours worked on the second job. Over 77 per cent spent 10 hours or less at their subsidiary employment, but the average hours spent at the main job were correspondingly higher than in the American case. Since 49 per cent of those interviewed gave income as their main reason for taking the extra job, and of these, two-thirds wished to raise their standard of living as opposed to taking a second job of necessity. There is every reason to expect this trend to continue, and become more important; this could reduce considerably the actual increase in leisure time.

Weekly hours worked is perhaps not the best indicator of the true work–leisure position of the typical worker. From the point of view of making the best use of non-working time, of more value than a marginal change in the number of hours of the week committed to work would be the number of days on which that work falls, the time of day it is undertaken, and the total holiday available during the year.

As yet there is little move towards a four-day working week, but this could be one of the most interesting developments over the next decade: a possible systematic rescheduling of working periods to leave an extra day clear from work. During the post-war period, the five-day week has become the norm for non-manual workers, leaving Saturday free for most service employees, and normally one other day for distributive workers, as evidenced by the spread of complete-day, instead of half-day, closures of shops.

For manual workers, the possibility of standardised working hours is less. Shift working tends to increase as a means of reducing manufacturers' unit labour costs, and this has obvious implications for the use of leisure time, particularly when members of a family are employed on different shift systems.

Holidays are normally fixed as part of national agreements, and major changes are relatively rare for most employee groups. Table 2.3 shows the basic pattern of paid holidays reported by the Department of Employment. It can be seen that three weeks is now the minimum accepted norm for the majority of workers. However, many employers provide for extra days paid leave as part of length of service rewards, etc., and the proportion enjoying these has risen from 4 per cent in

TABLE 2.3   Holidays with pay, 1951–70

	% Full-time workers having basic entitlement to annual holidays with pay of given duration			
	1951	1960	1966	1970
One week	28	—	—	—
1 to 2 weeks	3	—	—	—
Two weeks	66	97	63	41
2 to 3 weeks	2	1	33	7
3 weeks and over	1	2	4	52
	100	100	100	100

SOURCES   *Ministry of Labour Gazette, Department of Employment & Productivity Gazette, Employment Gazette.*

1950 to 25 per cent in 1970. It is possible that a major change in the standard annual leave could occur fairly soon, but the actual period of holiday is still likely to be most closely related to an employee's position and length of service. A more interesting question is the timing of holidays and changes in national or bank holidays. A movement away from traditional holiday fortnights to a more flexible holiday-taking system, and the growth of second holidays may be the feature of the next few years. Moves towards taking a one-week holiday over the Christmas–New Year period may be part of this trend.[23]

The evidence, although imprecise, does suggest that fears of a leisure explosion are unfounded. The argument, sometimes put forward, that this past evidence of stability leads to the conclusion that a major change is about to happen, also seems unwarranted when the length of this stability is considered. Some downward trend in working hours since the nineteenth century is evident, but in the broader historical context the hours worked by employees during the early adjustments to an industrial society appear furthest out of line with the norm. The change in the whole social and economic structure of society during this century has brought the concept of leisure to a greater proportion of the population and at the same time brought a reduction in the numbers attributable to a truly 'leisured class'.

Such features as the growth of second jobs and the increasing numbers of wives working for reasons other than need[24] are likely to have the reverse effect on the amount of time available for leisure activities. Two factors are likely to be more important, and more likely to result in increased demand, the improving economic position of people to enjoy what leisure time they have in more constructive ways, and probably of even greater importance, the spread of higher educational levels associated with more active leisure time. In such an environment, accessibility to leisure becomes all important.

Trends in the Supply of Leisure
The major problem here is to identify true supply measures which are independent of demand. Most figures relate specifically to the use of leisure facilities, club memberships, attendances, etc., and even the more independent figures – numbers of clubs, sports grounds, cinemas, etc. – must be assumed to be, at least in the long run, adjusted to local demand conditions. All the information in this section must be regarded in this light.

The cinema has been in a period of considerable decline over the past twenty years, concomitant with the spread of television into the majority of households, and whilst some 17 per cent of people in a sample in Oxford (discussed in detail in Chapter 5) had visited the cinema or theatre at least once in a given survey week, a national survey of leisure showed that, on average, only 1 per cent of all leisure periods were spent at the cinema or theatre.[25] Table 2.4 illustrates this trend in terms of both supply of cinema facilities and admissions.

TABLE 2.4   Trends in cinema, 1950–72

	1950	1954	1960	1964	1968	1970	1972
Number of cinemas	4580	4504	3100	2057	1631	1529	1450
Seating capacity (thousands)	4216.0	4151.2	—	2104	1672	1466	—
Admissions (million)	1366.3	1275.8	520.0	342.8	237.3	193.0	—

SOURCES   *Board of Trade Journal, Trade and Industry.*

It will be interesting to note whether the development of multi-cinemas, showing two or three films in the smaller auditoria of one large building, by providing a better choice of product, arrests this decline.[26] From the point of view of leisure travelling patterns it is unlikely that this will occur because of the concentration of these cinemas in the traditional cinema sites in city centres. They can be seen only as a supply-side response to falling demand, an attempt to cut overhead costs and encourage the remaining filmgoers to stay by improving general facilities. The spatial supply price of cinema to the individual thus continues to increase especially as the average admission charge to multi-cinemas was found to be higher than for single cinemas.

Recreation facilities in organised clubs have been well documented by Molyneux (1968) who has collected together information from many of the national organisations, sport by sport, on trends of affiliated clubs (see Table 2.5). All of these display a rising trend, with a particularly rapid rise during the early 1960s. A further notable

TABLE 2.5   Trends in organised recreation, 1950–68

Number of clubs affiliated to national associations

	1950	1951	1955	1956	1958	1960	1961	1962	1963	1964	1965	1966	1967
Archery	85				581				580		655		
Rugby union		914	1051			1152				1181		1229	
Judo						300	361	390	461	553	572		
Fencing						417	427	444		464	499	501	509
Squash			341	378					428	455	574	578	
Table tennis	6879	7142			6557				6917			7857	
Canoeing									174	236	272	291	300
Sailing					885			1071		1284	1333		1388
Rowing						400		434		463		477	

NOTE   Figures for rugby union and table tennis refer to winter season starting in each year.
SOURCE   Molyneux (1968).

feature is the more rapid growth of sports like judo, squash, and canoeing over the more traditional sports such as rugby, table tennis, etc. The Pilot National Recreation Survey showed how this trend may be expected to continue by comparing, for a list of 21 activities, the rank orders of the proportions of people reporting having taken part in the past, and those wishing to do so in the future (Table 2.6). Many

TABLE 2.6   Participation and desires in organised recreation

	% Having taken part in the past	Rank-order change from participation to desire
Team games	56	− 12
Tennis	36	− 7
Athletics	36	− 15
Bowls	13	− 1
Golf	12	+ 9
Sea sailing	17	+ 2
Inland sailing	17	+ 15
Subaqua	4	+ 11

SOURCE   *Pilot National Recreation Survey 1967*, Report No. 1 (British Travel Association – University of Keele).

of these desires must be recognised as wishful thinking on the part of the sample, and not just the absence of facilities. Two other activities with major rank-order changes were riding (+ 8) and motor sports (+ 9). Nevertheless, it is relevant to note that most of the 'growth' activities are both more specific in their location, and more extensive in their use of land area than the traditional sports. If the pressures from the demand side are realised into actual demand, then the spatial supply price of the relevant activities may be greater in the future than at present, because of this switch to more dispersed activities. It is unlikely that such facilities as yacht basins or golf courses could ever be so densely clustered as tennis courts or bowling greens.

Some interesting comparisons can be drawn between inner London and selected New Towns on the spatial dispersion of a range of facilities relative to the interviewed sample in the Government Social Survey study.[27] The figures (summarised in Table 2.7) must be treated with care; they are overall figures for the two groups of area and hide strong local variations, particularly within the New Towns group.

It is particularly interesting to note the contrast between relative provision of tennis courts and swimming-pools in the two areas, on the one hand, with that of golf courses, on the other. As Table 2.8 shows the participation rates are little different between the two areas. It should be remembered that the age structure of the population in New Towns is biased rather more to the younger age groups than in London, so that slightly higher rates for these activities would be expected overall. It is unfortunate that this is the most detailed data available on this question as it adopts a rather low cut-off point (2 miles) for consideration of sensitivity to accessibility changes, and only allows consideration of activities which are in reasonable spatial supply in most areas of the country. Even the most expansive of these activities, golf, is in reasonable supply in most areas, in spatial terms if not in the absolute provision of sufficient capacity to meet demand.[28]

This is an appropriate point to note that existing recreational facilities are often overcrowded, and club membership lists for popular growth sports like golf and squash have long waiting lists in some areas. With golf, in particular, it could be that the growth in car ownership has improved the accessibility of golf courses for a larger proportion of the population, and hence the pressure on existing facilities.

This issue does become particularly sensitive when applied to the natural resources of the coast and countryside. Increasing accessibility, in the form of improved roads, may lead to a destruction of natural beauty spots.[29] Research in the United States, by Clawson and Knetsch for Resources for the Future, has shown that visit rates per 1000 population to a particular Country Park decline at something greater than the square of the cost of reaching that Park.[30] They conclude that a 'given recreation resource within easy reach of a large number of people is potentially a much more valuable resource than a similar area located far from users'.

It is very difficult to provide adequate indicators of provision to the public of countryside resources. It is only comparatively recently that a concerted effort has been made to designate prescribed areas for public access in a joint bid to provide necessary recreational areas, and conserve the countryside, under the auspices of the Countryside Commission.[31] Tables 2.9 to 2.12 show the results of this work in terms of designated areas of conservation and public access for recreation of four major types. The growth of National Parks was the first develop-

TABLE 2.7   Distances to public recreation facilities

Distribution of addresses with respect to each facility (%)

	Tennis courts		Football pitches		Swimming pools		Bowling greens		Rugby pitches		Golf courses	
	Inner London*	New Towns†	Inner London*	New Towns†	Inner London*	New Towns†	Inner London*	New Towns†	Inner London*	New Towns†	Inner London*	New Towns†
Less than 1 mile	99	84	93	93.5	91	29.5	82	64	17.5	42	10	18
1 to 2 miles	1	12	7	6	9	39	18	32	32	34	22	34
2 miles and over	—	4	—	0.5	—	31.5	—	4	50.5	24	68	48

* Average of the London Boroughs of Westminster, Camden, Kensington and Chelsea, Hammersmith, Islington, Hackney, Tower Hamlets, Wandsworth, Lambeth, Lewisham, Southwark and Greenwich.
† Average of the New Towns of Peterlee, Hemel Hempstead, Basildon, Harlow, Stevenage, Welwyn, and Crawley.
SOURCE   Sillitoe (1969), Tables A.45 and A.46.

TABLE 2.8   Participation in public recreation facilities

% Participating at least once a month for part of year (summer or winter)

	National		New Towns		Inner London	
Activity	Males	Females	Males	Females	Males	Females
Tennis	5	5	7	5	5	6
Football	10	—	10	—	8	—
Swimming	17	8	18	13	17	10
Bowls	6	1	2	*	1	*
Rugby	2	—	3	—	2	—
Golf	6	1	4	1	3	*

* Less than 0.5%.
SOURCE   Sillitoe (1969), Table A.37.

TABLE 2.9   Development of National Parks, 1950–55

	1950	1951	1952	1953	1954	1955
No. in existence	1	5	6	7	8	10
Total area (sq. miles)	542	2843	3396	4076	4341	5258

TABLE 2.10   Development of Areas of Outstanding Natural Beauty, 1956–73

	1956	1957	1958	1959	1960	1961	1962	1963	1964	1965
No. in existence	4	5	8	12	12	13	13	17	19	20
Total area (sq. miles)	331	731	1107	1701	1701	1852	1852	2367	2717	3096

	1966	1967	1968	1969	1970	1971	1972	1973
No. in existence	22	25	25	26	27	28	31	32
Total area (sq. miles)	3761	4291	4291	4442	4464	4589	5367	5583

TABLE 2.11   Development of Country Parks, 1969–73

	Existing pre-1969	1969	1970	1971	1972	1973
No. in existence	9	17	29	52	83	99
Total area (acres)	7110	8386	10252	15953	24605	28282

TABLE 2.12   Development of long-distance footpaths, 1965–73

	1965	1969	1970	1971	1972	1973
No. in existence	1	2	3	4	6	12
Total length (miles)	250	343	510	678	899	1499

NOTES   A further 5 paths were at various stages of consideration in September 1973.
SOURCES   Tables 2.9 to 2.12 are derived from Countryside Commission (1971, 1972, 1974).

ment in the post-war period. These are all large tracts of country ranging in size from the largest, the Lake District, with 866 square miles to the smallest, the Pembrokeshire Coast, with 225 square miles. The Parks, which cover in all some 9 per cent of the total area of England and Wales, are all situated in the north and west. Although some are within easy reach of the main centres of population, most notably the Peak District, they probably cater more for holiday and specialist visitors (rock climbing, fell walking, pot holing, etc.), than for the average day tripper.

As a supplement to these ten basic areas of the country, further areas have been designated since 1955 as Areas of Outstanding Natural Beauty (A.O.N.B.). These have similar restrictions on development from a conservation standpoint, are found rather more to the south and east in areas away from the National Parks, and are generally smaller (the average size is 175 square miles against nearly 526 square miles for the Parks), although in size they range from 671 square miles (the North Wessex Downs) to 22 square miles (Dedham Vale on the Essex/Suffolk border). The A.O.N.B. cover a further 9.6 per cent of the total land area of England and Wales, though serving essentially a regional rather than a national function. Their dependence on natural characteristics does tend to make their distribution irregular. Nearly all the areas so far designated are based on coastal scenery or the chalk uplands, leaving many areas of East Anglia and the East Midlands some considerable distance from such a designated area.

At the more local level the Commission has been recommending for grants small areas under the heading of Country Parks. These are normally areas under the control of local authorities, although of the 99 in existence by the end of September 1973, some 20 were under the control of non-public bodies.[32] The average size of these parks is just over 300 acres, but again there is a huge variation from the 3784 acres of Clumber Park in Nottinghamshire to the 18 acres of Fell Foot in Westmorland. A further development at an even smaller level is that of Picnic Sites, often of only a few acres providing basic facilities for car users in pleasant areas, but normally without access to larger tracts of countryside. By September 1971, some 23 such sites covering nearly 454 acres had been opened and by September 1973 this had increased to 114 sites and over 1582 acres. Country Parks and Picnic Sites are often developed as special facilities within the confines of existing National Parks or A.O.N.B.

Hence something of the order of 20 per cent of the land area of England and Wales is under the auspices of the Countryside Commission. It is, of course, unlikely that the growth of the past few years will be maintained into the future since much of the work to date has involved confirming or bringing into the grant scheme well-established public recreational facilities. This is certainly true of National Parks and A.O.N.B., but there is still considerable scope for the development of local Country Parks and Picnic Sites which permit more intensive development of recreational facilities. In addition to these sites, but also well documented and widely publicised, are the many privately owned stately homes and wildlife parks – many of which cater specifically for children with attractions such as zoos, amusements, etc. On a smaller scale there are the many ancient monuments and buildings in both country and town areas preserved by the State, through the Department of the Environment or by subscriber organisations and trust funds of which the National Trust is the most important. In 1969 there were 378 sites in England and Wales listed in the *Ministry of Public Buildings and Works Handbook*, and 717 in the *National Trust Handbook*.

What are the implications of these developments for leisure travel? One of the problems in answering this question is to determine the extent to which the organisation of natural resources into a more formal site, complete with car park, toilet facilities, footpaths, etc. will generate new traffic, or divert existing traffic. Diversion could well take place away from the site rather than to it, because of objection to the changes.[33] Clawson and Knetsch distinguished between the demand for 'recreation experience' and that for 'recreation resources' (1966, pp. 33–6). The experience includes, in their definition, five phases which can be summarised thus: anticipation, travel to, on-site, travel from and recollection. Of these, only the on-site part constitutes demand for a recreation resource. Because of this, changes in the supply price of the resource may have little effect on the level of demand for the experience, as revealed in the amount of leisure travel.

Trends in Transport Usage
We have, so far, examined trends in the time budget constraint and in the supply of recreational facilities of various forms. It is now necessary to turn to evidence on the trends in travel for leisure purposes. It was stressed above, that obtaining a satisfactory unit of measure for travel is a difficult problem and that this is particularly acute in the case of leisure travel. Heterogeneity of purpose, and quality changes through time, make any data inadequate as a true measure. The major problem, however, in obtaining any indicator of time trends is the lack of time-series data on journey purposes. Only with the advent of the large-scale land use and transport surveys in the 1960s has detailed information become available on the purposes for which journeys are made. Since these apply to different specific areas it is not possible to build up a general series. Most trends must be inferred, therefore, from various sources of aggregate travel data, with two limited exceptions. Small-

scale travel surveys were undertaken by London Transport in 1949 and 1954, which together with the detailed information from the 1962 London Traffic Survey, provide some estimates of trends in the Greater London area. Secondly, the Ministry of Transport and the Government Social Survey set up a series of annual motoring surveys in 1960, which formed the basis of the more complete National Travel Surveys of 1964 to 1966; these provide a six-year series of car usage.

More information is, of course, available on the usage of recreational facilities from admission figures and on-site surveys. These, however, are inadequate for a comprehensive examination of trends in demand for two reasons. Firstly, they relate only to specific destinations, and thus do not give any indication of overall trends. Secondly, and more seriously, they are only concerned with revealed demand—those people who have actually visited—and not based on complete coverage of the entire population. On-site surveys can only relate to average generation rates per head of population in origin zones, assuming that origin information is obtained. Where figures are time series of admissions only, even this does not apply.[34]

The most complete national aggregate series available are those of estimates of passenger miles. Since the information for private travel has to be taken from roadside traffic counts, supplemented by average occupancy figures from the more detailed surveys, it is not possible to obtain simple journey figures for these modes of travel. Table 2.13 shows that the growth in total travel over this period is entirely the result of the growth of private travel. Rail travel has shown a slight

TABLE 2.13   Trends in aggregate consumption of transport, 1952–72

Passenger miles (thousand million)	1952	1957	1960	1965	1968	1970	1972
Rail	24.1	25.9	24.8	21.8	20.8	22.2	21.1
Bus and coach	50.1	45.9	43.9	39.2	36.9	34.8	34.2
Private	37.9	59.9	89.4	144.7	177.7	196.2	223.5
Total transport	112.2	132.0	158.6	206.7	230.6	254.4	280.1
Annual total mileage *per capita*	2287.2	2638.3	3112.7	3902.4	4306.8	4681.9	5163.3

SOURCE   *Passenger Transport in Great Britain 1972*, Table 1.

recovery from 1968 to 1970, but bus and coach travel continues steadily downwards. Even after standardisation for population change, the growth of annual transport consumption over this period amounts to an increase of over 100 per cent, a compound annual growth rate of 4.1 per cent. The increase in average annual mileage by private transport is even more startling, a compound growth rate of nearly 9 per cent per annum.

Some idea of how this overall trend may be broken down into the trends for the main journey-purpose groups of travel to and from work, travel in course of work, and other travel (shopping, recreational, social and pleasure), can be obtained for private travel for the early 1960s from the more detailed Motoring and National Travel surveys. As Table 2.14 shows the number of journeys for non-work purposes was growing much faster than for work purposes over the period 1961–5.

TABLE 2.14   Average weekly travel by car for main journey purposes, 1961 and 1965*.

	Mileage		Journey stages	
Journey purpose	1961	1965	1961	1965
To and from work	30.4	35.1	5.6	6.0
In course of work	30.4	18.8	2.4	1.4
Non-work travel	65.8	75.5	6.8	9.4

* There were slightly different recording procedures in the two surveys. The 1961 figure refers to recorded journeys by household *cars* in the sample. The 1965 figure refers to car driver journeys by *individuals* in car-owning households, adjusted for multiple ownership. The differences in course-of-work journeys for the two surveys are partly due to differing definitions for inclusion. Otherwise the figures are directly comparable.
SOURCES   Gray (1969); National Travel Survey 1965, unpublished tabulations.

The mileage consumption pattern is less clear. The trend for car-owners emerging out of this is of a gradually increasing average journey-to-work length, and a corresponding reduction in the average length of non-work journeys (Table 2.15). This is the pattern which might be expected with gradual residential decentralisation, and improving

TABLE 2.15   Average stage lengths for car journeys, 1961 and 1965

	Miles	
Journey purpose	1961	1965
To and from work	5.4	5.8
In course of work	12.9	13.4
Non-work travel	9.7	8.1

SOURCES   Gray (1969); *National Travel Survey*, 1965.

accessibility to recreational facilities.[35] This point illustrates well the need to consider both trip rates and mileages to obtain an adequate picture of changing consumption patterns over time. Applying these findings back to Table 2.13, and bearing in mind that in 1965 58 per cent of car mileage was for non-work purposes (about 83.9 thousand million passenger miles), the annual increase in mileage for these purposes must be of the order of at least 8 to 10 thousand million passenger miles in the period 1965–70. Using an average journey-length figure of eight miles and an average vehicle occupancy of 2.2 persons for such journeys, this yields an increase of some 450 million car journeys for non-work purposes a year in Great Britain (about 1000 million person journeys).

The London Transport Travel Surveys of 1949 and 1954 were primarily concerned with regular travellers, from the point of view of their captive market. The proportion of central bus journeys for work purposes increased from 61 to 67 per cent over this period whilst that for shopping and other regular non-work journeys went down from 30 to 22 per cent. On the Underground the proportion of journeys for these non-work purposes declined from 10 to 6 per cent. These figures do cover a fair proportion of such journeys, as 26 per cent of the sample reported regular journeys for theatre or cinema visits, 25 per cent for shopping, 7 per cent for sport and 23 per cent for other non-work purposes.

In 1954 information was collected on all journeys, regular and casual, and these figures can be compared with later surveys (Table 2.16). Very little change has occurred over the eleven-year period 1954–65. A slight

TABLE 2.16   Trends in journey-purpose usage of London Transport, 1954–65

% All journeys for each journey purpose

	Central bus			L.T. Underground and British Rail		
Journey purpose	1954	1962	1965	1954	1962	1965
Work	51	53	47	73	78	70
School	8	8	8	6	4	4
Shopping	11	21	19	2	6	7
Entertainment/Sport	⎫	6	9	⎫	4	6
Personal social	⎬ 30	7	13	⎬ 19	3	10
Other	⎭	4	2	⎭	5	3
	100	100	100	100	100	100
Average trip rate per person for all purposes	6.2	0.5	4.1	1.8	0.2	1.9

NOTES   1962 figures are based on a single average weekday, 1954 and 1965 figures on the whole of a representative week.

SOURCES   *London Travel Survey 1954, London Traffic Survey 1962*, Vol. 1, National Travel Survey 1965, unpublished tabulations.

fall in the proportion of total journeys for both work and recreational purposes has occurred, the increase being for shopping travel. The 1962 figures show slight overestimates for work and shopping because they relate to an average weekday, whereas the others cover the whole of a representative week. There is an amazing stability of the journey-purpose composition of rail traffic over this period. There was, however, a substantial fall in bus traffic, and taking the fall in the proportion of that traffic for recreational purposes as an indicator, much of the total loss must have been due to a declining demand for this type of traffic. On the Underground and railways the fall seems to have been more uniform across the different purposes.

It seems unlikely that the general decline in non-work travel by public transport will have had anything but a very minor effect on the total, since this decline is by far outweighed by the increase in private travel.

The Size of the Recreational Sector

To establish the magnitudes of leisure activities in general, Tables 2.17 and 2.18 use data from two surveys dating from 1965. In the former of these, the Planning for Leisure survey of the Government Social Survey (Sillitoe, 1969) information is available on frequencies of trips to public open spaces, parks etc., for other than specific recreational activities, organised sports etc., and of trips to country or seaside. Table 2.18 is drawn from the National Travel Survey of 1965, the most comprehensive source of data on all aspects of travel at present available in the U.K.[36] This excludes walking trips of less than one mile, and hence probably a large number of visits to local parks etc. Journeys of the type discussed in this section are classified as recreation, social, or pleasure according to the criteria outlined above.

It will be seen that, apart from work and shopping travel, with which we are not directly concerned in this study, we have as yet to consider

TABLE 2.17   Visits to public open spaces, country or seaside, 1965–6

| | % Making visits with given frequency | | | |
| | Public open spaces | | Country or seaside* | |
Frequency	Male	Female	Male	Female
Twice weekly	18	17	—	—
Once weekly	15	12	17	19
Once monthly	21	20	21	16
Less than monthly	16	19	11	15
Never	26	30	51	50
Visited for organised activity only	5	1	—	—
Average number of visits/person†	18	17	5.5	6.0

* Summer period only.
† During whole year for public open spaces, and during summer period for country or seaside.
SOURCE   Sillitoe (1969).

TABLE 2.18   Trip generation patterns in different types of area, 1965

Journey purpose	*Average number journey stages for each journey purpose (weekly)*			
	Greater London	*Other conurbations*	*Urban areas*	*Rural areas*
Shopping	2.3	2.3	2.4	2.6
Recreation	1.8	1.5	1.6	1.6
Social	1.8	2.2	1.8	1.9
Pleasure	0.8	0.6	0.7	0.8
Work	5.1	5.0	4.5	2.9
Other	1.4	1.5	1.4	0.1
Total Stages	13.2	13.1	12.4	9.9

SOURCES   National Travel Survey 1965, unpublished tabulations; Vickerman (1972a).

one further main category of travel, social travel. This, by definition travel for which the main purpose is to visit friends or relations, is *ipso facto* the most difficult category to analyse in the framework used above, yet it is of vital importance, accounting for some 15 per cent of all journey stages made. It is difficult because of its independence of specific locational factors. Prediction will depend on the ability to establish a much more complex set of socio-economic relationships and to project changes in the spatial aspects of these into the future. This must be regarded as beyond the scope of this study, but worthy of further research.[37] The crucial issue in question is the effect on travel of changing patterns of social mobility. Does the spatial dispersion of the extended family reduce travel, increase the consumption of passenger mileage, or divert social travel into relationships outside the family, and with what effect on movement patterns and the consumption of transport? Some more specific aspects of this will be covered in Chapter 5.

Conclusions

We now turn to draw some preliminary conclusions from this discussion of trends in leisure. There has undoubtedly been a considerable increase in the amount of travel generated for leisure purposes. There has been a parallel increase in both the provision of organised recreational facilities, and in recorded participation (with the exception of cinema attendances). But from where does this growth originate? In terms of economic theory does it represent a pure income effect, a response to price changes (either as an equivalent-variation real-income effect or a pure substitution effect), or is it evidence of a change in tastes?

Incomes have certainly risen to the extent that leisure activities are now accessible to a larger part of the community than hitherto. Possibly more people can now afford to overcome their workplace alienation so that leisure is compensatory and not just a spillover from the workplace.[38] However, it may be that a further type of what Wilensky (1960) has called 'underdog response' has developed, that of 'family-home localism'. The 'Affluent Worker' studies found evidence of increasing concentration on the nuclear family for leisure activities, and Gavron (1966) in her study of working wives, noted that for working-class groups, recreation is television-centred, and as many as 25 per cent of the wives in these groups claimed no friends outside the family.[39]

Leisure time, however, does not appear to have risen by a large amount. This is not to say that changes in the amount of leisure time are necessarily insignificant. Rationalisation of working hours, and the concentration of leisure into more useful periods – weekends, longer holidays, etc. – may have had a sizeable impact on external leisure activities for a small change in hours worked.

The only detailed work on the money price of leisure is that by Owen (1969b) on time-series data for the United States. Owen estimated the market price for recreation from admissions data for cinema, etc. and from prices of relevant leisure goods, television, radio, sports goods, etc. The expected complementary nature of the demand for leisure time and market recreation was identified.[40] Because of the essentially spatial nature of all external leisure activities, the true supply price must include an element of accessibility. This is particularly true for non-marketable activities, where the perceived time and travel costs are the price of the activity. The growth and spread of facilities for leisure evidenced above suggests a considerable reduction in the true supply price.[41]

A further element of supply price is the pure network effect of changes in transport facilities. The most important of these by far is the growth of car-ownership, car travel being the only feasible means of access to many facilities. Car-ownership is, of course, directly related to income changes, but its more relevant position in a travel demand model is as an accessibility or price factor. These are primarily income effects resulting from the lower supply prices, the equivalent variation of demand theory.[42]

Substitution would appear to have been largely a case of people changing between indoor and external activities, or possibly between nearby and more distant external activities as a result of falling relative prices as activities become more accessible.

Changing tastes in leisure have probably been just as important as changing relative prices, although it is impossible to identify the specific sources of changes in leisure patterns. Innovations like television have certainly altered choices in the entertainment subset of activities, although this is mainly a supply-price effect. Television itself, as a moulder of attitudes, may have stimulated demand for many growth activities independently of price.

Having set the scene in terms of magnitudes and trends in leisure activities and leisure travel, providing a definition of the subject matter, we must now turn, in subsequent chapters, to a more detailed examination of independent factors affecting the demand for these. First, however, it is necessary to establish the purpose for which the end-product of this examination is required, in order that the results are of the right form. The next chapter is therefore devoted to a brief discussion of future planning and project appraisal in the context of leisure and recreation.

3. The Economic Analysis of Leisure Projects

Before developing more specific models of the demand for leisure activities and leisure travel in subsequent chapters it is desirable to establish the overall framework within which these analyses can be more satisfactorily developed. This chapter has three main themes: the establishing of an objective or aim of the analysis, the similarities and differences of leisure activities and leisure projects from others for which such analyses have been developed, and the development of a rational framework for the economic appraisal of leisure projects.

Objectives

Precise definition of the ultimate objectives of the analysis is necessary in order that the results obtained, and the assumptions made, are compatible with the nature of the conclusions to be drawn. We are here concerned with examining the factors which influence the demand for leisure activities. As a forecasting model of possible consumer behaviour there are two main types of application. One is the estimation of likely trends in the use of existing facilities. This is largely a question of transport and facility demand as far as the planning process is concerned; given the existing pattern of land use, what changes in the amount and nature of trips to different sites can be expected? The crucial transport planning question here is likely to be the extent to which the answers for recreational or pleasure travel differ from those for the work journey, which by reason of both size and economic importance will be the primary capacity determinant. Hence, in conurbation areas the transport planning requirements can be met by adequate analysis of journey-to-work patterns whilst in rural or coastal areas volumes of non-work trip demands may be the critical determinants. For recreational site planning the issue is the future level of usage of particular sites and possible congestion which may arise here requiring additional management procedures.

The second use is in essence a reversal of the instrument and effect roles of land use and transport. The results must also consider the question of what sort of recreational facilities are likely to be demanded,

31

and where, and when, within a given transport network situation, and hence optimal locations of new leisure facilities and the resultant secondary feedback effects on to transport and other land uses can be considered.

This contrast can be phrased in a more relevant and interesting manner, however, which does question a basic assumption of the conventional land use–transportation study methodology. Implicit in the philosophy of these studies has been that land use is a basic policy variable around which the demand for movement and resultant transport policy revolves. Land use, therefore, becomes exogenous to the whole modelling process. A more rational approach to movement would need to consider the whole spatial structure of the relevant sectors of the economy in a general, rather than the above partial, equilibrium model, treating land use as an endogenous factor in the model. Whilst this does complicate the neat directional simplicity of the conventional model by introducing feedback effects, it does result in a more realistic approach. Although land use is, through planning legislation, a controllable policy variable, the general equilibrium approach illustrates more clearly the possible pressures for changes in land use and hence gives a clearer view of likely long-term changes.[1]

A further contrast which needs to be drawn is between the macro and micro planning applications of the results. The former is concerned with the overall growth of leisure activity, and the associated travel in the economy in question, be this national, regional or urban, and the implications for overall planning. The latter is concerned with the appraisal of specific projects as would normally be considered in a cost–benefit analysis framework. It is the specific case which is the more relevant to the discussion here and we shall concentrate on this in the development of the general principles in question.

The Cost–Benefit Analysis Framework

What are the requirements of the analytical framework? There are two basic dimensions to this, firstly the identification of beneficiaries, and secondly the evaluation of benefits received. We shall consider these in the context of social cost–benefit analysis which has become the accepted framework of analysis for problems of this type in which, for reasons of market failure, the financial rate of return on an investment is held to be an inadequate measure of a project's value to the community.[2]

Evaluation has been at the centre of many of the recent developments in cost–benefit analysis, in particular the response to the need to ascribe monetary values to non-marketable factors such as time and noise.[3] Whilst values have been forthcoming from this work which appear intuitively reasonable, and which seem to stand up in application, it has normally been necessary to introduce a form of quasi-marketability to obtain numerical answers. Thus noise problems have been evaluated, for example, through the impact on property values, and time through willingness to pay for greater speed or more accessible locations. There may be severe problems in this approach, the quasi-market introduced may have crucial imperfections in it and whilst yielding certain private valuations of noise or time does not give reasonable estimates of the true social cost or benefit. Time-evaluation studies, for example, show a consistently higher valuation of time by higher-income earners; thus a project benefiting a higher proportion of high-income earners will get a higher valuation of attributable time savings than an equivalent project benefiting more lower-income groups. Likewise a noise valuation based on property values can only reflect the valuations implied by those groups of the population who both own property and are able to consider moving.

There may be cases where this implicit weighting is valid in terms of reflecting social valuation of a project, possibly the higher valuation of time savings of high-income groups includes a valuation of the worth of their time to the community. Nevertheless, it is reasonable to expect that there is a divergence between the apparent private valuation and the true social valuation, and that this divergence is related to the ability to pay. Specific distributional factors do need to be considered more closely.[4]

Attempts have been made to avoid the quasi-market approach, notably by the use of subjective evaluations with the help of 'game' situations.[5] These tend to yield compatible results with imputed-valuation studies, which suggest that the imputation is normally correct. All this confirms, however, is that people on the whole act rationally, and that their *ex post* revealed action accords with their *ex ante* stated preferences. It does not overcome the social *v.* private-valuation dichotomy.

The bias towards evaluation is well illustrated in the literature, both in outlines of the theory and its applications. There are essentially four stages to the analysis: the concepts of benefits and costs; the question of shadow prices in cases where there is no market, or the market price is unsatisfactory; the establishing of an objective function; and the formulation of the basic decision rules for project selection.

Concepts of Benefits

Crucial to the whole philosophy of this type of analysis is that benefits can accrue to society or to individuals which are greater than that reflected by the relevant expenditure. Economists have long been aware that implicit in the assumption of a downward-sloping demand curve for a normal commodity, *DD'* in Figure 3.1, is that at a ruling price,

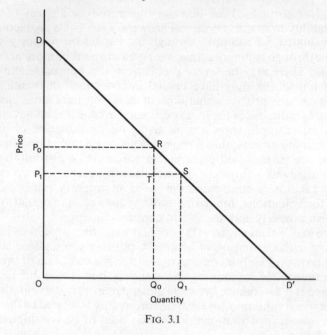

FIG. 3.1

say P_0, the purchasers of all units up to, but not including Q_0 would have been prepared to pay a price higher than P_0. The fact that they need only pay P_0 suggests that they derive an additional benefit free of charge.[6] This measure of, in Marshall's words (1920, p. 124), 'the excess of the price which (the consumer) would be willing to pay rather than go without the thing, over what he actually does pay' is known as the consumer's surplus.

If the price is reduced to a new level of P_1 then the size of this benefit is seen to increase on all the existing units which would have been bought at price P_0 by an amount represented by the rectangle $P_0 RTP_1$, and, in addition, the new lower price causes there to be a non-negative benefit over and above the valuation given by market price on an additional $Q_0 Q_1$ units now purchased, equal to the area of the triangle RST.

This analysis will hold if it can be assumed that the demand curve provides an adequate indication of the valuation by the consumer of each unit purchased. For the conventional Marshallian demand curve, like DD' in Figure 3.1, which relates quantities purchased to the price, to have this direct relationship to marginal utility implied by the concept of benefit valuation requires that the marginal utility of money should be constant. If this assumption is removed, then the thus-defined demand curve does not reflect the relevant valuation, and the concept of consumer's surplus becomes imprecise.[7]

Allowing for the presence of an income effect when price changes means that at the prevailing price P_0 a marginal-valuation curve can be defined, which – in order to maintain a constant real income – will, for a price fall, lie below the Marshallian demand curve and, for a price rise, lie above it (Figure 3.2).

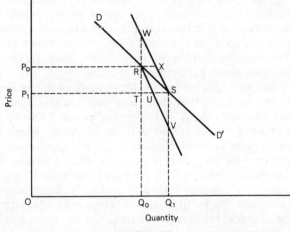

FIG. 3.2

Hence, for a fall in price from P_0 to P_1 a compensating variation in income of $P_0 RUP_1$ can be defined as that amount by which income would need to be reduced after the fall in price to keep the consumer just as well off as he was before the reduction. The demand curve, however, shows that $OQ_1 = P_1 S$ units will be bought after the price fall, and not only the $P_1 U$ which the marginal-valuation curve suggests. There is therefore, on this definition, an implied income loss equal to the area of the triangle USV for the US units where price is greater than their marginal valuation. A corresponding analysis using the marginal-valuation curve operative at the new price P_1 (SXW) shows the equivalent variation in income which would be necessary to make the consumer as well off as he has become after the reduction in price to P_1 in the absence of that change in price. We can note that the simple Marshall measure using the uncompensated demand curve RS will be the average of the compensated measures, i.e. the special case when marginal utility of money is the same at both income levels. Adequate evaluation of the change in benefit can be derived simply from knowledge of the demand curve in the Marshall case, the critical component is the triangle *RST*. Once a compensated demand curve is introduced we also require knowledge of the variations incorporated in the marginal-valuation curves, the relevant measurements now required being triangles *RUT* and *USV*, or the equivalent variations *RXS* and *RXW*.

Essential to either approach is the demand curve. If this cannot be adequately estimated over the relevant section, *RS* in the diagrams, then however accurate evaluation procedures are otherwise the total benefits will be grossly mis-estimated. Once some form of Marshallian demand curve is established its usefulness will depend on the extent to which income variations alter valuations. In projects where the proportion of individual incomes spent on the commodity or activity is high, or there are strong biases in the distributional or redistributional implications then there is much greater probability of error.

There is a danger in presenting the framework of the analysis in the simplified form above in that it focuses only on the problems in a certain minor area, section *RS* of the demand curve. All too frequently, however, in areas of transport and land-use planning, where the cost–benefit analysis of investment projects is the accepted common technique, an entirely new project is in question. In the terminology used in transport projects all the traffic is generated and none simply diverted from other routes or means of transport. At least in cases where there is an existing demand the point *R* can be observed; where there is no such existing demand the forecast is likely to be much less accurate because it is the position as well as the shape of the curve which has to be estimated.

Hence, it can be seen that the first priority is the estimation of a reliable demand relationship for potential users of a new project. This might involve the use of observed demands for existing facilities of the same type, transferring the relationship to the new case under certain assumptions. In many cases, however, it might involve the establishing of such a relationship for a new project, or in circumstances where the transference of a relationship estimated for another case might not be appropriate. In such cases a much wider concept of substitution will be necessary.

So far we have considered only the direct benefits to users implied by the demand curve, a full cost–benefit analysis requires consideration of spillover effects. These, the possible effects of the project on persons or organisations other than those directly involved as producer or consumer may be beneficial or detrimental, and may be accounted for in different ways depending on their nature. In the simpler case there is some fairly straightforward linkage between the primary activity and a secondary activity such that the effects (cost or benefit) on the latter need to be accounted for in the overall calculation. Care must always be taken in this case that the apparent secondary benefit is not just a redistribution brought about by the project.[8] The more complex case is one where these spillovers are less obvious and cannot be assessed in the direct manner. These normally involve a distortion in the market such that the market valuation in terms of ruling market prices is not a good estimate of a true social valuation. These are normally grouped under the heading of externalities and public goods, and are defined as there being non-independence of individual utility functions for the goods and services in question.[9] The correction implied by the presence of this form of spillover is either some form of compensation,[10] or the use of a shadow price which reflects social valuations better than the market price.[11]

This discussion of social valuation and shadow price does, however, beg a very important question. All economic prescriptions are based on some, usually implicit, objective function; in this area of analysis it is usually referred to as a social welfare function.[12] Only by establishing some objective of this type can any rational assessment be made of the effects of a project. It is at this point that this whole analytical framework faces its severest test. The critical point is the need to aggregate individual preference patterns, those neatly defined by economic theories of consumer choice, into a single function representing the preference pattern of the community as a whole so that unambiguously optimal decisions can be taken with reference to it. Does economic analysis lead to the possibility of social choice in any meaningful sense?[13]

In this brief overview of the definition of benefits, we have sought to identify the information required for any project appraisal, and the relative importance of different categories of information. The discussion suggests that of primary importance is the identification of beneficiaries, both in terms of numbers and their economic status. This is implicit in the theoretical importance of the social welfare function. Most practical studies seem, however, to honour this in the breach rather than the observance, and concentrate on valuations of the likely benefits. The main implication of this is the need to concentrate on derivation of an adequate demand curve, or series of demand curves, for the project in question. The particular importance of this is to provide an estimate, not just of the number of beneficiaries, but a classification of these beneficiaries by socio-economic strata. Valuation exercises can then be concentrated on the revealed most important variables, and where different valuations for different strata are applicable weightings can be applied to give a more realistic total benefit in the social welfare sense. In short, it is suggested that it may be more important to know who benefits than by how much. This appears from crude theory to be a less important and less interesting problem, but it is one which assumes greater importance and interest once put to the practical test.

Concepts of Costs

It will be obvious that there is a symmetry in costs and benefits. The items discussed above as benefits also involve costs to users and non-users both in the form of prices or monetary costs incurred less directly. For completeness we also need to mention the costs to the producer of the service or activity in question. Investments which facilitate a reduction in the supply price to the consumer will also involve a reduction in marginal operating costs and, if a price is charged, a possible increase in net revenues. Whilst a socially worthwhile project does not necessarily raise net revenues any increase which does occur is part of the total benefit which must be counted.

The change can be shown as in Figure 3.3. The demand curve DD' is as shown in Figure 3.2. $C_0 C_0'$ represents the marginal operating costs prior to the investment and $C_1 C_1'$ the new lower-cost curve after the investment. The change in net revenue is shown by $P_1 SC_1 - P_0 RC_0$.[14]

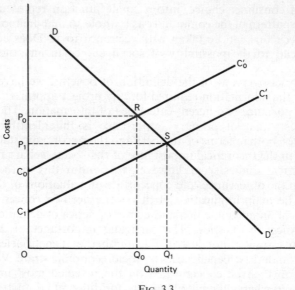

FIG. 3.3

The second point relating to operating costs is the need to consider social opportunity costs rather than just financial costs. This occurs where the price which has to be paid in the market, for resources used in producing the service, deviates–for reasons of market imperfections–from the true value of those resources as determined by their alternative use. Imperfections commonly arise as the result of imperfect competition in the resource market, leading either to scarcity because of withholding by the sellers of the resource or unemployment of the resource because of restrictions in demand by other potential purchasers without this being reflected in the price charged. They may also arise through government interference in the form of taxes or subsidies imposed for other than allocational reasons. The deviation could be positive or negative but in either case would involve a marginal social cost curve which differed from the marginal private (financial) cost curve. Such a problem would need to be overcome for the purpose of the cost–benefit analysis by employing a shadow price of the resource which reflects this true opportunity cost to the community and which therefore implies that the price charged to the consumer for the service or facility in question reflects the true costs of resources used.

The Application of Cost–Benefit in Leisure Projects
We now turn to discuss the way in which leisure and recreational projects can be analysed within the conventional framework.

We shall consider the costs and benefits under two main headings, those to users and those to non-users. The problems of defining operator costs will be left for the moment but reconsidered in Chapter 9. Of the two to be considered, user costs and benefits are the more straight-forward to identify.

User Costs
Direct costs to the user of a recreational facility are those on-site charges which need to be paid, admission charges, parking fees, etc., and the cost of access to the site. There may be additional items which are more difficult to classify, the cost of special equipment or clothing, or the payment of standing charges such as seasonal angling permits or boat mooring charges. All of these represent essentially capital outlays for regular users which render the marginal cost of this item for a specific visit zero. Given that special equipment is not site-specific it cannot reasonably be included in the appraisal of a particular site. However, it must be recognised that the provision of a completely new facility such as a local marina or ice stadium will have strong generation effects, and that in these cases some bias may be caused by disregarding these items. Standing charges for site use must, of course, be included. If use is solely by those having paid such charges then the most satisfactory procedure would be to consider the demand for 'membership' separately from the demand for facilities by members–

the relevant charges could therefore be included in their correct perspective.

A greater problem exists where there is a mixture of season-ticket holders and day by day users, a situation which is likely to be the most common. If the average number of occasions when the site is used by a season-ticket holder is known, then a representative average cost can be estimated from the two costs weighted by the relevant numbers of users.[15] It is, however, unsatisfactory to use such artificial prices when trying to estimate demand response. In particular, any change in the prices, whether this affects the relative costs of the two systems or not, may change the proportional usage of each, and hence the new artificial price is not known. For example, a 5 per cent increase in the costs both of a season ticket and of a daily charge may lead to different reactions. Amongst daily users there is likely to be a fall in demand dependent on the price elasticity. Amongst season-ticket holders, however, the outcome may be less certain; some will feel that their level of usage does not justify the purchase of a new season ticket and therefore switch to using day tickets for a smaller number of visits; others may increase their usage so as to reduce the effective cost per visit on the season ticket, possibly causing a diversion from other activities; others may be lost as customers altogether. The fact that switching between groups may occur makes it difficult to analyse them separately since they are not completely independent.

There is a more fundamental issue which needs to be considered, the nature of prices in recreation. As we have seen, any cost–benefit analysis framework which is attempting to assess an overall social rate of return on the use of resources must use prices which reflect the opportunity cost of that use accurately. Strictly, shadow, rather than market, prices should be used and if market prices are used, then the extent of their deviation from the true shadow price needs to be assessed. This calls into question the whole philosophy of the financing of recreation projects and, in particular, that substitutable activities can be financed in very different ways such that their relative market prices do not represent their relative shadow prices or resource costs.

There are three possible policies, that the full cost of the activity is charged to the user; that the user pays a nominal charge, the remainder being financed from other sources;[16] and that the user pays no charge, the facility being financed out of general taxation. The rationale for not charging full user costs to the user is a combination of non-marketability of certain leisure activities together with the presence of social externalities.

It is wrong, however, simply to classify such activities as public goods. Activities such as the appreciation of the countryside might not involve the possibility of exclusion, in that one person's consumption does not use up the resource, but individual consumers are rivals for its consumption at a particular time, and their presence can be detrimental to each other.[17] More specific and marketable recreational activities are more akin to private goods. Nevertheless, in all cases there are likely to be elements of externality which must be allowed for in the analysis, although it is possible that the external benefits of recreation to society may be eulogised more than objective analysis should allow. 'Outdoor recreation', say Clawson and Knetsch (1966, p. 267), 'is essential to a full and well balanced personal life...and thus the welfare of the whole nation is enhanced'.

The fact that there are external benefits, or that exclusion is not implied by the nature of the activity does not necessarily imply a zero charge. This arises because although the private marginal cost of the additional person is zero, the social marginal cost of his presence is above zero; this is the classic case of congestion. The case for charging therefore rests on the relationship between capacity and demand such that whereas the capacity of, say, the Lake District might not be exceeded at a zero charge, that of a sports stadium, swimming-pool, or golf course may well be. Whilst it is recognised that there is a social benefit from individual usage of recreational and cultural facilities, the policy of charging should be one which ensures maximum usage of existing capacity and the lowest level of frustrated demand, consistent with the social cost of resource usage.[18]

There is no easy classification of recreational activities. They cover the whole range of 'goods' from pure private to pure public depending on the degree of rivalness or excludability in the particular case. Even more problematical from the point of view of developing a simple framework for the economic analysis of such activities is that the same activity can be classified in a different way at different times depending on circumstances such as questions of capacity utilisation.

This makes the interpretation of charges in terms of payments for benefits received very difficult. If the charge is purely a congestion tax without any regard to the resource costs in question then serious distributional questions may arise. There is, for example, a danger that congestion taxes are based on valuations of time which are related to wage rates and hence only applicable to a certain section of the community. If the whole community has to bear charges based on this criterion there is an effective distribution of benefit away from non-wage, and low wage, earners.

Financing the provision of recreational facilities out of public funds may be a reasonable way of ensuring that such facilities are not solely available on an ability-to-pay criterion. However, to the extent that provision is out of local authority revenue, this must come mainly from rates which will be calculated on the basis of that authority's expenditure needs, and which are generally regressive in their incidence. In this way poorer sections of the community may have to bear an unreasonable proportion of the cost of providing and maintaining recreational facilities. Finance out of national taxation through grants to local authorities is more satisfactory.[19]

We have concentrated the discussion with regard to charging so far in terms of site charges for the actual use of the recreational resource in question. To the extent that benefit arises more from the entire experience, however, care must be taken that necessary expenditures incurred in the ancillary parts of the activity such as access to the site bear similar relationships to resource costs in different cases. If, for example, a council operates two swimming-pools, one in the town centre which has limited and expensive parking facilities, and one in a peripheral area which has ample free parking, then relative prices reflect relative resource costs and no great allocation problems arise. If, however, there is a standard charging policy for swimming-pool use when for similar reasons the resource costs of pool provision differ, there is a potential problem. The fact that councils need to use policies of cross-subsidisation between sites and facilities because of severe budgetary constraints is always likely to lead to problems in benefit estimation.

When the site charge is zero, and particularly in the case of sites of natural beauty, an even greater problem arises. Now the relative prices for the experience at particular sites are dependent solely on the access costs, and whilst simply applying standard vehicle operating costs and values of traveller time will produce reasonable estimates of relative resource costs for access they will not represent true relative resource costs of the sites in question. Assume that in terms of intrinsic natural beauty there is no perceivable difference between sites in any of the National Parks such that rational people are indifferent between them, that sites are spatially equally distributed in each Park so that the number of sites is directly proportional to area, and that visits are a function of distance from site. The Lake District has an area of 866 square miles compared with the Peak District's 542 square miles, but lies much further from any large centre of population (Leeds, Liverpool, Manchester, Teesside and Tyneside all being over 70 miles from Kendal on the edge of the Park) than the latter which is ringed by the urban areas of Manchester, Sheffield, Derby–Nottingham, and the Potteries, none of which are more than 20 miles from a choice of sites well within the Park's boundaries. The pressure on the Peak District's resources, and hence the marginal costs to society of their supply is clearly far higher.[20] Given its greater accessibility, however, the perceived costs to the visitor are much lower, and hence perceived private benefit greater.

The costs of access are all too often ignored in economic demand theory because of its normal assumptions of instantaneous consumption over time and space. In consequence, spatial theories of consumption have largely been disregarded. In the case of recreation, access costs are such a large and important part of the total cost of consumption that they cannot be ignored. Two distinguishable elements of access cost must be identified, money and non-money costs. Money costs are the actual costs of transport to the site and thus depend on the location of the site relative to the home, and the cost per unit distance for the relevant means of transport. The non-money costs are those involved in the expenditure of time on access. There is no reason to assume that time spent or saved on the activity itself and on access to the activity are valued equally. We shall need to develop more fully the role of time in the consumer demand function for leisure activities, and this is left until the following chapter.

Non-user Costs

Some non-user costs and benefits are directly attributable to individuals, i.e. of the nature of private goods, whilst others can only be assessed to society as a whole. Of the latter, we have already discussed the possibility of external effects in recreational provision affecting charging policy and finance of the facilities. There are three further factors in this area which require consideration: regional planning, environmental pollution and traffic movements.

Regional Planning. It must be recognised that any recreational project, large or small, has repercussions on both land-use and movement aspects of planning policy, whether at local, regional or national level. If overall strategies of planning have been established then any new project has to be analysed within this framework. If the project eases the attainment of planning targets then there are secondary benefits which must be evaluated, if the project tends to conflict then there are costs which must be allowed for in assessing the return.[21] There are three main headings under which these planning aspects can be assessed. First of all there is the question of overall strategy, the extent to which recreational facilities are embodied in a structure plan for a region or subregion, what needs are envisaged, and when and where. Secondly, there is the problem of specific planning variables at a local level, infrastructure, employment, resources and environment. And thirdly, there are interregional effects and national strategies.

Structure-plan considerations are not solely of a planning nature. Identification of needs and location of facilities consistent with overall strategy is a vital factor, but of equal importance is the timing of the facility's provision. This is a central feature of any economic appraisal in that provision too early or too late might result in the rate of return not meeting a satisfactory level. Advancing a project may involve current costs in excess of current user benefits for some years plus losses to competing facilities. Delaying a project may lead to a rise in construction costs plus a severe loss of benefits in the delay period due to congestion and associated external costs. The criterion for establishing optimum timing is not clear but it is a factor which must be considered explicitly.

The relationship of a project to the existing or exogenously planned infrastructure of an area is vital since it will determine the need for ancillary works associated with the project, such as access roads, parking, houses for employees, etc. This will be important in either rural or urban contexts, hence the construction of a swimming-pool as part of a recreational and sports complex of the type envisaged in the planning of new urban areas will benefit from being able to share common infrastructure with the other activities.

The employment potential of recreational projects themselves is not likely to be a major factor in their planning.[22] In the case of major projects, however, the consequent growth of tourism may be contributory in reducing rates of rural depopulation and preserving rural farming communities.[23] Whilst much of the benefit in such cases is strictly a private benefit there are undoubted social benefits arising as externalities from these. Archer (1973) has estimated that the likely employment multiplier resulting from tourist expenditure in Anglesey is about twice the size of that to be expected from general expenditure.[24] However, when these are split into direct and indirect effects this difference can be seen to be simply a reflection of the labour intensity of the tourist industries, particularly catering. Job creation was estimated as 4.35 per £10,000 expenditure in tourist industries compared with 1.90 per £10,000 generally, but the indirect effects were virtually identical in each case at 0.48 to 0.49 per £10,000. The lesser secondary effects in the case of the tourist expenditure means that the more conventional employment multiplier of total jobs created to each direct job is only 1.11 compared with 2.58 for general expenditure. Very little besides the direct employment creation needs to be taken into account therefore.

A parallel study by Sadler *et al.* (1973) has shown that this finding also applies broadly to indirect income effects in the local economy; apart from the directly connected sectors of distribution and recreational services only agriculture appears to receive any noticeable benefit.

Discussion of general income effects leads us to a consideration of the indirect impact on resources other than labour, which in the case of recreational projects will essentially involve natural resources. There are two main questions at stake here – the joint development of resources and recreational facilities, and conflicts between recreation and resources. The former of these is most easily seen in the case of water-resource development and examples of these are already well established as case studies in the literature.[25] In this case of joint development, what would otherwise be classed as externalities are being effectively internalised in a joint product. Problems of identifying the source of remaining external effects may arise if there is a possibility of separate development such that rates of return for the separate cases are needed in order to take a final decision on the project. For example, if the traffic generated by recreational use of the facility leads to local external costs which cancel out benefits from the provision of water, or if the secondary benefits to local residents from catering for tourist traffic are weighed against their loss of land in the reservoir scheme. In many of these joint development schemes it must be tacitly recognised that severe distributional questions may arise.

This is the main issue at stake when we consider conflicts. The primary benefits accrue to the tourist largely as a free good, the main costs are the secondary external effects on local resources. This is one major reason for the need to identify the distribution of costs and benefits carefully.

Although we have seen above that agriculture may benefit to a limited extent through the income generating effects of recreation, it can also suffer through loss of land or harsher planning regulations in areas of natural beauty, where, in any case, the economics of farming may be less amenable to the imposition of additional costs. Greater total losses may, however, accrue through the more marginal external effects caused by a greater throughput of people in rural areas, damage, noise and pollution being the offending items.

Finally in this area of local planning considerations comes the least tangible, interrelationships with the environment. In many respects the sources of the problems are similar to those discussed above with reference to resources. The essential difference, however, is that the resources in question will not be in, nor potentially in, any specific alternative use. Hence the costs will be entirely social in nature. The fact that they do not fall on particular individuals' private 'cost curves' does not mean that distributional problems will not arise, however. Differential incidence will occur between groups, according largely to location, but the cost will be of the nature of a public 'bad' to all within that group.

The third heading is that of interregional effects and national strategy. Since planning tends to be essentially a local function[26] the basic pressure occurs at this local level, and the primary consideration in terms of overall structure planning and local planning factors will be carried out within the context of the local authority concerned. Even regional planning has only developed in the U.K. since 1961, and in a more formal guise only since the establishing of the Economic Planning Councils and associated Boards in 1965. The role of these is limited, however, to the production of broad objectives for each region, advising on the national policies affecting the region and on the application of such policies within the region, plus general exhortative functions to the local authorities in the region; a role described by Cullingworth (1970, p. 292) as 'regional stocktaking'. This gap in the planning framework means that the detailed implementation of government policy is inefficient and a proper balance of planning development is not achieved. Government grants may be distributed on the basis of a national view of regional needs, but the machinery cannot channel these adequately at a local level. Similarly, proposals emanating from a local level are not adequately sifted to produce a coherent regional structure before being passed up to central government level.[27] To some extent recreational proposals manage to bypass the system by coming under the auspices of the Countryside Commission for grant purposes, but this could still mean some problems at the planning level. The fact emerging is that the conflicts and consequent possible inefficiencies in planning recreational activities could be placing sizeable costs on areas outside that of direct involvement, or leading to a distortion in the overall national or regional patterns of recreational provision which in itself represents a cost which needs to be allowed for.

Environmental Pollution. We need to make a more formal analysis of the whole pollution question than discussed under the more limited heading of local planning factors above, and in particular to establish the framework for measuring pollution spillovers. Pollution is used here as a general term for all deleterious influences on the environment which can also be considered harmful to other people. The main categories relevant to recreation are noise, litter and, where appropriate, contamination of water supplies or the creation of fire hazards. Recent developments in the economic analysis of pollution problems such as that by Victor (1972) have adopted a materials balance approach to the use of resources and production of waste, using input–output analysis as the basic technique of analysing economy–environment interactions.

This type of analysis allows identification of the sources and sufferers of environmental pollution, but still leaves the problem of placing a value on such spillovers. Here a number of problems arise. Firstly, does the external cost fall directly and identifiably on individuals or not? If the former case applies then the externality is of the form of a private good entering into the sufferer's utility function, and its handling in theoretical terms is more straightforward. If this is not the case, then it cannot be analysed directly in terms of its interference with utility-maximisation.

Theoretical analysis of these problems assumes the former of these two cases. Externalities become potentially relevant in welfare economics when the parties concerned are motivated to trade over the externality. Given the aim, assumed in welfare economics, to attain a Paretian optimum, where no person can be made better off without *ipso facto* making someone else worse off, such potentially relevant externalities can be further identified as Pareto-relevant if the trading would improve the welfare of one party without harming that of the other, allowing for a compensation criterion. As we have already seen, however, the nature of the compensation required to restore an individual to his former welfare, or to raise him to a new level from attaining which he is being restrained, is vague. Each definition has its merits, *qua* theoretical definition, but the answers in a practical exercise will differ. In terms of the problems under review here, we are saying that the compensation required to restore an individual to the level of utility he enjoyed before a new recreational project gave rise to spillovers deterimental to his well-being will differ from that amount he would be prepared to pay to avoid the sufferance, and these both from the compensating variations of the provider of the facility.

Now it is true that some average of these amounts will be a good estimate of the Marshallian consumer's surplus being lost or gained, but it is still not clear that the average variation is correct in this case. But how are the amounts to be measured anyway? Does an individual know what he would accept as reasonable compensation for a loss of utility, given that his marginal utility of money will not be as neutral as the theory would imply? Is there not an even bigger divergence in the before and after compensations caused by the fact that in reality the sufferer and inflictor are not in most cases in the equal bargaining position assumed in the theory.[28] This point has been typified by arguments over noise compensation with regard to the Third London Airport. It has been claimed that whereas an individual might view the necessary compensation to be paid by the airport authority (or inducement to live by the airport) as infinite, his own capability for bribing the airport authority to stay away is, in comparison, virtually nil.[29] This does hinder the nice workings of the theory towards a Pareto improvement, but in practice may be a rather misguided adherence to the principles of the perfect-competition assumption. If collusion amongst the sufferers becomes possible then the feasibility of bribing the polluter to stay away increases. Collusion of this type is most practicable in terms of action through the Government using taxation and/or physical or legal controls.

There is an analogy in some respects to the marginal-cost pricing rule which suggests that the marginal user, of a full train for example, must pay the full cost of the extra carriage or train, all subsequent users up to the new capacity being free-riders. However, the marginal user cannot normally be identified. If a train is due to depart at a certain time, then arriving passengers for that train cannot be ordered; if more arrive than there is space, each is contributing equally to the overload and the marginal cost of additional capacity must be shared. The same applies to a congested road, and in the pollution case; since such factors as noise are not privately tradeable the cost of bribery necessary must again be shared, and this can be achieved most satisfactorily institutionally.

We are still left with the question of how to measure the utility loss which requires compensation when there can be no market in the externality in the conventional sense. The usual procedure to overcome this is by establishing a quasi-market, viewing people's behaviour in an attempt to avoid the externality as a proxy for this trading, the most common approach being through property values. The analysis of this relationship has been much discussed recently with reference to the noise problems associated with airports.[30]

There are two immediate problems with a property-value approach. The valuation is only operative if the person moves. The market does not identify a loss to those who stay except in terms of the imputed value of their assets. Secondly, it can only be applied to those with property assets to value – once again the question of distribution is to the fore. Basically, however, we need to consider three groups of people: those who move because of the disbenefit they would suffer from staying, those who were moving anyway but lose from a reduction in asset values, and those who stay but suffer both the reduction in asset values and the continuing disbenefit of the pollution. There are four values which are required to enter on the costs side, the depreciation in asset value (i.e. house prices) (D), removal costs (R), the loss of consumers' surplus caused by being compelled to move, which is judged to be equivalent to the difference between subjective and market values of the vendor's house (S), and the compensation necessary for noise annoyance disbenefit (N).

Then for the three groups, the natural movers suffer only D, and the noise movers $D + R + S$, both of these also suffering N for the time until they move; the stayers suffer N. When it comes to estimation, natural movers will migrate according to regional trends and can thus be eliminated. For the remainder the decision depends on the relative sizes of N and $(D + R + S)$; when N is greater the person moves, when N is smaller he stays. However, N and D are related since overall it is assumed that D will reflect some average level of perceived N. Estimates of D are made from house prices and related to some physical index based on survey methods which reflects N, in the case of noise this being the Noise and Number Index (N.N.I.), a composite number reflecting the average peak loudness of the noise source in decibels and the number of occasions on which it occurs per unit of time. Estimates of S are made from a social survey.

This is, on the surface, a fair enough approach, given the assumptions made. The difficulty is that there is little *a priori* grounding for these. All that can be asserted is that the choice of residence, and the consumer's surplus derived from it will be affected by the environmental pollution; this, in effect, shifts the demand curve for houses and hence causes price depreciation. What can be observed is some index of the degree of pollution, the price change and a certain amount of migration. Beyond this, all assumptions are tenuous. We must ask whether depreciation does reflect median noise annoyance (as assumed by Roskill's research team), whether everyone for whom N exceeds $(D + R + S)$ will in fact move. This last point is related to the question of the accuracy of an individual's assessment of S, and again the asymmetry between what an individual will regard as fair compensation for sufferance, and what he is willing and able to pay to avoid it. A further point of difficulty is the trend in the degree of pollution through time. This is not only one of predicting the future degree, but also of determining trends in public reaction; does, for example, the initial depreciation understate or overstate the ultimate market equilibrium position? And what of those purchasing property in the area? They are assumed neutral in the analysis since they are willing to pay the going price for the property, which implies that they are indifferent to the existing degree of pollution. This is not necessarily so and they could be gaining or losing according to whether they are insensitive to the source of pollution or more sensitive than they believed. It must also be remembered that the general trend is towards increasing environmental pollution, whether this is from noise, waste, fumes, etc; the search for a pollution-free area may thus become more difficult.

The above discussion shows clearly that although it may be correct to suppose that there exists a definite relationship between property values and the actual or expected degree of environmental pollution resulting from a new project, there is a little *a priori* grounding for specifying any particular relationship. Again some basic rule of thumb may have to be adopted, but it is important that the criteria used are made explicit and the problems with the particular one adopted are not ignored.

Traffic Movements. We have concentrated so far on aspects of the recreational facility in terms of of the site itself. If we are to consider the effects of the activity as a whole we must also assess the traffic implications. The external effects of traffic movements in connection with the new facility reflect the degree of interference it will have on other facilities in the area. This interference can arise in two ways. One is the interference with, or even diversion of, traffic from competing facilities. This is to be distinguished from the true substitution effect due to better facilities at the new site or improved accessibility. It is an additional diversion of traffic because of unforeseen circumstances which make the revealed relative accessibility differ from that perceived *ex ante*. Since it amounts to forced diversion the valuation of its cost is likely to be higher. The second aspect is interference with movement to and from non-competing activities. These are worth identifying separately because the valuations of interference with traffic for other purposes are likely to differ considerably, for example in such factors as the valuation of time losses.

The possibility of achieving realistic and meaningful evaluations of this item must be recognised as being low. Nevertheless it is probable that sizeable secondary costs will be falling on existing users of the transport network which should, in principle, be allowed for. There is an important element of feedback to our first consideration of regional planning factors at this stage. It must be determined what the impact of a new facility on the usage of existing or planned infrastructure is to be, and hence that the choice of a particular site, or even the decision to build at all, is not suboptimal to the most efficient usage of that infrastructure. The extent to which attributable costs to infrastructure users can be identified is thus a test of the adequacy of the overall regional planning structure.

An Evaluation Procedure
Having established the main points to be considered in the appraisal of a recreational project, we now have to establish the most satisfactory means of making some empirical estimates for evaluation purposes. What is required is an objective function which reflects those items discussed above which correspond to the community's economic response to the planned facility. In terms of simple economics this is a demand curve, as outlined in the first part of this chapter, but the considerations of the previous pages have shown that it needs to be a more general expression of the implied demand relationship. The way of formulating this relationship, and of deriving empirical estimates, is, in itself, a difficult task. The essential distinction which has to be made in this, as in most other equivalent economic exercises is whether to use an aggregate or disaggregate approach. Do we concentrate on estimating the aggregate level of demand or on the micro-economics of individual consumer behaviour?

Most previous studies, following largely on the work of Clawson, have adopted aggregate approaches.[31]

In the following chapter we shall proceed to develop an economic model of individual recreational behaviour which is shown to be superior in terms of both its theoretical logic and its basis for empirical estimation. However, whilst it is reasonably straightforward to develop user demand models to fairly high levels of sophistication on both theoretical and empirical levels there is always a danger that non-user aspects are ignored in this. For this reason evaluation procedures, in terms of the monetisation of particular benefits, have been largely overlooked in the remainder of this study to avoid the impression that a complete project evaluation has been performed. In the following four chapters we concentrate on the derivation of user demand curves. The wider issues are returned to in Chapters 8 and 9.

4. Consumer Demand for Leisure and Recreation

The discussion of a procedure for evaluating projects in the recreation sector has highlighted the need for a rigorous examination of a theory of individual consumer demand for such facilities. This lies at the heart of this study and in this chapter we shall establish the framework of the analysis; subsequent chapters are concerned with the empirical evidence and testing of this framework.

Two points must be stressed from the outset. Like any economic theory, that presented here is a simplification which abstracts from reality. Its role is not to reproduce exactly both decision processes and the resulting actions, but to gain insights into likely behaviour patterns from a series of simplifying but reasonable assumptions and from these to produce estimates of the resulting actions with a given degree of statistical confidence. Secondly, even a simplified theory of consumer behaviour is likely to produce a model which is too complex for readily available data or easy projection on an objective basis, and hence a second stage of simplification into an operational model will be necessary. The operational model is discussed in detail in the following two chapters but it is, nevertheless, thought worth while to produce the more detailed theoretical model as a first step so that simplifications introduced are made explicit and placed in context of an overall view.

Goods, Activities and Movement
The initial problem is to decide what constitutes the entity for which we wish to estimate the demand. In Chapter 2 various concepts of leisure were outlined; the primary distinction must be that between time and activities. We are not concerned here with the demand for leisure time *per se*; although this is an important subject it is beyond the scope of this study. It is likely that the demand for leisure time is, to a certain extent, derived from that for leisure activities, but for our purposes it is sufficient to regard leisure time available as exogenously determined in the labour market and by such factors as home and workplace location. The important assumption here is that in the short run the amount of

leisure time available is relatively fixed, both in terms of the total time budget and its position in the day.[1]

The Demand for Activities

Time and income can be taken as a 'dual currency' budget constraint on the demand for leisure activities. But activities are not goods of the type on which conventional consumer demand theory is based, and an analysis of the demand for activities cannot be tackled in the same way. Demand theory is essentially a derivation of a theory of value and whether one takes the line of a Walrasian general equilibrium, or the more common Marshallian partial equilibrium, the implication is of the equilibrium solution being determined by exchange in the market place through a balancing of direct utility received from the good or goods in question with a budget constraint. However, a leisure activity is not a tradeable entity in the normal way. A rate of exchange of one activity for another can, it is true, be established for any one individual, but this is only a necessary condition for the conventional approaches. To be sufficient it would appear that inter-personal trade is essential and one cannot exchange a tennis match, or attendance at a football match, or a walk in the country. It is possible though to trade some of the elements of the activity, the racket, the match ticket, the monetary cost of reaching the country, and so forth. The time involved both in the activity itself and in the travel to it can be traded also, usually in the labour market. Thus we see that we have three components – goods, time and travel – which are inputs to the production of an activity. The goods can be exchanged for other goods or money, the time and effort involved for money through work or, for the individual himself, for another activity, and the travel for both its time and goods elements. It would seem, therefore, that production theory, rather than demand theory, may offer a more satisfactory approach to the problem.[2] Once the nature of a production function for the activity has been established the demand for the various inputs can be derived, all of which are tradeable in the conventional way. There are thus three separate but interrelated demand functions, for recreational goods, for travel and for leisure time, this latter giving a feedback into the labour-market determination of the time budget constraint.

The implications of this approach are even wider than our immediate concern of leisure activities since all of a consumer's behaviour can be resolved into an activities structure. The distinguishing features of each activity will be the nature and relative sizes of the inputs. The peculiar feature of the typical leisure activity is that the output is consumed as it is produced, it is thus analogous to the case of service industries although the 'end-product' is even less well defined.

Before formalising the hypothesis concerning leisure activities in more detail it may aid understanding of this approach to give some examples of activities within this framework. First of all, how do we deal with conventional durable goods? All goods as such in this analysis are intermediate goods in the production of the final activity. This accords well with the view of durable goods as investment goods which provide a flow of services, and also with the attributes approach to consumer theory in which goods are not required for their own sake but only for the services which they provide.[3] Hence a refrigerator is the goods input to a food storage service or activity, the use of which will involve the consumer in effectively zero inputs of time and travel. A television, however, is an input to a leisure activity in which the input of viewing time will also be important. In this case we can also observe an interrelationship (complementarity) between the demands for the inputs since if there is a severe time constraint the consumer will not wish to purchase a set which he has insufficient time to view, or at least if his viewing time is limited he may decide to purchase a cheaper set; once the set has been bought, however, there is every incentive to substitute time from other activities into television viewing. A visit to a cinema will involve a goods input in the sense of the purchase of a ticket entitling the holder to enjoy cinema services, the time input spent actually watching films, and additionally a travel input in reaching the cinema. On the other hand, a walk in the country would involve a virtually zero goods input,[4] but a high time and travel input.

A slightly difficult case is that of shopping activities which are essentially intermediate activities, servicing main activities. The goods purchased during shopping are outputs of the shopping activity which serve as inputs to final activities. The demand for shopping will therefore be derived from the demand for goods as inputs to other activities; each goods input implies a certain amount of shopping in terms of time and travel although, of course, shopping is not exclusive to single activities, there being strong externalities between several bundles of goods.[5]

The analysis could also be extended to cover work activities. These involve the same inputs except that the goods input becomes negative since payment is received rather than made. The minimum inputs of goods, which will exist for all activities as a sort of technological constraint will be even more rigid in this case, being institutionally determined. This limits the amount of trading implied between work and other activities but does allow the flexibility of some trading at the margin through non-contractual overtime or the absence in some occupations of established hours of work. In this way the activity system becomes closed with an endogenous income budget constraint which is more realistic than the assumption of a totally exogenous one with no work–leisure substitution possible. The exogenous constraints are then solely those which are beyond the individual's personal control, the total amount of time available and agreements on standard working practices and on the times at which certain facilities will be available.

An Activities Model

The pattern of activities undertaken may thus be represented by a matrix of the following order, each identifiable activity A_1 to A_k involving the input of goods X_1 to X_m, time L, and travel T, which is a composite of a goods element (money cost) and time.[6] Any number of these inputs may take a zero value as long as at least one is non-zero.

$$
\begin{aligned}
A_1 &= f_1(X_{11}, X_{12}, \ldots X_{1m}, L_1, T_1) \\
A_2 &= f_2(X_{21}, X_{22}, \ldots X_{2m}, L_2, T_2) \\
&\;\;\vdots \\
A_k &= f_k(X_{k1}, X_{k2}, \ldots X_{km}, L_k, T_k)
\end{aligned} \tag{1}
$$

This system produces its own internal constraint for total expenditure such that if Y is the amount earned from the work activity, i.e.

$$
Y = p_w L_w \tag{2}
$$

for a given expenditure of work time, L_w and wage rate of p_w per hour. An exogenous element for unearned income, I, can be added, it being reasonable to assume this is independent of other terms in the model. Hence if p_1 to p_m are the prices of goods inputs X_i, and c is the unit cost of travel,[7] then

$$
\sum_i \sum_j p_i X_{ij} + \sum_j c \cdot T_j \leqslant Y + I \tag{3}
$$

If H is the total time available in a day or week or whatever period is chosen for anaysis, then the time constraint can be written

$$
\sum_j L_j + \sum_j T_j = H \tag{4}
$$

The time constraint is an equality because if all activities are specified there can be no time saved over for a later period. The income constraint can be an inequality because of the possibility of saving, although if this is the case there is no reason why this constraint should be as rigid in the other direction as implied, current spending need not be limited to current income. This raises the whole question of the consumer's choice between current and future activities. The simplest solution is to disregard this aspect of the model and make further simplifying assumptions, but it must be recognised that this is taking a purely short-run view of leisure activities.

There is a further problem in the definition of both Y and H in the case of non-occupied persons who have no fixed income-earning hours. Nevertheless, persons such as housewives do tend to have a committed time similar to persons working, but they will also normally have a greater flexibility in timing this commitment. Income is much more difficult when it is being used as a constraint. Use of a household base so that activities are summed over all household members would permit the use of a household income constraint which would make sense in the context of many leisure activities. However, it could not be applied to households with no income-earning member, and would leave additional difficulties with the time constraint which cannot simply be summed to give a total household time constraint. The total amount of time available will remain constant regardless of household size, it is only the economies of scale and externalities between household members which can be regarded as effectively altering this. Difficulties of organising activities may indeed increase with the size of the household because of differing commitments of time, and the effective result may be a decrease in the time budget available.

Finally, we need to stipulate some form of objective function for the solution of the activity system. Use of a production function suggests criteria analogous to output- or profit-maximisation. The problem is not, however, as simple as the production decision facing the individual firm making a single product. The technical relationship between the inputs is not as straightforward; in particular it is not always true that an increase in the use of one factor will be at the expense of another for a given quantity of output. Furthermore, the individual has to take decisions not only on the correct technical combination of factors in the production of each activity, but also exercise his preferences in terms of the most desirable combination of those factors, and indeed of the combination of activities themselves.

The obvious approach is to combine the activity production function, representing the technical possibilities, with a utility function, representing consumer preferences. Becker (1965), for example, specified a utility function of the form:

$$U = U(A_1, \dots A_m) \tag{5}$$

where each A_i had a production function of the form:

$$A_i = f_i(X_i, L_i) \tag{6}$$

X_i and L_i being the goods and time inputs respectively.

Equations (5) and (6) can be combined to give a function of the form

$$U = U(X_1, \dots X_m, L_1, \dots L_m) \tag{7}$$

This collapsing of the two relationships into one means that the activity concept is essentially redundant. In fact in a later development De Serpa (1973) has argued that the concept has tended to obscure the real issues of the time allocation problem. Certainly there has been a tendency to accept this fusing of the production and utility concepts rather too readily, so that whilst maintaining lip service to Becker the utility function has been specified entirely in the form of equation (7). One exception is a formulation by de Donnea (1972) who explicitly partials all the derivatives of the utility function, e.g. $\frac{\partial U}{\partial A_i} \cdot \frac{\partial A_i}{\partial X_i}$, but his formulation is otherwise such as to make this mathematically identical to the straightforward collapsed form $\frac{\partial U}{\partial X_i}$.[8] Evans (1972) has adopted a rather different methodology where the utility function does have an activity-based argument, but the activity is measured in units of time, other inputs being introduced as limiting constraints.

De Serpa (1971) has taken the most different line. In his formulation the activities concept is forsaken for a basic utility function of the form of equation (7), utility being derived not via activities but directly from the consumption of goods and the amount of time spent in consuming them.[9] The technical constraints of the production function are retained in a 'consumption constraint' which specified the minimum input of one factor, e.g. time, necessary to consume the other satisfactorily. An inequality of the form

$$L_i \geqslant a_i X_i \qquad (8)$$

satisfies the need to limit the input substitution possibilities. This approach does depend on the assumption that utility derives from the inputs themselves, rather than from the activity which would not hold, for example, if the implicit production function were not linear homogeneous of degree one, i.e. if increasing returns to scale exist. It is not difficult to think of situations in which the individual's enjoyment of an activity increases at a faster rate than the time devoted to it or the goods used. Even in cases such as book reading or rounds of golf which De Serpa (1971, p. 830) uses to illustrate consumption constraints of the form of equation (8), there is a conflict between a technically possible minimum and a choice variable. Whilst it is preferable to complete at least nine holes of golf or finish a chapter of a book, it is not technically impossible to spend less time.

This problem is most likely to affect the analysis of domestic activities which may be regarded as filling in otherwise useless bits of residual time between primary activities. In total they are a positive contribution to total utility, with a minimum acceptable level of participation, although in terms of the allocation of time through time they are not subject to any binding technical constraints. Hence we must recognise the existence of both technical constraints and choice constraints operating simultaneously.

The Travel Input

If we now widen the analysis to include the travel element many of the points made above are compounded. If the travel element can enter into the utility function, either directly or through the activity production function, this will imply both substitution possibilities between goods and the money cost component of travel, and activity time and the time component of travel. Furthermore, it will involve implications as to the direct derivation of utility or disutility from the activity. With this in mind we must consider the travel component in more detail.

In the formulation of equation (1) a simple single-equation production function for each activity was assumed which reflects the goods, time and space components. Following the pattern of equation (8) a technical constraint, specifying the minimum travel input to permit an activity to take place can be introduced. For example,

$$T_i \geqslant b_i X_i \tag{9}$$

would reflect the travel input relative to the necessary goods input, which would depend on the spatial distribution of sites for the activity. However, it is clearly not as simple as this implies. For many activities, only that part of the goods input which is fixed in space should enter. For example, once purchased, a set of golf clubs has no travel requirement but the course fee for a given round of golf does. Thus equation (9) requires recasting in terms of a vector of goods inputs, each with its own travel requirements.

Nor is it only the goods inputs which have a travel requirement. Evans (1972) has suggested a relationship between travel time and activity time, that as activity time increases so will the travel time considered feasible. This formulation again raises the problem of involving preferences instead of being a purely technical relationship.

More than this, the nature of travel relative to the activity will differ between activities. In many it is a disutility, a part to be minimised, and which arises not through choice but because of a spatially dispersed economy.[10] In other activities, however, travel is an essential and intrinsic part of the activity; the reluctance of Sunday motorists to leave their cars testifies to this. One further aspect of travel is that a single travel input can be used as a common input to a number of separate activities. The activity system as set up in equation (1) would thus require a large number of activity linking constraints to reflect this.

These observations suggest a logical development of the system. Firstly, a classification of activities according to the nature of their travel input. For those where it is part of the activity proper, pleasure travel, the input is directly into the activity and travel time is indistinguishable from other time spent in the activity. For other activities where travel is only an enabling input, the travel component becomes an intermediate activity involving 'goods' (i.e. travel cost) and time inputs. One intermediate activity can service several final activities, and objectively the consumer's preference is to minimise the amount of resources, money and time expended on these activities. A series of technical constraints can express the intermediate activity requirements of each primary activity.

The Value of Time
It is not proposed to develop the theory of time valuation as such since it lies outside the primary purpose of this study. It is nonetheless of crucial importance in two respects. Firstly, consideration of the literature on time valuation does enable us to highlight many of the points developed in a more general context in the preceding section, since the behavioural implications are more clearly demonstrated at the margin. Secondly, although this study is not designed to produce empirical estimates of any monetary values of time, such valuations will be important in any appraisal exercise of investment projects in the sector.

There are two rather separate problems which must be considered. The theoretical question is to ask in what sense the concept of a value of time is meaningful and moreover what relevance can be attached to relationships derived from time-explicit activity models of the type discussed above. If such a concept does exist theoretically, it must, secondly, be considered whether empirical derivation is possible and, possibly of greater importance, whether observed trade-offs between time and money accord with the theoretical concept.

The Concept of Valuing Time
In its simplest form the 'value' of time is taken to be its implicit price. Hence leisure time is valued at its opportunity cost which, at the margin, is the income foregone. This is essentially a labour-market analysis which derives from the early work of Robbins (1930), but is found later in the empirical work of Mincer (1962 and 1963). Early studies of time valuation in the travel context carried forward this opportunity-cost concept with the additional assumption that such factors as imperfect labour markets and standard working weeks, which limit the choice at the margin, would lead to the wage rate being a biased estimate of the true opportunity cost.[11] Subsequent develop-

ments, both in the general theory of time allocation,[12] and the specific case of travel-time valuation,[13] have shown that this bias is not just the result of imperfections, but is the expected result of a model of consumer choice.

The specific results are highly dependent on the exact formulation of the model. For simplicity of exposition, no attempt has been made to translate these alternatives into the form of the model discussed in the previous section. Essentially these models all involve the maximisation of a conventional neoclassical utility function which has time explicitly included as an argument, as well as goods. The utility function is assumed to have the usual properties of convexity and differentiability, and is maximised subject to constraints of time and income. Hence in a simple case the objective is to maximise

$$U = U(X_i, L_i) \tag{10}$$

subject to the two constraints

$$Y = \sum_i p_i X_i \tag{11}$$

$$L = \sum_i L_i \tag{12}$$

By the use of the technique of Lagrangean multipliers the following first-order conditions for a maximum can be derived:[14]

$$\frac{\partial U}{\partial X_i} = \lambda p_i \tag{13}$$

$$\frac{\partial U}{\partial L_i} = \mu \tag{14}$$

The multipliers λ and μ can be interpreted as the marginal utility of money and time respectively, and the ratio μ/λ, the marginal rate of substitution of time for money, is thus an implied value of time. Johnson (1966) and Oort (1969) both split time into work and non-work components, thus obtaining marginal utilities of work time and non-work time, the income constraint thus being a function of work time and the wage rate. Thus we have

$$U = U(X_i, L_i, W) \tag{15}$$

where L_i refers to non-work activities and W to work.

The constraints to the maximisation of this utility function can be written as

$$p_w W = \sum_i p_i X_i \tag{16}$$

$$H = \sum_i L_i + W \tag{17}$$

Maximisation of (15) subject to (16) and (17) yields the following first-order conditions:

$$\frac{\partial U}{\partial X_i} = \lambda p_i \tag{18}$$

$$\frac{\partial U}{\partial L_i} = \mu \tag{19}$$

$$\frac{\partial U}{\partial W} = \mu - \lambda p_w \tag{20}$$

Substitution gives

$$\frac{\partial U}{\partial L_i} = \frac{\partial U}{\partial W} + \lambda p_w \tag{21}$$

which can be interpreted as the marginal utility of non-work time being less than the marginal utility of the income foregone (λp_w, where λ is the marginal utility of money) by the implicit marginal disutility of the work time which would be required to earn it $\left(\frac{\partial U}{\partial W} \text{ being assumed negative} \right)$. Rearranging the equation can yield alternative ways of expressing this relationship.[15]

Dividing through equation (21) by λ yields an expression for the marginal rate of substitution of time for money:

$$\frac{\partial U}{\partial L_i} \cdot \frac{1}{\lambda} = p_w + \frac{\partial U}{\partial W} \cdot \frac{1}{\lambda} \tag{22}$$

Hence the value of time is shown to be less than the wage rate by the marginal rate of substitution between work and money.[16]

We have thus shown that an alternative specification of the utility function, which frees it from the rather unconvincing assumption that the marginal utilities of leisure and work are 'mirror images of each other',[17] leads to the conclusion that the valuation of leisure time will always differ from the wage rate, not just as a result of imperfections in the market.[18] However, it is not clear that this yields a meaningful concept of the value of time. *A priori* we should expect that subjective valuation of time would differ between activities, yet its marginal utility will always be μ for all i in this model. Further than this, it leads to rather tortuous justifications for the meaning of the total differential with respect to time, the marginal utility of time in the aggregate.

Oort (1969, p. 281) shows that the total differential $\dfrac{dU}{dH}$ is equal to the

partial with respect to any i, $\dfrac{\partial U}{\partial L_i}$. He argues that on this basis the

individual's valuation of an exogenous change in circumstances, such as the opening of a new facility closer to his home, or the reduction in travelling times as a result of transport improvements, is identical to his valuation of a 'God-given increase of the day from 24 to 25 hours'. This is a very unsatisfactory conclusion, it leaves the marginal valuation of time the same in any use, and equal to a quantity with no operational meaning.

Watson (1971) follows the suggestion of Evans (1972) that μ/λ refers to the marginal valuation of 'time in general', which is associated with the 'value of life'. This leads them to a rather fruitless definition of 'pure leisure time', which is spent doing 'absolutely nothing'. This is meaningless, both in any *a priori* sense, and in the context of the model which specifically adds up the time spent in activities (doing something) to equal the total time available. Watson comes to the rather unsatisfactory conclusion that μ 'merely reflects that a time constraint is in operation' and that the individual will use this as a cut-off point, only undertaking activities which have a marginal utility greater than μ, equating the ratio of this excess utility to the cost of the activity at the margin.

To overcome this problem what has to be recognised is that μ, like λ, is the marginal utility attached to an increase in the amount of a scarce resource, independently of its allocation. Like the marginal utility of money, the marginal utility of time (as a resource) does not require an operational significance, it is a shadow variable implicit in behaviour. If we require a valuation of time spent on any particular activity we require an additional specification of the production 'technology' of the activity in question, i.e. an explicit reference to the potential value of time in that activity.

De Serpa's suggestion (1971) that a simple inequality, the time consumption constraint, should be introduced to the model, reflecting the minimum possible amount of time necessary for the consumption of a unit of a particular X_i overcomes this difficulty. With the addition of the constraint

$$L_i \geqslant a_i X_i \tag{23}$$

maximisation of equation (10) yields the following first-order conditions in place of equations (13) and (14),[19]

$$\frac{\partial U}{\partial X_i} = \lambda p_i + K_i a_i \tag{24}$$

$$\frac{\partial U}{\partial L_i} = \mu - K_i \tag{25}$$

and the additional condition

$$K_i(L_i - a_i X_i) = 0 \tag{26}$$

$$\text{i.e.} \quad K_i = 0 \text{ or } L_i = a_i X_i$$

This last condition, equation (26), is interesting because if the time consumption constraint is not binding, i.e. $L_i > a_i X_i$, then K_i must equal zero, and if K_i is not zero the constraint must be binding, the minimum possible time being spent on the activity.[20] To interpret the implications of this analysis, consider equation (25) which represents the marginal utility of time in activity i. Dividing throughout by λ to express this in monetary terms gives

$$\frac{\partial U}{\partial L_i} \cdot \frac{1}{\lambda} = \frac{\mu}{\lambda} - \frac{K_i}{\lambda} \tag{27}$$

Hence the marginal value of time in activity i differs from the marginal resource value of time, μ/λ, by an amount determined by the activity specific parameter K_i. Only in the case where $K_i = 0$ will the two be equal, and this event will normally arise when the time consumption constraint does not bind, i.e. the individual is choosing to allocate more time than necessary to the activity.

To appreciate the significance of this more fully, it is useful to rearrange equation (27) as

$$\frac{K_i}{\lambda} = \frac{\mu}{\lambda} - \frac{\partial U}{\partial L_i} \cdot \frac{1}{\lambda} \tag{28}$$

K_i can be interpreted as the marginal utility of saving time from the ith activity since it is a Lagrangean multiplier, just like λ and μ, and hence measures the change in the objective function, U, resulting from a marginal relaxation of constraint (23). K_i/λ is thus the value of saving time from i, which is the difference between the resource value, μ/λ, and the value in the consumption of i.

The main advantage of this formulation is that it yields an objective and empirical value of time – people can be observed saving time, and trading time for money. This meets the objections raised against the earlier evaluation exercises which in fact were measuring time savings but referred to these as the μ/λ element, the resource opportunity cost. This aspect of time valuation has been criticised by Tipping (1968) with regard to earlier studies. There was, he maintains, a confusion between activities where time may be perceived as having a positive utility 'the time which is spent in enjoying the consumption of goods and services' and those where people would gain positive utility from a reduction in the time spent. The classification of activities according to $K_i = 0$ or $K_i > 0$ enables this distinction to be made. It is likely that, with the exception of pleasure travel, most travelling and such activities as shopping will fall into the latter category and hence display positive value of time saving. Thus we have an objective criterion for the classification of primary and intermediate activities for the model of the previous section.

De Donnea (1972) has reached essentially the same conclusion from a rather different basic model which includes a utility function incorporating activities, and a 'satisfaction' function of time spent in them, as the arguments. Activities have a production function depending on goods and time. Hence time appears twice, once as a technological input and the other time in a form which reflects how enjoyable or not the spending of the time is. A result similar to equation (28) is derived, which de Donnea interprets as showing that the marginal value of time as an input to the production of an activity is equal to the marginal value of time (μ/λ) less 'the marginal value of the (dis)satisfaction produced by the circumstances under which time is spent'.[21]

Travel Time in the Economic Model
Having shown the method by which a meaningful and acceptable concept of time valuation can be derived, one further extension of the models can be considered, the separate identification of travel time within such a model. The main problem of introducing travel time explicitly as a separate argument in the utility function is the implication that utility is directly derived from the time spent travelling, or conversely that it always yields disutility. De Donnea (1972) is forced into a number of unsatisfactory assumptions about the behaviour of total utility with respect to an increase in travel, essentially that the quality of the activity will increase as distance is increased. The model will also yield positive values of travel time. Some alternative approaches have been investigated by Mansfield and Watson (1971) particularly with regard to the more general problem of what the utility formulation implies about the possibility of trading off, not just time between the activity and the travel, but both of these with the goods in question.

Both a straightforward utility approach and an activities approach have problems. The former tends to allow the possibility of too much substitution between time, goods and travel, whilst the latter runs into the problem of too-fixed production relationships. De Serpa (1973, pp. 406–7) has rightly pointed out that there is a danger that the model establishes only the technical alternatives without any reference to consumer preferences.

The general model of consumer behaviour developed by Evans (1972, pp. 14–16) is slightly different in its concentration entirely on activities, defined solely in time units, which form the argument to the utility function. The goods or income-earning elements in each activity then form a constraint, as does total time and an activity linking constraint, which, for example, links travel activities to their associated activities. This does sidestep some of the above issues quite neatly, but leaves a utility function dependent only on the time spent in activities. This leaves out the possibility of the same activity having different quantities or qualities of goods inputs, independently of the time spent, which would normally be expected to influence the production function.

This approach through the value of time essentially confirms the broad outlines of the framework presented in the first part of this chapter, a compromise solution between a pure utility and a pure activity production function approach.

Estimating Values of Time
The empirical question of time values has already been introduced. The main point to be emphasised is that traders are valuing time savings (K_i/λ) rather than the marginal value of time as such (μ/λ), and hence the ratio of time and cost coefficients, which is traditionally used[22] is strictly not a value of time as such, as often interpreted. A further point which emerges is that the revealed value of time savings does differ between modes which tends to lend support to the de Donnea (1972 and 1973) thesis of incorporating the circumstances under which the time is spent, i.e. comfort etc. However, some recent work by Collings (1974) has suggested that this could arise from a specification error in the formulation of the relative time and cost variables, particularly if a ratio form is used.

The main difficulty with trader analyses is that they depend only on the small subset of observed traders. Factors other than time and cost are usually suggested as explanation for these choices, as by de Donnea, but even more difficult are the apparently irrational behavers who expend more of both resources.[23] This concentration on the trading subset can lead to biased valuations of possible time savings by those not in a position to trade. De Serpa (1971) has suggested a possible way of obtaining a valuation for all groups by use of the demand function for travel implicit in the formulation of the utility model. Demand is a function of the value of time savings, money price and income (from the equilibrium conditions for utility-maximisation) and hence by rearrangement the value of time savings can be expressed as a function of the time and price elasticities, adjusted by the rate of change of the value of time savings with respect to both money price and income.

A parallel approach to valuation via the demand function rather than through a choice model was developed by Gronau (1970) using the original Becker formulation. This defines price, in a straightforward price–income determined demand relationship, as a composite of money and time prices. The time–price element devolves to finding a value of k in the term $kw_i T_j$, where w_i is the wage rate of the ith group and T_j is the travel time to the jth destination, which maximises the overall fit of the demand function to the data. The 'value of time' term is thus kw_i which is equivalent to the ratio of the time to the price elasticities. This formulation thus omits the additional adjustment of the time price with respect to money price and income implicit in the utility-derived demand curve. This assumption of the existence of k does contradict the empirical finding of choice studies that the value of time savings as a proportion of the wage rate does vary with income.[24]

The Demand for Travel – An Economic Model

The discussion in this chapter has shown the importance of the travel element in consumer behaviour in the recreation sector. Those activities which involve movement are also, in general, those involving large outlays of finance in the provision of recreational facilities, and they are those which are likely to have the greatest associated externalities. Whilst other social scientists may thus be more interested in the activities *per se*, the economist's overriding concern is with the use and allocation of resources. For this reason we are justified in concentrating on the movement aspects of leisure for the remainder of this study. Moreover, since it is travel activities which are likely to involve the most binding time constraints – and hence the ability to provide the intermediate activity, travel, will be a major constraint on the consumer's activity pattern – consideration of the travel for leisure and recreation provides an effective means of analysing the overall demand for leisure and recreation activities. From an empirical point of view it may often be easier to measure movement than the revealed demand for an activity *per se*.[25]

A relationship describing the demand for any good which appears in a consumer's utility function can be derived from the equilibrium conditions for a utility maximum. This will express demand as a function of those other variables appearing in the constraints to utility. In the activity model discussed in this chapter demand for an activity will be a function of income, time, and both own and relative prices for goods and time.[26]

For any activity in the marketable recreation sector there will be one commodity (X_{ki}) in the activity production relationship which represents the site demand, for example an entry fee. Solving the demand function for this commodity, which will be exclusive to the kth activity, will yield the potential demand for that activity. The intermediate travel activity necessary to satisfy this potential demand will be defined by the relative locations of available destinations. The potential demand for movement is translated into an actual demand for travel by attempting to maximise the effective demand for the activity subject to the resource and consumption constraints involved in the travel activity. Demand for travel will thus be a function of the same variables as for any activity, with the added condition that the consumption constraint will be binding.

Whilst this two-stage model for each activity has great advantages over the single-equation formulation, it will be clear that the normal effective demand curve for an activity implied by it is similar. In general terms the demand is a function of available resources, own and relative prices, and own and relative spatial supply prices.

The solution is not, however, as simple as this suggests since the intermediate activity cannot be treated as the homogeneous entity the theory implies. The presence of different modes of transport with differing characteristics, and of different routes within each mode, serving the same ultimate destination, are the main sources of heterogeneity. These differing characteristics will also lead to differing perceptions of movement costs, and hence spatial supply prices, between different consumers. For example, there will be very different perceptions of supply price by those with a car available and by those relying on public transport. This will not only affect the absolute level of spatial supply prices but also, given the differing levels of public transport service to different destinations, the relative costs of reaching alternative destinations, and hence the distribution of trip making.

Considerations of this type suggest that it may be extremely difficult to derive any empirically meaningful intermediate travel activity in terms of actual costs and times. Consistency may require the use of more general aggregate indices, such as distance, to obtain objective measures. Any specific mode determined measure is liable to be influenced by the subjective preferences of the consumer.

The demand for travel has thus been shown to be only a theoretical concept, implicit in consumer behaviour, but not readily identifiable. What then of the demand for transport, i.e. the demand curve faced by transport operators, or for road space? The abstract theoretical model suggests that this is at a second stage of derivation, i.e. derived from the demand for movement, which is itself an intermediate activity. Once the consumer has perceived the travel necessary to satisfy the demand for activities, he then translates this into a demand for each mode of transport, depending upon the relative prices, money and time.

However, we have seen that these transport characteristics are those actually perceived as travel characteristics so that this splitting of the decision process is not perceived by the consumer. This derived demand thus includes an important feedback to the primary demand. If this is so, there is an additional problem of possible non-identification of the demand relationship. This arises because at the individual-mode level there can be zero supply to certain consumers which will have a direct bearing on the possible level of demand, potential demand at zero supply (infinite price) being undefinable.

This discussion leads to the conclusion that the demand for each individual mode will require separate estimation rather than as a derived demand from that for travel in aggregate. The separate demand models will, however, require careful construction to retain as much as possible of the basic constraints discussed in this chapter.

In the remainder of this chapter we shall assess previous approaches to the construction of recreation demand models in the light of the above discussion.

Approaches to the Demand Model

The Clawson Method

The method of forecasting suggested by Clawson (1959) and further developed by Clawson and Knetsch (1966) concentrates on the travel-cost component of recreation. A basic distinction is made between the demand for the recreation resource (i.e. the site for the activity in question) and that for the whole experience including travel to and from the site and any other utility generating aspects of the activity such as anticipation and recollection. What is actually observed from data on site visiting or travel movements is the revealed demand for the whole experience.

The reason for concentrating on travel costs is that these provide the only source of variation in supply price in a cross-sectional study, the cost of the resource is constant but that of the whole experience is uniquely determined for each individual by his location relative to the site. Hence an initial demand curve can be derived from the distance decay function relating number of visits to distance from the site. Translation of distance into monetary terms by the use of standard vehicle operating costs data or fares and standard values of time provides the normal price–quantity relationship.

For most practical purposes such as project evaluation, what is actually required is the demand function for the resource rather than for the whole experience. This final demand curve is derived from the latter by imputing the demand response to variations in travel costs to variations in the direct money costs of the facility, admission charges, parking charges, etc. If the existing facility charge is zero then the demand for the resource at a zero price is the sum of the demands from each travel cost zone ($QE = OA + OB + OC$ in Figure 4.1). The demand at any non-zero price can then be estimated from the experience demand curve by adding this price to the travel cost and observing the demand at that total cost (e.g. $QD = OA + OB$).[27]

The Clawson method has the great advantage of simplicity and this has led to its fairly widespread use as the technique for estimating recreation demand.[28] The assumptions of the approach are, however, very suspect on a number of grounds and whilst previous authors have expressed reservations the ease of use has been felt to outweigh any disadvantages. Here we argue that the criticisms strongly outweigh any advantages, and the method will produce inaccurate and possibly misleading results.[29]

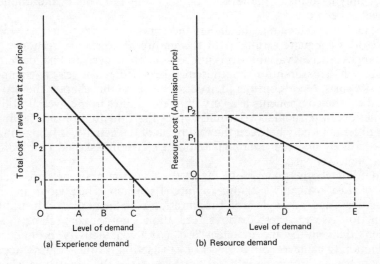

FIG. 4.1

The first drawback is the partial approach of the method, considering only a single site in isolation. This is particularly difficult where the method is being used to predict the use of a new site from data for a comparable existing site. Whilst diversion effects can be allowed for, no account is taken of the effect of the lower aggregate supply price of recreation in an area resulting from the increase in supply, and hence the generation of new demand may be underestimated. In other words the demand curve does not allow adequately for the income effect of new developments, particularly in a situation where demand may be frustrated by lack of supply. The only attempt to allow for complementarities between sites is that by Mansfield (1971b) who used an intervening-opportunities approach but only in the special case of adjacent sites.

The second problem is in the translation from the initial experience demand to the final resource demand. There are two stages to this: firstly the monetising of the distance decay relationship and secondly the assumption that the response to site charges will be the same as that to travel costs. The monetising is conventionally achieved, as mentioned above, by the use of extraneous information. The problem here is that the important variable is consumers' perception of costs rather than engineering data.[30] Implicit in the distance decay function is the response to perceived changes in monetary and time costs. Common (1973) has demonstrated clearly the errors this can give rise to, not only in terms of the level of demand but in terms of the implied level of benefits.

Having obtained a realistic demand curve for the experience, which provides adequate estimates of the nature of consumer response to changes in access variables, it is not reasonable to derive a final demand curve on the assumption that those price elasticities also refer to changes in site costs. As we considered in detail earlier in this chapter the travel and on-site components are very different entities in the overall utility function. In particular we would expect the valuation of time savings to differ markedly between the two parts of the activity, it being much more likely that the time consumption constraint should be binding on the travel part.

Ultimately the main problems of the Clawson approach are those associated with any attempt to model consumer behaviour in the aggregate under a single broad assumption as to the nature of the utility function. As we suggested above, recreation is not the same thing to all men – different people in effect use a different activity production function to achieve similar levels of satisfaction. In this context many may regard travel as an integral positive part of the experience whilst others treat it as an undesirable necessity. In the terminology used above, it may be either part of the primary activity or a secondary, intermediate activity occasioned by demand for the former. The Clawson approach masks these important differences which we shall need to highlight during the remainder of this study.

An Econometric Approach
One attempt to model recreation demand in a conventional econometric way through an equilibrium model is that by Cicchetti, Seneca

and Davidson (1969). Their primary concern was that most demand forecasting ignored supply and could not use price variation because of the availability only of cross-sectional data. In particular this concentrated only on the response to changes in socio-economic factors and consequently limited the range of possible policy alternatives which could be assessed by the model.

The solution proposed was the introduction of a supply of recreation to the consumer function with a lag structure to make the system recursive and eliminate any identification problem. Implicit in the demand function is an information and learning concept, the lag structure making demand in period, t, D_t, a function of the supply price in period $t-1$. Supply price can be represented partly by location or accessibility (e.g. distance d_{t-1}) and partly by facility characteristics of size and quality (q_{t-1}). Such a demand curve can be formulated as:

$$D_t = f_0(d_{t-1}, q_{t-1}, Z_t) \tag{29}$$

where Z_t refers to current socio-economic status.

The supply function for period t is then written as

$$S_t = g_0(d_t, q_t) \tag{30}$$

The market clearing price for period t, P_t can then be expressed as

$$P_t = h(d_t, q_t) \tag{31}$$

where for equilibrium

$$P_t = P_t^D = P_t^S \tag{32}$$

where P_t^D and P_t^S are the demand and supply prices respectively.

From (29) it can be seen that

$$D_{t+1} = f_1(P_t^D, Z_{t+1}) \tag{33}$$

and

$$S_t = g_1(P_t^S) \tag{34}$$

Rewriting these equations with price as the subject and equating for equilibrium permits derivation of a reduced-form equation for demand.

Cicchetti *et al.* estimated the reduced-form equation using a two-step analysis to determine initially the probability of a given individual participating in an activity and then secondly the degree of participation.

The main contribution of this approach is its explicit recognition of the supply characteristics as an influence on revealed demand. The method as applied in the study in question is still rather crude in its means of measuring such factors and it has concentrated on outdoor activities using specific sites which are easily identifiable and usually have no close substitutes. A detailed discussion on ways of measuring the supply-price factors is deferred until Chapter 6.

Nevertheless we are still left with an inadequate recognition of the distinction between site and experience demands and a failure to allow explicitly for variations in the activity production function.

Conclusion

In the course of this chapter, we have outlined various alternative ways of approaching consumer demand for recreation. In the first part a theory of consumer behaviour in terms of activities and time allocation has been established together with the implications this has for ascribing monetary valuations to time savings. The rationale for this approach has been that recreation is characterised and distinguished from many other activities by the need for the consumer to use large inputs of time and travel relative to that of money in participating. It has been shown that a key to the understanding of overall demand for recreation is in its spatial content, through the demand for travel.

Previous approaches to recreational modelling in the context of economic appraisal have been assessed in the light of these basic guidelines.

The following two chapters extend the discussion, with a view to formulating empirically testable models. The analysis is divided so that we firstly discuss activities in general, investigating the factors influencing participation and the degrees of interrelatedness between activities, and secondly the impact of supply-price variations on mobility.

We must recognise from the outset, however, that many of the requirements for a model laid down in the above analysis cannot be met at this stage. Nevertheless they remain as explicit limitations of the results which have been obtained.

5. The Determinants of Recreational Activity Patterns

Before considering more detailed forecasting models for the movement aspects of leisure and recreational activities, it will be helpful to look at some broader determinants of activity patterns. In order that we may both understand the underlying structure of demand and interpret these results in a more relevant light, it is useful to develop some simple models of consumer preference with regard to the activities themselves.

The purpose of the analysis of this chapter is fourfold. Firstly, we shall consider a simple model of activities subject to income and time constraints to identify the main determinants of variations in activity patterns. Secondly, we must consider the split, and possible differences between domestic and external activities. Thirdly, any differences between activities with differing degrees of commitment can be assessed. Fourthly, but ultimately of considerable importance for the analysis, some assessment of substitutability and complementarity between different activities will be necessary.

A Model of Recreation Activity

The Data
There were no readily available data from a large-scale survey which included the detailed information required on activity patterns as well as the necessary details of the provision of recreational and other services. Detailed time budget data would have permitted a more thorough examination of the activity patterns *per se*, but at a much greater cost in view of the complexity of such data, and to the exclusion of factors not normally considered within studies of time budgeting. It was necessary to undertake a small survey as part of a detailed study of the relationships between recreational movements and the recreational infrastructure in a single urban area. The details of this exercise are reported in Chapter 8, but it is useful to present the general findings on activity patterns which emerged at this stage, although it must be

stressed at the outset that the activities model was not the main purpose for which the survey was designed. Adequate testing of an activities model of the type discussed in the previous chapter would require a much larger-scale data collection exercise.

Owing to limited resources[1] the survey undertaken was on a small scale. A postal distribution and return method was used which is subject to considerable loss of response and error. Whilst the method proved to be not entirely satisfactory it did yield a usable response from 858 individuals in 436 households in Oxford.[2] Within its limited objectives the survey did achieve reasonable results and provided useful insights into behaviour and the variables influencing decisions. The data would not support aggregation or acceptable forecasting exercises.

Model Structure

It is not our purpose to produce a complete model of the activity system assessing which influences determine levels of which activity. Many of these influences will be outside the sphere of the economist and certainly not amenable to deterministic modelling.[3] In any case our ultimate objective is not a detailed model of the determinants of leisure activities but of movement for leisure and the demands for particular recreation facilities. For this reason the analysis has been restricted to participation in terms of frequencies rather than the intensity of participation in terms of time spent. The latter is of interest from the point of view of time budgeting but of rather less relevance to this study where we are concerned with the potential aggregate demands placed on transport networks and recreation sites. For organised recreation the time spent is usually technologically or institutionally determined although it should be recognised that the length of stay will have important effects on the pressure of demand on natural-resource-based facilities. What is required from this particular analysis is an understanding of the relationships and interrelationships involved, and the relative importance of different possible explanatory variables so that the basic potential demand influences can be identified from the transport or site-based influences and eliminated from the analysis.

Any attempt to build a deterministic model will have to face the difficulties expressed in Chapter 4 of activities which do not explicitly enter any objective function of the individual and yet collectively can influence the perceived total level of satisfaction. A first stage is thus a classification of activities.

In Chapter 2 we referred to the possible distinctions between work and leisure, non-active and active leisure, committed time and free time as a possible hierarchy of classifications. Within the short run any deterministic model can only cope with the final category of activities, where the individual is free to allocate resources, money and time, between competing ends according to the sort of criteria discussed in Chapter 4. For many purposes it will, however, be desirable to investigate the factors which lead to varying commitments of otherwise free time to the category of committed activities. The influencing factors can be divided into three broad groups – economic status, family structure and social status.

Chapter 4 has discussed a theoretical economic model in detail, from which we have seen that both money and time budgets will be important. We would therefore expect both income and the amount of non-work time available to be important determinants of activity patterns. There may be some definitional problems here, however. In particular it will be necessary to decide whether total household income or individual income is the relevant determinant of individual behaviour patterns. For non-working household members the former may be the more appropriate, but for income earners the latter is likely to play an important role.

Even greater difficulties will occur with the time availability concept. Non-working persons do, of course, have certain amounts of highly committed time, for example full-time housewives and working wives will have highly committed parts of non-working time. Nevertheless, despite the degree of commitment, there is a greater freedom in scheduling and reallocating committed leisure time than for that committed to an income-earning activity. Secondly, but just as great a problem, is the household aggregation question with respect to time. Direct summation over all household members is obviously meaningless, but on the other hand a larger family will generate economies of scale in the use of time. In particular, savings may occur in time allocated to committed activities such as housework and shopping which may increase the free time available. However, the more people with committed time the more difficult the scheduling of family activities may become. The staggering of working hours and, in particular, night-shift working illustrate this problem well. Any sort of deterministic modelling of such a system thus becomes a highly complex programming problem.

The solution adopted here has been to retain the individual's time commitment as a basic variable in influencing individual leisure patterns, but also observe closely the influence of household size on that pattern. This leads us directly to the question of family structure which will, in practice, be interrelated with effective time availability.

Evidence from an international study of time budgets (Szalai, 1972) shows that employed women have, on average between 10 and 40 per cent less free time than employed men, and up to 76 per cent less free time than non-employed women. Women, both working and not working, have up to 40 per cent less free time than men on Sundays.

Most of the difference between men and women is made up by housework.

There may be a more basic factor influencing leisure patterns however, the reason for which married women commit their time to income-earning activities. Several studies have investigated this point[4] and although these tend to agree that the overwhelming reason is financial, there is no concensus as to what this means. The main alternatives, all with rather different implications for leisure are the aim for financial independence; to raise the gross income of the household with a view to raising its material or social circumstances; or out of sheer necessity to maintain a satisfactory income level. The study by the Government Social Survey (Hunt, 1968) found that for manual worker groups those families with working wives had both an income and a standard of living above that of the groups as a whole (i.e. the second alternative), whilst in non-manual groups those with a working wife had, on average, a slightly below-average standard of living (the third alternative).

Within a particular economic and family structure, stage in the family life-cycle and the ages of individual family members will be of great importance. These will affect both the amount of time which will be available and the way it is likely to be used. The main contrasts in the degree of home-centredness of activities will be between young and old,[5] but variations are found right through the age range.[6]

Much more information is available about the influence of social factors external to the family on leisure and recreational patterns. The adequacy of the traditional classification in terms of social class has been questioned if the objective is to group individuals of similar social behaviour. Wilensky (1960) has put forward the three propositions, that social behaviour depends on 'class', that advancing industrialisation and urbanism render traditional class distinctions inadequate discriminators of life styles and social integration in the 'growing middle mass', and thirdly that specific variations in environment, the work situation and the individual's experiences of mobility, education, etc. will lead to important differences in life style.

The work place, in terms of type of job and type of industry, will have important influences on leisure patterns. Considerable research has been carried out by sociologists on different groups and has identified, for example, the strong work motivations in the leisure patterns of professional and executive groups which can affect recreation, social activities and community activities (politics, social work, etc.).[7] Occupational milieu is therefore of just as great importance as economic status or class loosely defined.

Personal mobility and involvement in activities, particularly those of a social nature, private (visiting or entertaining) or public (politics, trade unions, community work) will also depend on two further social factors. The degree of integration into a community is most likely to depend on the extended family structure, the network of relations in an area.[8] Social mobility may also depend on actual mobility in a residential context, persons who move tend to be those of higher educational groups but also have less time to be absorbed into a community structure.[9] This type of mobility, characterised in the aggregate by residential turnover and at an individual level by length of residence in an area, may thus have influence in more than one direction.

A Basic Deterministic Model

Having thus discussed the nature of the factors which are likely to influence activity patterns we can formulate a simple deterministic model. The individual's activity pattern will depend on economic status, family structure and social and community status. As a first attempt a linear multiple-regression model will be used to estimate this structure.

The aim of this model is essentially to identify the most important single factors, those explaining the largest part of the variance in activity patterns. Since a single-variable definition of activity patterns is not possible a series of representative activities was selected, and the model estimated for the level of involvement, in terms of occasions per week, in each of these. Table 5.1 gives details of the list of activities and Table 5.2 details the explanatory variables.

TABLE 5.1 Levels of participation in selected activities

Variable	Description	Mean value	Variance
Y_1	Membership of public social organisation (clubs, etc.)	0.44	0.25
Y_2	Number of visits per week to public social organisation	0.38	0.45
Y_3	Enrolment on part-time educational course	0.07	0.07
Y_4	Number of visits per week to cinema/ theatre	0.20	0.23
Y_5	Domestic entertaining during week	0.54	0.25
Y_6	Number of personal social visits per week	0.85	0.65
Y_7	Number of eating/drinking trips per week	0.47	0.53
Y_8	Number of pleasure trips per week	0.30	0.30

NOTES Variables Y_1, Y_3 and Y_5 refer to proportions of the sample (being binary-valued) and thus can be interpreted as probabilities of undertaking the activity in question. The remaining variables are average frequencies of participation over the whole sample.

SOURCE Oxford Survey data; Vickerman (1972b).

TABLE 5.2   Explanatory variables of activity patterns

Variable	Description	Units	Mean	Variance
X_1	Employment status – Full-time employed	Dummy	0.49	0.25
X_2	Employment status – Part-time employed	Dummy	0.12	0.11
X_3	Employment status – Full-time Student	Dummy	0.07	0.06
X_4	Weekly gross income	£	15.57	268.42
X_5	Daily normal hours worked (incl. overtime)	Hours	5.22	21.00
X_6	Overtime hours worked	Hours	0.24	1.04
X_7	Nightshift worked	Dummy	0.04	0.04
X_8	Days free from work	Days	3.90	7.27
X_9	Travel time to and from work	Minutes	23.45	759.52
X_{10}	Occupational S.E.G. – Professional and managerial	Dummy	0.04	0.04
X_{11}	Occupational S.E.G. – Non-manual	Dummy	0.28	0.20
X_{12}	Occupational S.E.G. – Supervisory and skilled manual	Dummy	0.14	0.12
X_{13}	Industry group – Vehicles	Dummy	0.11	0.09
X_{14}	Industry group – Printing and publishing	Dummy	0.03	0.03
X_{15}	Industry group – Distribution	Dummy	0.05	0.04
X_{16}	Industry group – Professional and scientific services	Dummy	0.21	0.17
X_{17}	Sex – Male	Dummy	0.48	0.25
X_{18}	Household status – Senior member	Dummy	0.78	0.17
X_{19}	Age	Years	44.19	308.11
X_{20}	Household size	Number	2.98	1.66
X_{21}	Length of residence	Years	9.24	32.73
X_{22}	Relations	Index	2.54	5.68

SOURCE   Oxford Survey Data; Vickerman (1972b).

The list of activities in Table 5.1 is not meant as a completely inclusive list of all possible activities. With the exception of entertaining, which was included because of its reciprocal nature to visiting, no domestic activities were included and amongst the external activities, shopping, visits to libraries and to churches (except as included amongst religious-based public social activities) and attendance at marketed sporting events were the main activities excluded. However, the objective was to obtain a representative and fairly wide coverage of different types of activity and this is given in the table.

In Table 5.2, variables X_1 to X_9 reflect the essentially economic status variables; X_{10} to X_{16} are the more precise socio-occupational classification; and X_{17} to X_{22} are the family-structure variables.

The form of the model estimated over the 858 individuals for whom data was available was therefore

$$Y_i = \alpha_i + \sum_j \beta_{ij} X_j$$

for each of the i activities.

The Determinants of Activity Levels. 1 Aggregate Approach

First of all a word of caution is necessary about the regression results. As will be obvious from the nature of the dependent variables and their average values (Table 5.1) the range of possible values each variable can take is very limited – in three cases the variable is binary. This can lead to some problems in estimation because of violation of the assumption of homoscedastic error terms.[10] The binary case results in further difficulties in least-squares estimation leading to possible losses of efficiency in the estimators.[11] One way round this is by use of non-linear techniques, such as the logistic function, which is a more explicitly probabilistic formulation. In the event a linear formulation approximates the logistic without too great a bias within the probability range (of Y occurring) of 0.2–0.8.[12] Examination of Table 5.1 shows that only variable Y_3 violates this condition and of the non-binary variables only Y_4 fails to meet this criterion on translation into a zero–non-zero form (with a value of 0.17).[13]

Our main concern was with the structure of the explanatory equations and hence the main criterion was to be a significance of coefficients rather than simply a high level of explanation in terms of R^2. The regression procedure adopted maximised R^2 subject to a 10 per cent significance level of all coefficients in the model. The basic results for the total sample are given in Table 5.3

One amendment to the formulation of the model was necessary for variable Y_2 (level of club visiting) since it was necessary to remove the influence of club membership on visiting from the other explanatory variables. If this were not done the variation in Y_2 attributed to each of the significant X's would include their influence on Y_1. The simple approximation used here for ease of computation was to include Y_1 as an explanatory variable for Y_2. Additionally, club membership, as a more highly committed activity was felt to have a direct influence on other activities, both through the possible effect of this time commitment and also through its probable social consequences. It was, therefore, allowed to enter the other equations as an explanatory variable. A control of the equations estimated without this variable was also carried out to test whether its collinearity with other variables, particularly its own most important determinant (X_{22}, relations) would bias the results. These tests showed virtually zero bias in the coefficients of the relevant variables with or without Y_1 present as an independent variable. Since variable Y_3 (part-time educational courses) performs a similar function in both time and social contexts, similar tests were made with this as an explanatory variable for Y_4–Y_8 with significant results for Y_6 (social visiting) and Y_8 (pleasure travel).[14]

Whilst none of the equations can be considered as good they do yield some interesting findings. We can observe four main features of

TABLE 5.3   Basic regression results – Activity model

$Y_1 = \quad 0.20 + 0.31\, X_3 + 0.004\, X_4 + 0.34\, X_{13} + 0.21\, X_{14} + 0.05\, X_{22}$ $\qquad R = 0.377$
$\qquad\quad (4.72) \quad (3.51) \quad\; (5.99) \quad\;\; (2.08) \quad\;\; (6.84)$ $\qquad F = 28.23$

$Y_2 = -0.13 - 0.26\, X_{14} + 0.10\, X_{17} + 0.01\, X_{21} + 0.81\, Y_1$ $\qquad R = 0.636$
$\qquad\quad (2.32) \quad\;\; (2.89) \quad\;\; (3.60) \quad\;\; (22.40)$ $\qquad F = 144.85$

$Y_3 = \quad 0.06 + 0.01\, X_8 + 0.10\, X_{11} + 0.07\, X_{16} - 0.01\, X_{19}$ $\qquad R = 0.256$
$\qquad\quad (2.11) \quad (4.54) \quad\;\; (3.06) \quad\;\; (2.69)$ $\qquad F = 14.96$

$Y_4 = \quad 0.36 + 0.40\, X_3 - 0.001\, X_9 + 0.26\, X_{10} + 0.13\, X_{11} - 0.002\, X_{19}$
$\qquad\quad (5.76) \quad (1.90) \quad\;\; (3.08) \quad\;\; (5.53) \quad\;\; (1.86)$
$\qquad\quad -0.01\, X_{21} - 0.02\, X_{22}$ $\qquad R = 0.347$
$\qquad\quad\;\; (2.70) \quad\;\; (2.60)$ $\qquad F = 16.62$

$Y_5 = \quad 0.68 + 0.14\, X_3 - 0.13\, X_{13} + 0.08\, X_{16} - 0.09\, X_{17} - 0.03\, X_{20}$
$\qquad\quad\;\; (2.01) \quad (2.19) \quad\;\; (1.94) \quad\;\; (2.49) \quad\;\; (2.46)$
$\qquad\quad -0.02\, X_{21} + 0.04\, X_{22} + 0.13\, Y_1$ $\qquad R = 0.331$
$\qquad\quad\;\; (6.47) \quad\;\; (5.66) \quad\;\; (3.62)$ $\qquad F = 13.06$

$Y_6 = \quad 1.42 - 0.28\, X_{15} - 0.20\, X_{17} - 0.01\, X_{19} - 0.09\, X_{20} - 0.01\, X_{21}$
$\qquad\quad (2.26) \quad\;\; (3.95) \quad\;\; (5.23) \quad\;\; (4.36) \quad\;\; (1.82)$
$\qquad\quad +0.09\, X_{22} + 0.20\, Y_1 + 0.17\, Y_3$ $\qquad R = 0.396$
$\qquad\quad\;\; (7.52) \quad\;\; (3.84) \quad\;\; (1.75)$ $\qquad F = 19.74$

$Y_7 = \quad 1.36 - 0.03\, X_8 + 0.15\, X_{13} - 0.21\, X_{18} - 0.01\, X_{19} - 0.08\, X_{20}$
$\qquad\quad (2.80) \quad (1.84) \quad\;\; (3.71) \quad\;\; (6.85) \quad\;\; (3.90)$
$\qquad\quad +0.15\, Y_1$ $\qquad R = 0.367$
$\qquad\quad\;\; (3.15)$ $\qquad F = 26.52$

$Y_8 = \quad 0.21 + 0.11\, X_{16} + 0.14\, Y_1 + 0.12\, Y_3$ $\qquad R = 0.168$
$\qquad\quad (2.34) \quad\;\; (3.85) \quad (1.74)$ $\qquad F = 8.27$

NOTES   Figures in parentheses are t-statistics, all significant at 5 per cent level.
$\qquad\quad$ F-ratios all significant at 0.01 per cent level.

the statistical analysis which are illustrated by reference to summary tabular presentations of the material.

(i) Firstly, economic variables are virtually non-existent. Income occurs only once as a significant influence, but most of these activities are ones with low or zero direct user costs for the facilities. Income is significant for the one activity, club membership, where costs may be important in terms of membership dues or equipment. The pattern of participation by people in different personal income groups is shown in Table 5.4. More interesting is the lack of importance of the time variables which, given the low prices and lack of apparent financial constraint is particularly surprising (Table 5.5). The only time factor of any significance is the commuting-time variable as a determinant of variations in cinema visiting. This is the one activity where freedom of time scheduling is limited and which, in terms of the discussion of Chapter 4, has a significant minimum time consumption constraint. Although not highly significant the coefficient does display the expected negative sign.

TABLE 5.4 Income and recreational participation

| | % Sample participating by weekly income | | | | | | | | |
| | Part-time workers | | | Full-time workers | | | | | |
Activity	Less than £10	£10–19	£20 and over	Less than £20	£20–24	£25–29	£30–39	£40–54	£55 and over
Club membership	37.1	26.7	40.0	46.9	41.2	58.7	61.7	45.0	57.1
Club visit*	73.9	50.0	40.0	55.6	63.6	53.2	58.8	66.7	41.7
Cinema/Theatre	6.5	23.3	—	21.3	16.9	12.3	11.2	36.8	33.3
Course enrolment	3.2	13.3	20.0	9.6	11.7	9.6	8.2	13.2	9.5
Entertaining	59.7	60.0	70.0	55.3	46.8	52.0	44.9	68.4	52.4
Social visiting	61.3	76.7	70.0	58.5	57.1	65.8	65.3	63.2	42.9
Eating/Drinking	30.6	36.7	40.0	43.6	29.9	38.4	50.0	39.5	42.9
Pleasure trips	27.4	30.0	40.0	20.2	29.9	32.9	24.5	47.4	33.3

* Refers only to those in the sample who were club members.
SOURCE: Oxford Survey data; Vickerman (1972b).

TABLE 5.5 Daily hours worked and recreational participation

| | % Sample participating by hours of work | | | | | | | | |
| | Employed persons | | | | | | | Not employed | |
Activity	Less than 4 hours	4–7 hours	7–8 hours	8–8½ hours	8½–9 hours	9–10 hours	10 hours and over	School or college	Other
Club membership	39.7	50.0	29.5	61.1	55.2	50.8	50.0	58.6	31.7
Club visits	62.1	69.4	66.7	56.9	51.7	57.6	51.6	61.8	64.3
Cinema/Theatre	13.6	45.2	37.7	16.8	10.5	15.4	11.7	46.4	11.0
Course enrolment	5.5	6.9	13.1	8.4	9.5	6.2	11.7	—	4.4
Entertaining	56.2	59.7	52.5	60.0	48.6	47.7	51.7	65.5	54.4
Social visiting	64.4	63.9	60.7	66.3	58.1	50.8	65.0	68.9	55.8
Eating/Drinking	31.5	45.8	41.0	48.4	36.2	36.9	35.6	51.7	21.1
Pleasure trips	31.5	22.2	21.3	32.6	24.8	30.8	30.0	20.7	22.6

SOURCE Oxford Survey data; Vickerman (1972b).

Table 5.6 illustrates the variations in participation rates for working

TABLE 5.6   Travel time from work and recreational participation

% Sample participating by journey time from work

Activity	Less than 5 min	6–10 min	11–15 min	16–20 min	21–30 min	Over 30 min
Club membership	46.6	53.2	60.9	40.6	48.1	50.0
Club visits	70.4	58.1	61.4	48.3	63.5	51.4
Cinema/Theatre	25.9	30.4	20.9	20.3	12.0	14.3
Course enrolment	6.9	11.4	8.7	7.2	7.4	8.6
Entertainment	58.6	49.4	55.7	47.8	63.0	50.0
Social visiting	60.3	72.2	62.6	60.9	61.1	47.1
Eating/Drinking	37.9	41.8	41.7	40.6	33.3	38.6
Pleasure trips	22.4	32.9	24.3	30.4	25.9	22.9

SOURCE   Oxford Survey data; Vickerman (1972b).

members of the sample with different travel times from work. Slight differences have emerged between this pattern and the distributions with respect to travel times *to* work. The one presented here is the more relevant because recreation activities are more likely to take place after work than before and hence the travel time from work is the more binding constraint on levels of participation. It is nevertheless interesting to bear in mind that there is an asymmetry in the two journeys (Table 5.7). Part of the tendency for journeys home to be longer may be explained by the greater use of that journey for combining other purposes such as shopping and in this way save travelling time for other, more profitable, activities.

TABLE 5.7   Distribution of sample with respect to access to and from place of work

% With given journey time

Activity	Less than 5 min	6–10 min	11–15 min	16–20 min	21–30 min	Over 30 min
Journey to work	12.4	18.8	26.5	14.4	19.2	8.7
Journey from work	11.6	15.8	23.0	13.8	21.6	14.0

SOURCE   Oxford Survey data; Vickerman (1972b).

It is suspected, however, that the time effects may have been lost in this overall data set within employment status and other such variables. A more detailed analysis of subsets of the data such as for different employment status groups is necessary before any conclusion is drawn. (ii)   The results do show clearly that socio-occupational classifications are much better indicators of activity participation than these economic factors. Table 5.8 examines the influence of the socio-economic groupings (S.E.G.'s) used by the Registrar-General, which reflect the nature of employment status. Whilst no overall trend in levels of

TABLE 5.8   Socio-economic group and recreational participation

% Sample participating in each S.E.G.

Activity	Employers/ Managers/ Own account workers	Professional	Non- manual	Supervisory and skilled manual	Semi- skilled manual	Unskilled manual
Club membership	42.9	43.7	47.1	60.2	53.2	41.4
Club visiting	86.7	50.0	48.2	61.1	73.5	66.7
Cinema/Theatre ✓	8.6	37.5	23.6	8.5	6.4	6.9
Course enrolment	8.6	6.2	16.1	3.4	1.6	—
Entertainment	51.4	56.3	56.2	50.0	45.2	51.7
Social visiting	65.7	56.3	64.9	57.6	54.8	55.2
Eating/Drinking	51.4	34.4	41.3	32.2	40.3	31.0
Pleasure trips ✓	42.9	31.2	30.6	22.9	22.6	34.5

SOURCE   Oxford Survey data; Vickerman (1972b).

participation amongst workers in the different groups can be identified, there are important differences in the relative importances of individual activities between groups. We can note, for example the greater importance of cinema and theatre visits amongst professional and intermediate and junior non-manual workers whilst the latter and, to a lesser extent, employers/managers, etc. are the most likely to use part-time educational courses. On the other hand it is the unskilled manual workers who tend to make use of club facilities although amongst club members the employers/managers are the most loyal attenders.

An even more distinct pattern emerges from consideration of the industry of employment of workers (Table 5.9). We can observe, for

TABLE 5.9   Industry of employment and recreational participation

% Sample participating in each Industry group

Activity	Vehicles	Paper/ Printing	Transport and public utilities	Distributive trades	Professional/ Scientific/ Financial services	Public admin.
Club membership	82.4	65.2	53.7	33.3	40.6	41.5
Club visits	57.9	33.3	50.0	64.3	50.7	58.8
Cinema/Theatre	13.2	17.4	7.3	15.4	23.3	26.8
Course enrolment	5.5	13.0	7.3	2.6	16.1	12.2
Entertainment	40.7	60.9	63.4	51.3	61.7	43.9
Social visiting	58.2	65.2	65.9	43.6	66.3	48.8
Eating/Drinking	47.2	47.8	36.6	38.5	35.6	34.1
Pleasure trips	25.3	34.8	34.1	12.8	33.3	39.0

SOURCE   Oxford Survey data; Vickerman (1972b).

example, the high club enrolment of workers in the vehicle and publishing sectors, but the contrasting levels of attendance by those groups. Workers in transport and the public utilities appear to have rather low rates of participation in most activities, but the least active appear to be those in the distributive trades.

This is a very interesting finding. There are obviously important differences in standards of pay and hours of work between the groups whether we consider the socio-economic or the industrial classification. However, these may not be adequately measured just by income or hours of work variables. Working evenings or a night shift reduces recreational activity, for example on an external activity such as the cinema only 7.9 per cent of such workers recorded visits compared with 20.6 per cent of other workers, and even on a domestic activity such as entertaining the figures were 42.1 per cent and 54.7 per cent respectively. On the other hand workers working overtime often appeared to be more likely to participate in these two activities than did other workers.

The economic factors are thus very complex and bound up inextricably with the social factors making the occupational milieu. Whilst this hinders the construction of an empirical economic activity model it does have the advantage that socio-economic status can be adequately represented by simple and readily available indices without the need to collect complex data on times, incomes etc. A cross-classification by employment status and industry provides a very precise measure of the apparent influences on recreational activity.

(iii) Family and social network factors stand out as consistently important. The influences vary as may be expected but it is the relations network which dominates the pattern. Several of the activities are quite strongly related to age (Table 5.10), and increasing household size seems to reduce the level of social activities, possibly in that there

TABLE 5.10   Age and recreational participation

	% Sample participating in each age group					
Activity	*15–20*	*21–30*	*31–40*	*41–50*	*51–65*	*Over 65*
Club membership	53.3	44.0	45.2	55.5	45.7	29.8
Club visits	71.9	56.5	55.3	53.1	58.7	79.5
Cinema/Theatre	31.7	26.9	22.0	17.1	9.1	3.8
Course enrolment	11.7	9.3	8.9	11.0	5.1	—
Entertainment	50.0	64.2	58.5	48.0	53.8	47.3
Social visiting	63.3	72.5	59.3	59.6	60.4	42.0
Eating/Drinking	55.0	46.6	35.0	36.3	29.4	9.9
Pleasure trips	20.0	30.0	32.5	30.1	25.9	14.5

SOURCE   Oxford Survey data; Vickerman (1972b).

is greater scope for domestic entertainment, but more likely because of the influence of younger children. No particular conclusion can be drawn about the influence of length of residence but the sample did tend to be a rather stable one, nearly 50 per cent having been at the same address for at least ten years.

(iv)   Finally, the two activities allowed to interact with the other five display considerable influence, particularly with the social activities. Complementarity and substitutability are considered in more detail later in this chapter but we can note here that the more committed time activities tend to be complementary in that they are associated with increasing levels of involvement in social activities. It would thus seem that their social influence is greater than their economic influence through the using up of the time resource.

Hence this rather crude first appraisal suggests that there is little evidence of a binding time constraint on activity levels. Social factors dominate and only in the one case of a pronounced time consumption constraint does time really show any importance.

The Determinants of Activity Levels. 2 Disaggregate Approach
The complexity of the interrelating influences has proved a barrier to satisfactory identification of an economic activity model. Obviously the marginal influence of variables such as income and time availability cannot be estimated adequately over such a wide range of individuals of whom some are working full-time, some part-time, and some not at all. Whilst these differences have been allowed for, the estimated elasticity with respect to each constraint variable is an average and not, therefore, an accurate indicator of the effects of relaxing those constraints for the groups which find them binding.

There is an unmanageably large number of ways in which the sample could be subdivided to effect the desired aim of achieving greater homogeneity amongst the separate groups considered. Homogeneity in this context implies reducing the variance in certain dimensions of the data to emphasise particular features. A useful subdivision is that according to employment – full-time, part-time or not in employment.

We have already considered the data relating to income and time for the working groups in Tables 5.4 and 5.5 respectively. Reconsidering the income relationship in Table 5.4 suggests that splitting the data is a useful advance. It tends to show, for activities other than those connected with clubs, that there is an income constraint on lower-income earners since a positive relationship emerges. For full-time workers, however, the relationship is much less clear. Definite non-linear relationships can be identified for cinema/theatre visiting in which the middle-income groups are the least active, and social visiting in which these groups are the most active. However, as was suggested previously the low cost of most recreational activities would lead us to expect a low income elasticity; it is only at low income levels that the cost of the complete activity (particularly the travel component) may prove to be a seriously binding constraint.

Hours worked do already reflect the division of the data, albeit expressed in the form of a continuous variable. However, a closer examination of Table 5.5 suggests some discontinuities which would mask any attempt to estimate an overall relationship. If we omit the column referring to those working for less than 4 hours and place less weight on the 4–7 hours group there are again, as for income, some pronounced non-linearities. Club visiting, course enrolment, entertaining and social visiting all show a reduction in participation by those working in the 8–10 hours group relative to those working shorter or longer total hours.

All of these apparent economically influenced trends may, however, simply be related to changes in economic status which are associated with changing family structure or stage in the life cycle and it is these social factors which are the more fundamental determinants of recreational involvement. To simplify the comparisons a selection of four activities out of the seven considered has been taken for this stage of the analysis.

Four social determinants can be considered for the three main subgroups of full-time and part-time workers, and those not employed. Those in full-time education were excluded as they formed a very small proportion of the sample which was restricted to persons over the age of 15. The four determinants, all of which displayed some significance in the deterministic model are age, household size, the presence of an extended family structure in the area, and length of residence. Of these the age distributions of participation for the subgroups showed little improvement on the pattern of Table 5.10. Differing relative importances of activities did emerge between the groups but the age profile of participants for each group showed no clearer relationship than that of the overall sample. The remaining three variables are worthy of further consideration, however.

The size of household has already been discussed as a problem variable in terms of interpretation. It has both economic and social influences and may be seen either as a constraint on recreational activity because of the greater cost of family participation and the greater problem of time scheduling with increasing size, or as a boost to individual activity because of the economies of scale the larger household permits, particularly in the execution of essential household activities, thus freeing more time for general leisure pursuits. Table 5.11 confirms this rather inconclusive view. With the exception of part-time workers there is evidence of a fall-off in activity from members of larger

TABLE 5.11 Size of household and recreational participation

% Sample participating by size of household

Activity and Employment group	1	2	3	4	5 or more
Cinema/Theatre					
Full-time	23.1	18.6	16.2	19.6	16.3
Part-time	14.3	7.9	4.8	20.7	16.7
Not employed	7.9	9.3	12.5	16.7	8.3
Entertainment					
Full-time	42.3	55.0	59.6	47.1	36.7
Part-time	85.7	60.5	61.9	55.2	63.6
Not employed	42.1	51.8	69.6	58.3	41.7
Eating/Drinking					
Full-time	46.2	39.3	37.4	49.0	24.5
Part-time	28.6	28.9	38.1	27.6	58.3
Not employed	18.4	19.4	21.4	31.2	12.5
Pleasure trips					
Full-time	30.8	30.0	24.2	30.4	30.6
Part-time	28.6	26.8	28.6	17.2	33.3
Not employed	7.9	20.4	19.6	41.7	25.0

SOURCE   Oxford Survey data; Vickerman (1972b).

families and particularly so for those not in employment. The reduction in activity levels in middle-sized families is probably more the result of the stage in the family life-cycle than the size *per se*. The larger families are more likely to have junior members in employment and hence the tendency for the activity levels of these groups not to fall off so dramatically.

The measure of the extended family has been grouped from the cumulative index based on a hierarchy of relationships into four mutually exclusive groups, those without any relations in the immediate study area, those with primarily parental relations (including some with both parents and children not living with them), those with primarily descendant relations (children, grandchildren, etc.), and those with no parental or direct descendant relations but with other relations. Table 5.12 summarises the levels of participation for these groups. This index is seen to be a much better discriminator of the life cycle and its associated influences than is family size, or age. Column three of the table shows consistently lower levels of participation than other groups except for the expected activity, entertaining. Column one, those without relations, reflects the overall lower involvement of in-migrants, usually younger people, except in the one activity of cinema and theatre visits, and a slightly higher propensity for enrolment on part-time courses.

TABLE 5.12   Relations in area and recreational participation

Activity and Employment group	No relations	Parents/ Grandparents	Children/ Grandchildren	Other relations
	% Sample participating in each group			
Cinema/Theatre				
Full-time	28.1	17.5	7.8	13.2
Part-time	17.2	20.0	2.9	6.2
Not employed	15.7	19.2	4.9	5.6
Entertainment				
Full-time	42.1	59.1	56.2	50.6
Part-time	58.6	60.0	67.6	75.0
Not employed	51.4	67.3	59.8	48.1
Eating/Drinking				
Full-time	35.1	44.5	31.2	42.2
Part-time	37.9	44.0	26.5	25.0
Not employed	15.7	32.7	18.3	22.2
Pleasure trips				
Full-time	28.1	34.3	15.6	32.5
Part-time	24.1	44.0	23.5	25.0
Not employed	22.9	32.7	13.4	25.9

SOURCE   Oxford Survey data; Vickerman (1972b).

The final test is the effect of length of residence as a further measure of the degree of establishment in the local community. Table 5.13 reveals

TABLE 5.13   Length of residence and recreational participation

Activity and Employment group	Less than 1 year	1–2 years	2–5 years	5–10 years	Over 10 years
	% Sample participating by length of residence				
Cinema/Theatre					
Full-time	25.0	36.0	22.6	15.4	12.7
Part-time	22.2	42.9	23.1	15.0	3.7
Not employed	21.7	20.0	16.7	7.7	8.8
Entertainment					
Full-time	72.9	72.2	56.4	47.7	43.6
Part-time	55.6	57.1	61.5	70.0	57.4
Not employed	65.2	86.7	66.7	56.4	48.9
Eating/Drinking					
Full-time	50.0	44.4	43.5	36.9	34.8
Part-time	33.3	57.1	46.1	30.0	29.6
Not employed	26.1	13.3	25.0	17.9	22.6
Pleasure trips					
Full-time	27.1	33.3	25.8	36.9	27.6
Part-time	22.2	42.8	38.5	40.0	22.2
Not employed	39.1	26.7	22.2	25.6	21.2

SOURCE   Oxford Survey data; Vickerman (1972b).

that this variable actually yields the most regular pattern for all the subgroups. The relationship is not linear, there is a tendency for a rise in participation over the first few years followed by a steady decline. This does improve on our initial conclusion from the aggregate sample that the effect of length of residence was unpredictable.

Conclusion

This analysis of the determinants of levels of recreational participation has presented a useful empirical background for later discussions. Totally satisfactory results could not be expected from such a simple model and the data available. However, a valuable finding is that fairly straightforward indices, those usually available in any household survey data, are the most satisfactory determinants of variations. Useful first approximations can be made without the need to collect complex time budget data. This also confirms the view of Chapter 4 that much can be gleaned from a model of mobility in the absence of a complete activities model.

Domestic and External Activities

Although we have suggested that a detailed analysis of all activities is not essential we must consider the basic division between external and domestic activities and any possible reasons for variations in the extent of these groups of activities. This is important because of the repercussions on planning which only arise from those activities external to the home.

To a certain extent we can approximate to this by identifying the consistent themes in the preceding analysis. Hence, such factors as increasing family size, age and lack of a well-established social network would all lead to a higher than average degree of domestic-centred leisure. The generally positive coefficients of the socio-occupational variables used would also suggest that the less-skilled manual workers, and particularly those in the less-organised industrial sectors, will be more home-centred.

This is consistent with the conclusions from the aggregate trends in Chapter 2. There it was suggested that these groups are more inclined to regard leisure, in Engels terms, as a 'spillover', carrying the alienation of the workplace into the home, rather than as 'compensatory' for the pressures of work. Wilensky (1960) also identified this 'underdog response', characterised as 'family-home localism', and Gavron (1966) found supporting empirical evidence. The 'Affluent Worker' studies of Goldthorpe and others (1969) found similar contrasts in the groups of workers living on new estates.

This is not a sufficient analysis, however, because it does not allow for the variations in time availability or problems in time scheduling which many families may find constraints on external activities. The large family may have severe time scheduling problems if family leisure activities are to be undertaken. Similarly, workers working overtime or on night shifts may have not only less leisure time but also less useful leisure time.

As a simple test of some of these interrelationships, four variables from the preceding analysis measuring time availability were related to the other economic and social variables. Table 5.14 gives the results of this exercise for the complete sample.

TABLE 5.14 Variations in time availability

Total hours worked $(X_5) =$

$$0.58 + 7.84\, X_1 + 3.61\, X_2 + 6.82\, X_3 + 2.18\, X_7 + 0.53\, X_{13}$$
$$\quad (31.82) \quad (12.96) \quad (17.02) \quad (5.46) \quad (1.87)$$

$$+ 0.74\, X_{15} + 0.65\, X_{17} - 0.13\, X_{19} \qquad\qquad R = 0.859$$
$$\quad (1.86) \qquad (3.22) \qquad (2.39) \qquad\qquad F = 298.75$$

Overtime hours worked $(X_6) =$

$$-0.13 + 2.17\, X_3 + 0.01\, X_4 + 0.16\, X_{18} \qquad\qquad R = 0.505$$
$$\quad\ (16.71) \quad (3.43) \quad (2.06) \qquad\qquad F = 97.45$$

No days free $(X_8) =$

$$7.0 - 2.48\, X_1 - 3.46\, X_2 - 3.04\, X_3 - 0.23\, X_5 - 1.09\, X_{10} - 0.66\, X_{15} \qquad R = 0.822$$
$$\quad (11.01) \quad (17.54) \quad (11.01) \quad (10.42) \quad (3.86) \quad\ (2.56) \qquad F = 295.50$$

Total travel time $(X_9) =$

$$0.01 + 4.21\, X_1 + 4.39\, X_2 - 2.87\, X_3 - 0.02\, X_4 - 0.53\, X_{16} \qquad R = 0.602$$
$$\quad (14.80) \quad (15.67) \quad (8.98) \quad (2.76) \quad (2.55) \qquad F = 96.85$$

Naturally the employment status variables account for most of the variation in time availability. This influence having been removed, quite significant effects of the socio-occupational variables can be identified. Employees in Standard Industrial Classification groups Vehicles and Distributive Trades work longer normal hours and the latter have less days completely free from work, as also do professional and managerial workers. Night-shift workers also appear to work considerably longer hours than corresponding day-shift workers. Overtime in this context was not strictly defined as hours paid at overtime rates because this would exclude many people (mainly salaried staffs and professional and managerial workers) who are not directly paid for working over normal hours. A looser formulation of hours worked outside normal hours was adopted, which would include work done at home and that done outside college hours by full-time students. The result is that students do have the largest commitment outside normal hours, although this is presumably flexible in terms of its scheduling. The other two significant factors are status in the household (overtime is more characteristic of household heads), and income. The causal direction of this latter variable is unclear; to the extent that overtime is paid, income will be determined by overtime working, but it is also possible that overtime loosely defined is dependent on status within an organisation for which income is a proxy.[15]

In view of the fairly predictable conclusions which emerge from the data it seems reasonable to conclude that much of the variation in the domestic–external split of recreational activity will remain a random element. Individual preferences for one form or another of recreation will not vary systematically with any socio-economic influence.

Committed Activities and Short-run Flexibility

The other basic distinction in activities (apart from the external–domestic split) is that between activities where the individual has a high degree of commitment and those where there is a high degree of flexibility possible in the allocation of time in the short run.

We have already looked at one aspect of this briefly when considering the determinants of activity levels. Club membership was shown to be associated with higher levels of participation in a range of activities, and commitment to a part-time educational course was also associated with higher levels of social visiting and pleasure travel. In some respects this finding may be thought to contradict the expected result, greater commitment leading to a reduction in the time available for other activities and hence a lower level of participation. However, we must remember that we have been concerned here with frequency of participation and not intensity, so that the actual time spent may be reduced. The positive relationship identified is not necessarily a causal one, the two factors may be independently related to other character-istics; more-active people are also more likely to indulge in a greater number of organised activities.

There may be a further point here in that committed activities do not only involve a commitment of time, that time is also committed at a particular point in time. This reduces the short-run flexibility of the consumer to reallocate time between activities and hence to alter the consumption pattern. The likely effect of this has been shown to be a higher valuation being placed on savings of time in such circumstances. With such a premium being placed on time, much greater care is likely to be taken in its allocation. We can thus expect that persons with more committed time may be more efficient in their use of available time as well as having greater demands placed on that time. These two factors combine to give the results found here.

It may be noted that this finding accords with the views expressed by Linder (1970) that as society acquires more leisure time through shorter working hours, improvements in transport and time-saving innovations in the home, people also become more conscious of being short of time. Genuine free time, idleness, the time devoted to hedonistic pursuits, has been reduced.

An example of the effects of reduced flexibility in the allocation of time in the short run because of the restriction of activities to particular points in time is best seen in the case of cinema visits. This is the inverse relationship between the amount of time spent travelling to and from work and the level of participation in this activity. The time spent on the work journey is indicative of both a reduction in the amount of time available for non-work pursuits and of an increase in the likely travel cost (money and time) for organised market recreation, such as the cinema, which tends to be concentrated in the more accessible parts of urban areas. These more accessible areas also tend to be where employment opportunities are concentrated so that journey-to-work times may be good indicators of journey times for this type of recreation. It is interesting that cinema visits are the only type of recreation considered here for which such a time factor is identified as a significant determinant of the level of participation.

There is no immediately obvious distinction between the determinants of the more committed and the less committed activities. It can be noted that similar levels of explanation are achieved for both groups of activity but rather more efficiently in the case of the committed activities, in the sense that fewer significant explanatory variables are necessary to achieve the equivalent performance of the model. Most of the variation in participation in the committed activities is attributable to the occupation and industry of employment variables. It seems therefore that it may be easier to achieve a reasonable predictive model for such activities in terms of readily available socio-economic data. A larger part of the variance in participation in the less committed activities is independent of these basic determinants and likely to be determined in the short run by a more stochastic process.

Complementarity and Substitutability

We have been aware throughout this discussion that each activity cannot be considered totally independently of all the others. Some activities are complementary in that a change in participation in the one leads to a parallel change in participation in the other, whilst other activities may be better regarded as close substitutes if the response is in the opposing direction.

As a basic means of assessing the interrelationships between participation levels in the activities considered, Table 5.15 presents the zero-order correlation matrix of these. The correlations obtained from the total sample are seen to be very low suggesting that there is no strong

TABLE 5.15 Correlation matrix of activity participation (Total sample)

		Y_1	Y_2	Y_3	Y_4	Y_5	Y_6	Y_7	Y_8
Club membership	Y_1	1.000	0.621*	0.038	−0.039	0.117*	0.177*	0.152*	0.129*
Club visits	Y_2		1.000	−0.024	−0.075*	0.007	0.088*	0.092*	0.034
Cinema/Theatre	Y_3			1.000	0.047	0.023	0.081*	0.077*	0.079*
Course enrolment	Y_4				1.000	0.106*	0.076*	0.185*	0.050
Entertainment	Y_5					1.000	0.312=	0.076*	0.134*
Social visiting	Y_6						1.000	0.159*	0.200*
Eating/Drinking	Y_7							1.000	0.175*
Pleasure trips	Y_8								1.000

NOTES   Variables Y_1–Y_8 as defined in Table 5.1.
An asterisk denotes a value significantly different from zero at the 5 per cent level.

SOURCE   Oxford Survey data; Vickerman (1972b).

overall pattern of interrelationship between activities. However, it will also be seen that all but eight of the correlation coefficients are significantly different from zero on the basis of the standard statistical test. Furthermore, all but one of these significant coefficients are positive, the exception being that between club visits and part-time educational course enrolment.

Our first conclusion is, therefore, that there is no evidence of strong substitution effects between activities. The positive coefficients point to complementarities which are significant but weak.

Secondly, we can note that the only significant substitution effect is between activities which have been classed as being committed. We may therefore conclude tentatively that the expansion of free-time activities can be done without the fear that any such expansion will take place only at the expense of other similar activities. However, the development of activities which imply a commitment of time may only take place at the expense of other such activities. We may note that many of the growth leisure pursuits are in fact ones implying such a commitment because of their club organisation or the high initial cost of equipment.

Thirdly, the correlations indicate that the strongest positive relationships are between the essentially social and pleasure activities. The social factors already noted as determinants of variations in individual activity participation levels are also reflected in asymmetries in the correlation matrix. For example, the differing strength of the relationship between entertaining and eating and drinking out from that between the latter activity and social visiting.

Finally, it should be noted that this has been only a preliminary look at a key problem. Much more research needs to be carried out on defining the markets for individual activities and the extent to which they interrelate.

Conclusions

The purpose of the analysis of this chapter has been to further our understanding of some of the basic relationships between the socio-economic background and the nature and extent of recreational activity. The nature of available data and the fact that a complete definitive model of time budgeting was not central to the main theme of this study led to the adoption of the more impressionistic approach used here. This approach has yielded two important results however.

It has been shown that a considerable amount of the variation in activity levels can be explained (in a statistical sense) by straightforward indices of socio-economic status, and that a relatively minor additional amount is attributable to more precise factors of time and money. This suggests that adequate model building could be obtained without the need to resort to expensive large-scale data collection exercises which would, in any case, cause severe problems of accurate collection, and helps to justify the approach adopted here of concentrating on movement data.

Secondly, the analysis above has provided a form of selection of the possible range of socio-economic variables to be used in our more general demand analysis, incorporating spatial supply prices, in the subsequent chapters. In addition to identifying the main factors which may have an impact on the potential demand for activities of certain groups, this may help in the interpretation of the estimated models.

The analysis has also been extended to cover the nature of substitution and complementarity between various activities, which will also have important implications for our further analysis.

We must now turn from this rather abstract consideration of potential demand to the construction of a more robust model incorporating the spatial supply price of activities. The importance of this topic warrants the devotion of the whole of Chapter 6 to a detailed discussion of this model.

6. The Demand for Leisure Travel–Constructing an Operational Model

We have seen the problems associated with the construction of an activities model as the basis of the study of demand for leisure and recreational activities. We have also rejected the straightforward approach of modelling demand on the basis of site visitors as begging some of the most important questions.

The travel for such activities has been seen to be the key variable, however, in a number of ways. The bulk of activities which either require some form of planning or which will be influenced indirectly by other planning decisions are those taking place away from home. Characteristically the travel component is a major input to such activities. Furthermore, travel for such purposes is becoming an increasingly important part of total movement and thus understanding of the nature of such demands is increasingly important for transport planning.

Leisure mobility has been shown to have three basic determinants, the structure of consumer preferences (as investigated in Chapter 5), the potential of a given location (normally that of the home residence) for leisure activities, and the characteristics of accessibility, comfort, convenience, etc. of the transport network.

In this chapter, we shall develop this basic model and illustrate its relationship to other approaches.[1] We shall also discuss in some detail the problems of defining some of the key concepts of potential, attraction and accessibility, and examine the role of car-ownership.

A Basic Travel Demand Model

Trip Generation Approaches
We have established a basic hypothesis of trip making for the individual which can be represented as:

$$T_i^{kp} = f(S^p, P_i^{kp}, A_i^{kp})$$

where T_i^{kp} is the number of trips made by person p from location i for activity k in a given period; S^p is a vector of socio-economic characteristics determining the preference pattern of p; P_i^{kp} is a vector determining the potential for activity k of p's location i; A_i^{kp} is a vector of relevant accessibility indices relating to the transport networks linking p's location in i with sites for k.

There are two important issues to be resolved in translating this into an estimable, operational model. Firstly, the economic derivation of this model from the normal utility-maximising framework has implications. We must remember that travel is an intermediate good. The revealing of an individual's preferences will depend primarily on the activity for which the travel is an input, and the choice of a particular journey is part of the secondary production decision. The importance of this is in the formulation and interpretation of the demand model since the observed effects of particular influences may be partly reflecting the utility derived from participating in the complete activity and partly the desire to produce the activity in the most economical way. Whilst the former may lead to the desire to maximise the number of trips for a given purpose subject to income and time constraints, the latter may relate to an additional desire to minimise travel inputs.

The second issue is partly an independent one but is also implied directly by the formulation of the objective function, that of aggregation. There are a number of dimensions to the aggregation issue as we have discussed briefly in Chapter 2 in the context of defining a homogeneous transport product. Consideration of mode of transport and destination is particularly important because these are the dimensions into which flows are ultimately disaggregated in conventional transportation models. We must also consider the degree of aggregation in the unit of observation, whether we remain with the individual, the theoretical basis, or resort to aggregation because of the zero observation bias in the behaviour of individuals. Obviously the more disaggregated the product is made the more significant will the zero weighting of observations become.

The usual way around this problem has been aggregation of observations into geographical zones. Some previous attempts have been made to build in sensitivity of total trip generation to locational/ network characteristics in single equation econometric studies of travel demand, notably by Quandt and Baumol (1966) for inter-city travel and Kraft and Wohl (1967) for more general intra-urban applications. Both of these models were based on aggregate flows between origin–destination pairs. Aggregate trip production models in the conventional hierarchical procedure have conventionally yielded very high levels of explanation (in terms of the coefficient of multiple determination, R^2). These levels are a little lower in the single equation inter-zonal transfer models, but still in a very acceptable range, 35 to 63 per cent for the urban models and as high as 87 per cent for the inter-urban models.

There are two reasons for this apparently highly satisfactory performance. The aggregation to zonal level of the trip-making pattern averages out much of the variation in the dependent (trips) variable, and therefore leaves less to explain. Secondly, most of the variance is explained by aggregate variables which have little or no behavioural significance, the particular offenders being zonal population variables. Other variables such as income, population density, or car-ownership are difficult in an aggregated model. Car-ownership particularly is often used as a dummy shift variable which is assumed to be independent of other explanatory variables, whereas, since car ownership is normally itself explained in terms of those same independent variables, this is likely to lead to biased estimates of coefficients. In fact car-ownership may be better regarded as a variable to classify a population into more homogeneous subsets, rather than to explain marginal variations in travel.

The problem of the population variable has often been solved in such models by expressing the aggregate dependent variable as trips per head in the origin zone. This tends to reduce the level of explanation by removing a very significant variable, but is argued to yield a more easily interpreted equation. It does, however, introduce a further possible source of bias in that it assumes neutrality of origin-zone size, mathematically it would constrain the exponent of population in a classic gravity formulation to be unity. Since zonal population (or any other 'mass' factor used) is likely to be strongly related to zonal potential, which will in turn influence trip making, this assumption of neutrality or independence is unjustified.

Interpretation of these models raises problems on two fronts. One arises from the pattern of significance of the coefficients of the independent variables, those variables which can be interpreted as behavioural tend to yield low significance in spite of high levels of overall explanation. It thus becomes very difficult to use the models to predict changes in levels of mobility as a result of changes in economic factors such as incomes, prices, or travel times. The other problem is closely related, that it is extremely difficult to interpret such coefficients in a genuinely behavioural context. There is, for example, no obvious *a priori* relationship between an average measure of income and an average amount of trip making, although there is between an individual's income and his own trip making. An aggregate formulation may not identify changes in distributions unless more sophisticated variables than simple arithmetic averages are used. Achieving a high level of explanation does not necessarily imply achieving a greater degree of understanding of the relationships in question.

The question of interpretation and aggregation was at the centre of the development of category analysis as a basic approach to trip generation (Wootton and Pick, 1967). Category analysis starts with the formulation of a basic behavioural model, a certain limited range of variables is hypothesised to influence individual travel patterns. The population is then classified according to the variables selected, for example, a cross-classification by car-ownership (3 groups), income (6 classes), and household structure (6 groups) yields 108 household groups. Trip data reveals a representative (average) trip rate for each of these groups or categories. The distribution of trip making within each category will suggest the most representative average figure to be used – mean, median, or mode – although if the data revealed a high standard deviation of trips or was very skewed this would suggest the need for further subdivision, each category being assumed homogeneous.

The forecasting exercise with category analysis is then one of predicting the structure of the population in terms of the categories used, and using the appropriate trip rates to predict travel. Although it does bypass the aggregation problem this approach is subject to the same limitations as any cross-sectional regression analysis based on individual data. In particular, the cross-sectional approach fails to identify any dynamic trends in behaviour, and assumes that people in a given class will always behave the same, regardless of their progress through time, or their relative position in the class structure. The lack of statistical estimation is an additional problem, however, no confidence limits can be placed around any forecasts, and the importance of different explanatory variables is not assessed statistically.[2]

There is a further criticism of category analysis which is rather more fundamental: its restriction to consideration of socio-economic influences on travel behaviour. Although there is no theoretical reason why potential and accessibility factors should not be used in the classification, it is often very difficult to incorporate more than a small number of variables (four or five) because of the implication for cell sizes resulting from any reasonable size of sample.[3]

One useful development which has occurred as a result of the demands of the category analysis technique, and which is equally appropriate for forecasting by any means, has been the research into methods of predicting the future distributions of certain key variables such as income and car-ownership. Too frequently in complex statistical modelling the problems of forecasting the key independent influences into the future take second place to the structure of the model itself.

Therefore, it would seem that criticism of the more conventional regression approaches to trip generation analysis has probably concentrated wrongly on the statistical technique involved rather than the level of aggregation. Once data disaggregated to the individual decision-making unit is available, regression analysis is a perfectly acceptable statistical tool.

In the preceding paragraphs, we have concentrated on the issues concerning aggregation over the decision-making units. We are, however, still left with an aggregation question concerning the decision variable, the dependent variable of any regression model. The single-equation model discussed above for inter-urban travel was concerned with the generation of trips by individual modes, but only for specific links of the network. The dependent variable thus took the form T_{ijm} where i and j refer to the origin and destination of the trip, and m the mode of transport used, compared with our original formulation of T_i^{kp}. The intra-urban model as developed by Domencich and colleagues (1968) does consider separate journey purposes and is therefore represented as T_{ijm}^k. It is thus clearly seen that our derivation from the economic model represents in effect aggregation over destinations and modes (although we shall consider the merits of modally dis-aggregated models later in this chapter).

The main reason for this is that it makes total trip making responsive to network changes or other changes in the supply of particular activities, rather than taking an independent look at each link in a network. Wilson (1973) has shown clearly the advantages of this approach in the context of entropy-maximising transport models.

One further point which arose in the discussion of the measurement of trends in leisure travel in Chapter 2 can also be raised in this context. We have treated the decision variable so far as number of trips, but we know from the economic derivation that this is inadequate because of its failure to account for differences in trip lengths, besides qualitative differences in trips made under different conditions, for example by different modes. The real economic decision variable which will capture this is expenditure, or more precisely, generalised cost to embrace both monetary and non-monetary outlays. The development of models of expenditure flows is an important future research objective. Two practical problems arise, however, the greater difficulty of collecting accurate expenditure data relating to both on-site activity and travel, and the problem of divergence between objective and perceived costs. For this reason, we shall choose not to use the direct expenditure approach but employ a half-way stage of considering total mileage generated as a dependent variable. This has the advantage of being an objective measure for all transport modes, although it still hides some qualitative differences.

It is not possible to replace the T_i^{kp} measure with either expenditure (E_i^{kp}) or mileage (M_i^{kp}) since these do not distinguish frequency variations which will be important in planning both the supply of facilities and the transport network. Obviously all three are related, and since we have assumed that utility-maximisation implies a solution value for E_i^{kp} rather than T_i^{kp}, then we can postulate that T_i^{kp} is a function of E_i^{kp}. This suggests rewriting our original model as:

$$E_i^{kp} = e(S^p, P_i^{kp}, A_i^{kp})$$
$$T_i^{kp} = f(E_i^{kp}, S^p, P_i^{kp}, A_i^{kp})$$

There may be problems in introducing E_i^{kp} (or its surrogate M_i^{kp}) into the argument of the trip frequency function since variations in these may be the result of residential location decisions. It is not reasonable to assume that households necessarily achieve locational equilibrium with respect to leisure activities as such a step seems to imply. In practice we shall adopt the procedure of considering separate equations for T_i^{kp} and M_i^{kp} in the form of our original model, for each k.

Distribution and Mode Split Approaches
We have criticised the conventional hierarchical trip generation – distribution–modal split – approach for its failure to incorporate feedback from the factors involved in the P and A vectors of our basic trip generation model. More specifically we have criticised the trip generation submodel for being too aggregated in terms of the units of observation. On the other hand we have also criticised those single-equation models of trip making which have tried to integrate spatial and modal price variations into a basic trip generation framework for disaggregating too far with respect to the decision variable.

A model for total trips has been outlined but this is of little value on its own for most specific planning decisions. Some means of allocating trips generated to links of a transport network, to particular modes of transport and to specific destinations are required.

In a situation where the total production of trips has been made specifically sensitive to distributional and modal split characteristics, what has been termed an elastic trip generation model, conventional distribution and mode split procedures, using either gravity- or entropy-maximising models can be applied.[4] These models are designed to allocate flows of traffic to specific links of a network given total trip productions of each zone (O_i) and total arrivals in each zone (D_j).

A basic gravity formulation allocates traffic to links, T_{ij}, by

$$T_{ij} = a_i b_j O_i D_j g(C_{ij})$$

where $g(C_{ij})$ refers to a generalised cost function[5] for travelling from

i to j. a_i and b_j are calibrating factors determined by iterating the model to balance flows such that the following constraints are met:[6]

$$O_i = \sum_j T_{ij}$$

$$D_j = \sum_i T_{ij}$$

$$a_i = \left[\sum_j b_j D_j g(C_{ij}) \right]^{-1}$$

$$b_j = \left[\sum_i a_i O_i g(C_{ij}) \right]^{-1}$$

C_{ij} will depend on the availability and characteristics of the modes of transport available, in practice being a weighted average of the generalised costs (C_{ijm}) for each mode m, available on that link. Modal split of T_{ij} can then be determined straightforwardly by allocating traffic according to relative characteristics,[7] viz.

$$\frac{T_{ijm}}{T_{ij}} = \frac{g_m(C_{ijm})}{g(C_{ij})}$$

If we maintain the disaggregation by journey purpose then $O_i^k = \sum_p T_i^{kp}$. For the same reason as discussed for the generation model there are good reasons for not considering trips aggregated over all persons in this way, but maintaining disaggregation to the individual level is not a practical proposition, both because of the sheer number of observations and the very high proportion of zero values which will occur. A suitable intermediate stage is to consider zonal aggregations only of person types and calibrate separate models for each person type. Hence we would aggregate to $O_i^{kr} = \sum_{p \in R(r)} T_i^{kp}$ where r refers to the person type in question, $p \in R(r)$ indicates aggregation over all persons p who are included in the set of type r. A simple application of the person type procedure is the separate consideration of car-owners and non-car-owners, but any socio-economic variable could be used for classification. *A priori* reasoning should suggest those groups which might display very different reactions to variations in attraction and accessibility which will determine distribution.

Thus we can write a partially disaggregated model as

$$T_{ij}^{kr} = a_i^{kr} b_j^k O_i^{kr} D_j^k \exp(-\beta_i^{kr} C_{ij}^{kr})$$

where

$$a_i^{kr} = \left[\sum_j b_j^k D_j^k \exp(-\beta_i^{kr} C_{ij}^{kr}) \right]^{-1}$$

$$b_j^k = \left[\sum_i \sum_r a_i^{kr} O_i^{kr} \exp(-\beta_i^{kr} C_{ij}^{kr}) \right]^{-1}$$

This shows clearly that the generation factor b_j^k is dependent on purpose and person type, as well as generalised cost which is itself variable with respect to k and r. The attraction factor a_i^{kr} has been left determined only by journey purpose, and thus dependent on aggregation over all person types except for the variation allowed for by generalised cost. We must look at the role of the attraction factor in more detail before accepting this formulation.

Let us recall the logic of the model. We started with a model of trip generation based on individual behaviour and, as yet, undefined concepts of potential and accessibility. From this we can aggregate to an appropriate level to obtain total zonal trip productions of the form O_i^{kr}. However, total trip arrivals in the various zones, D_j^k, have not at this stage been determined. Moreover we have postulated a concept of attraction as perceived by consumers which influences their total mobility yet constrained the distribution of trips by means of a calibrating factor which makes attraction implicitly depend on the number of trips made to a zone. If we wish to concentrate on the impact of destination opportunities on both total mobility and the distribution of trips, we must free the model of this limitation. This will further enable us to test the impact of variations in the supply of facilities in particular locations.

Thus the model becomes a singly-constrained interaction model with only a trip production constraint.

$$T_{ij}^{kr} = a_i^{kr} O_i^{kr} W_j^k \exp(-\beta_i^{kr} C_{ij})$$

where

$$O_i^{kr} = \sum_j T_{ij}^{kr}$$

and

$$a_i^{kr} = \left[\sum_j W_j^k \exp(-\beta_i^{kr} C_{ij}^{kr}) \right]^{-1}$$

The W_j^k are weights expressing the attraction of j for activity k. There is no reason why variations in attractiveness as perceived by different groups of people could not be introduced. The attraction factor a_i^{kr} is a combined attraction–accessibility index, and as we shall see later in the chapter this formulation can be used in the context of a generation model as well.

One final important modification can be mentioned. The one advantage of the doubly-constrained model is its effective capacity constraint on destinations. Whilst this has not been thought to be a useful measure of perceived attraction, in cases where this capacity constraint may be binding it may be advantageous to calibrate both singly- and doubly-constrained models in parallel to estimate any b_j^k

parameters. If the capacity of destination j is given as $\bar{D}_j^k$ then in effect cost penalties can be imposed whenever $\sum_r \sum_i T_{ij}^{kr} = \bar{D}_j^k$, and traffic redistributed accordingly.[8]

We must now turn to the problem of allocating traffic to modes. The integrated distribution–modal split approach simply involves disaggregating the distribution model further to deal with T_{ijm}^{kr} terms, thus producing a separate interaction model, with its own parameters for each mode. However, we must recall that the generalised cost term C_{ij}^{kr} has been synthesised from individual-mode generalised costs C_{ijm}^{kr} The integrated model places an extra burden on the parameter β which must reflect both the distance decay element and the response to modal cost element. For this reason it seems desirable to separate the two processes.

Wilson (1973) has suggested a market-share approach to allocating distributed traffic to modes. The share of mode m in the market for travel from i to j by person type r for purpose k is:

$$M_{ijm}^{kr} = \frac{T_{ijm}^{kr}}{T_{ij}^{kr}}$$

where

$$\sum_m M_{ijm}^{kr} = 1$$

Now the actual cost of travel from i to j is independent of person type and purpose, this is the mode's pure cost (m_{ijm}) although we know that C_{ij}^{kr} is some function of the m_{ijm} for all modes combined. There is therefore an expenditure constraint which can be written as:

$$\sum_m M_{ijm}^{kr} . m_{ijm} = E_{ij}^{kr}$$

The solution is obtained by maximising an entropy function of the form

$$Z_{ij}^{kr} = -\sum_k \log M_{ijm}^{kr}!$$

subject to the constraints of expenditure and market shares summing to unity to yield

$$M_{ijm}^{kr} = \frac{\exp(-\lambda_{ij}^{kr} . m_{ijm})}{\sum_m \exp(-\lambda_{ij}^{kr} . m_{ijm})}$$

λ being a Lagrangean multiplier relating to the expenditure constraints and hence an indicator of the sensitivity of modal split to costs, now independently of the distribution parameter β.

This approach is reasonable in cases where the choice of destination is a higher-order decision than the choice of mode as for the work journey. There may be severe doubts whether the choice of destination is independent of the choice of mode in this way in the case of recreation, and it may be that mode choice is a higher-order decision than destination choice. In these circumstances the market is best thought of, not as trips on specific *ij* links to be shared by available modes, but as recreation trips by car or by bus to be shared amongst available destinations.

A Mode Generation Approach
If the mode choice decision is placed ahead of that concerning destination it seems logical to combine it with the decision whether to travel at all – the generation decision. In such circumstances modes of transport are assumed not to be perfect substitutes in the same market.[9]

Separate demand models for each mode have been used in developments of the single-equation models relating to specific links. These have shown that estimates are sensitive to the number of modes available to the extent that even the separate consideration of two operators within a single mode, each with identical modal characteristics, can lead to an artificial creation of total traffic.[10] This is an analogous problem to that of route choice where one mode offers more than one possible route between two points. Wilson (1970, pp. 31–4) has demonstrated the distorting effects this can have on the model's results.

Our original trip generation model is now rewritten as:

$$T_{im}^{kp} = f(S^p, P_i^{kp}, A_{im}^{kp})$$

where the accessibility factors linking *i* with sites for *k* are made more specific.

The main problem is that specific mode characteristics of cost or time cannot be used in this formulation which is independent of particular *ij* links. Some form of aggregate index will be necessary but there is a danger that such an index may imply equal relative modal services on all the links serving one particular origin zone, whereas in most circumstances certain links, such as those to city centres in urban areas or those to higher-order centres in an inter-urban context, will have markedly better levels of public transport service relative to the private car.

Again we conclude that the best approach is not determinable on *a priori* grounds. Further research on comparing the results obtained from a mode generation–distribution model sequence with those from an elastic trip generation–distribution–modal market-share model is obviously necessary. In Chapter 7, we shall consider some empirical results for mode generation models alongside those for total trip generation models; further comment is delayed until then.

Attraction and Accessibility

Having outlined our preferred model, we must now concentrate on some of the more detailed specification of the approach. It has been clear throughout this discussion of modelling procedures that the crux of the approach suggested, at all levels, is in the definition of attraction and accessibility. These are terms which are easy to use conceptually but much harder to achieve workable definitions of in practice.[11] In the course of the chapter, we have introduced the potential and accessibility vectors in the argument of the generation model, P_i^{kp} and A_i^{kp} respectively, and identified an implicit combined attraction–accessibility index, d_i^{kr}, in the singly-constrained spatial interaction model. It is more convenient here to consider in turn three concepts – of attraction, accessibility and level of service – which have been referred to in the course of the argument and to relate these back to the requirements of the model when appropriate.

Attraction

The rationale for our making a separate examination of attraction, independently of attraction implied by trip flows in the construction of an interaction model, is the need to identify its exogenous influences. We need some measure of attraction as a planning parameter so that the effect of changes in levels of facility provision on both the generation and distribution of trips can be assessed. There are two problem areas: one is the definition of a suitable parameter, the second is incorporating this in the model structure.

There are two essential requirements of any index – that it should be a readily measurable planning parameter and that it should make sense in terms of consumer perception. The former criterion is easily met in the case of work journeys by data on employment opportunities, and for shopping such parameters as aggregate floor space and turnover have been used in various studies.[12] These indices also make some sense in the context of consumers' preferences in the aggregate, inter-urban flows for example, but a more precise examination of behaviour reveals severe aggregation problems in another dimension. Retail turnover, for example, does not discriminate between retail outlets in different trades but rather between forms of organisation.[13]

A more precise index dependent on consumer preference rather than commercial organisation would be expenditure-based weights. Expenditure is related both to turnover and to frequency and/or importance of visit within broad subdivisions of retailing but it can be derived independently of a specific location or interaction model by using sources such as the *Family Expenditure Survey* (Department of Employment, annual). Alternatively, national or regional figures for average levels of trip generation could be used if these were available on a sufficiently disaggregated (by purpose) basis. The important modification is that the weights are based on standard figures for commodity groups rather than the number of journeys made to any specific destination. Once again a more rational disaggregation has been achieved.

Attempts to derive more sophisticated indices of perception using techniques such as the semantic differential scale based on general environmental considerations have not been particularly successful at adding to levels of explanation of variation in trip patterns beyond that provided by more conventional indices. One of the more interesting findings has been the good performance of indices based on the counting of a number of predefined 'key' stores each with a relative weight.

Thus the exogenous attraction weight, W_j^k of the singly-constrained interaction model involves both the number of establishments, N_j^k, and a locationally independent weight, e^k; $W_j^k = e^k N_j^k$, and from this an aggregated index of zonal attraction can be derived:

$$W_j = \sum_k e^k N_j^k$$

Obviously the problems of using this formulation in the case of recreation are much greater. Expenditure weights can only be derived for the limited sector of marketed recreation activities and thus particular problems may arise when there is a need to aggregate these with non-marketed activities to produce an index of zonal attraction. The use of exogenously derived frequency of visit rates may be of greater value here. The equivalent of a key-stores concept could also be used in connection with activities such as professional sport or the cinema although we should note that even for a given site the attraction of the product offered may vary considerably through time with such features as the quality of the opposing team or the film in question.

For recreational activities using natural-resource-based facilities the problem is particularly severe. Most previous studies have only considered single sites and therefore avoided this question. Mansfield (1969) referred to the construction of a relative attractiveness index in this context but argued that it can be assumed constant and independent of the time and cost of travel factors in the short run, and hence unimportant in considering the single-site case. In any event the sort of factors often considered as contributing to attraction – car parks, toilet facilities, and so on – may not be seen by many potential visitors as enhancing sites; these really serve as means of managing existing demand.

Attraction in these cases is not so much what a site does but how it does it. Natural beauty or even the particular attraction of a specific golf course may be largely in the eye of the beholder, yet overall a certain concensus can be achieved on at least relative orderings of scenery, amenities, and so on. Fines (1968) has reported on one example of a practical attempt to classify the countryside on an objective basis, but such exercises are subject to many practical as well as conceptual objections.

However, it may be that highly sophisticated measures of perceived attraction are not required. We suggested that the best index of attraction is provided by an expenditure- or frequency-based weight. We know that both on-site expenditure and visit rates are low for recreation in comparison with other activities, and particularly so when locations are taken into account. For this reason simple counts of facilities may provide acceptable indices of attraction, $W_j^k = N_j^k$, and the burden of discrimination between sites is placed on accessibility.

We have concentrated the discussion on the attraction weights in the interaction model context. In the trip generation context it is not possible to consider attraction independently of accessibility because of the need to aggregate over all possible destinations. For this reason the relevant vector was described as relating to potential rather than attraction; this is discussed in more detail below.

Accessibility
It was suggested above that the structure of costs and the nature of the demand for recreation activities will make accessibility the more crucial parameter. Moreover, even when a separate index of attraction can be derived, it will be necessary to place this in a relative spatial context by deflating attraction by a measure of accessibility.

We have already derived such an index from the spatial interaction model in the form of the calibrating factor a_i^{kr} which is best distinguished as a combined attraction accessibility index. In general terms:

$$a_i^{kr} = \left[\sum_j W_j^k f(C_{ij}^{kr}) \right]^{-1}$$

which is the inverse of what is usually termed economic potential, after the work of Harris (1954) and Clark (1966). Hansen (1959) also used this potential concept as an index of attraction, the total pull exerted on an individual at location i by facilities for k located at various points j, taking into account the distance from i to j.

A similar conclusion can be reached if we start with a concept of pure accessibility along a network. Aggregate accessibility is the sum of the accessibilities to all other points on the network. If we start with accessibility expressed simply as linear distance we can use the index suggested by Shimbel (1953):

$$Z_i = \sum_j d_{ij}$$

If comparisons between networks of different dimensions are required, for example locations in different urban areas, average accessibility could be written as

$$A_i = \frac{1}{n} \sum_{j=1}^{n} d_{ij}$$

where n is the number of possible destinations. These indices are inversely related to the usual concept of accessibility in that low values imply good accessibility. A more common formulation is to consider the inverse of distance and moreover to introduce a non-linear response to distance. The gravity model has used power functions of distance so that we can now write aggregate accessibility as

$$A_i = \sum_{j} d_{ij}^{-\beta}$$

where β is either imposed or more normally calibrated on interaction data.[14] A more common approach is to use an exponential function as discussed above so that:

$$A_i = \sum_{j} \exp(-\alpha\, d_{ij})$$

where α is again calibrated from spatial interaction data. Other writers have gone beyond this to suggest that Gaussian and other non-linear functions give better representations of observed distance decay functions.[15]

At this point, we have defined accessibility as if we were considering the classic featureless plain of location geography. To produce an index of aggregate accessibility which has any behavioural significance for trip generation or distribution each destination needs to be weighted according to the opportunities available, that is by the W_j elements discussed previously. Furthermore, it can also be argued that the links of the network themselves are not homogeneous so that linear distance is not a good approximation to the true deterrence. Such features as capacity (and hence congestion), level of service, quality, comfort and convenience as well as access to the main network itself will all be important. For this reason the concept of generalised cost is normally used instead of distance, this being defined to include elements of these additional features.

The main problem which has been noted is the need to impose the parameter of the deterrence function, the α and β of the formulations used above, or to calibrate this from interaction data. This naturally leads to forecasting problems with any model since the interaction must be known before the parameter can be derived, the parameter being a balancing factor rather than an estimated coefficient with given confidence limits. Since the parameter does not derive from a behaviourally based model, we can have even less confidence than usual about predicting forward with the existing parameter, especially in view of our expectation that the pattern of trip making will be very sensitive to changing accessibility, particularly if non-marginal changes are involved. This criticism applies mainly to the use of such accessibility measures as an influence on trip generation, the P_i^{kp} vector of the basic model. Whilst the interaction model does present a more satisfactory way of producing a deterrence parameter than the imposition of an arbitrary value it is felt that careful sensitivity testing is called for if any confidence is to be placed on forecasts from such a model. What has been very clearly illustrated is the feedback effect, the dependence of the trip generation model on distributional behaviour and in particular the deterrence parameter.

Level of Service
There are two aspects of accessibility independent of the combined attraction–accessibility index, which require a more detailed considera-tion: level of modal service and individual accessibility to transport networks.

We have referred to the construction of aggregate measures of accessibility because of the need to consider total pull and total mobility in the context of the trip generation model. There is an implication, however, that equal relative levels of service by each mode exist to all possible destinations, whether we use crude distance measures or weighted generalised costs. Public transport modes, unlike private transport, do not normally give reasonably constant levels of service in all directions. Improvements in the provision of facilities or in the network, such as the speeding-up of services, will have unequal impact on public transport trip generation depending on the direction in which they occur. To look at this another way, possible redistributions of traffic are more seriously constrained if public transport modes are involved. The consideration of separate-mode generation models helps to some extent here as an accessibility index for a single mode can more easily incorporate such changes than an index aggregated over modes. In the latter case any change affecting the relative generalised costs of the modes on any one link implies a change in the weights for constructing the aggregate generalised cost. Even in the single-mode generation case some concept of the relative price of substitute modes is called for. This remains a rather unsatisfactory area of the model.

Accessibility to the network is mainly a problem with public transport modes although pressure of demand on a household car when there are several drivers may also present similar problems. An obvious measure is the time or cost of reaching an appropriate bus stop or railway station, and the likely length of wait. This is an important modification to the basic accessibility index which must be considered separately because of the different implicit valuations of time spent walking or waiting, from that spent in transit.[16] Again we can note that this accessibility to the network is likely to vary with destination, especially if we introduce the further aspect of a need to change vehicles or mode *en route*. All of these must be added as cost penalties to the accessibility of each destination before aggregating the index. It is these additional dimensions of accessibility which are implied in the separate A_i^{kp} vector of the basic trip generation model.

Conclusions – Some Approximations
We have discussed the construction of some precise indices of attraction and accessibility in some detail, but it must be recognised that these are demanding in terms both of data and computation. Often simpler and more aggregated indices will have to be used as will be seen in Chapter 7. Some guidelines for the use of such approximations are given here.

Attraction and accessibility will not only alter the trip-making patterns of residents of an area but may, in the long run, determine the character of the area itself such that measures of the nature and type of dwellings or even population density can be indicative of such features. Likewise the concentration of many facilities in major urban areas, or within a single urban area towards the centre, means that crude accessibility measures relative to this single destination can give a reasonable approximation to the variations in aggregate accessibility. Hence the lack of suitable detailed data need not prevent the introduction of some index of attraction and accessibility into a model although forecasting will become a more tenuous exercise because of the longer-term adjustments to equilibrium implied in the aggregate surrogates.

In the context of levels of service, aggregate zonal indices of bus miles per hour standardised by zonal area or population can also be indicative of the basic pattern of service provision.

Car-ownership
This is really a part of accessibility, but is such an important variable, and has so often been misused that it is worth separate consideration here. It is an obvious candidate for use as an explanatory variable in a trip generation model, particularly as it is associated with major differences in travel patterns, and indeed leads to good levels of fit, but can it legitimately be used in this way? First we face the multi-collinearity problem; car-ownership and other socio-economic variables, income, occupation, etc. obviously affect travel patterns, but these socio-economic variables can also determine variations in car-ownership patterns, and hence possible bias is introduced into any

estimates. Secondly, it must be recognised that, although there is a clear association between car-ownership and mobility, the causality is not so clearly established. The car-ownership decision may be the result of a particular demand pattern for mobility which makes a car essential, and although it can be argued that it is only the ownership of a car which enables the consumer to reveal his preferences, there is the likelihood of a least-squares bias being introduced.

The usual criticism of forecasting from cross-sectional analyses is particularly relevant here: there is no reason to suppose that a person becoming a car owner immediately adopts the same mobility pattern as an existing car owner of otherwise identical characteristics. The mere fact of his not owning a car implies different valuations being placed on time, convenience, etc. and whilst the decision to own a car will relieve certain constraints on travelling and lead to a new mobility pattern it is most probably a different sort of pattern from that of the existing owner. Ownership of a car in many rural areas may be forced on a person because of the decline in the level of service offered by public transport modes rather than as a result of any change in preferences on the part of the consumer.

For these reasons the most satisfactory approach is to consider car-owners and non-car-owners as distinct groups of the population and to estimate independent equations for each group. Hence the forecasting procedure requires a model of car-ownership to define the relevant groups for whom the separate travel forecasting models can be used. This does mean that we can expect the common explanatory variables to take different coefficients, for example, income elasticities may differ between the two groups because of rather different cost constraints. If it turns out that there is no significant difference between coefficients for the two groups, this will provide more rigorous justification for treating them together than exists at present. Even in zonal aggregate models there is a case for attempting separate estimation of models for two car-ownership groups rather than relying on average zonal car-ownership levels, if data will permit – given that they form, in effect, separate markets.

We must also consider the consequences of this split for mode trip generation modelling. Here the implication is that car ownership affects not only total mobility through car usage, but also usage of other modes. This is an important point which illustrates very clearly possible errors in a conventional modelling procedure. One point is mainly a psychological factor, the mobility granted by car availability leads to the adoption of a different reference standard of accessibility. This will be particularly relevant for those members of a car-owning household for whom the car is not available. What is not clear, however, is how this will affect the usage of other modes since two conflicting arguments can be raised. The greater potential mobility may on the one hand simply lead to a shift outwards in the demand functions for all forms of transport. However, if it is found that travellers are more price (in its widest sense) sensitive the relative price of the alternative mode compared with car may appear much worse, and consequently reduce the demand for non-car modes below that of comparable non-car-owners.

This illustrates a particular advantage of the mode generation model over a total generation–modal split procedure. It indicates clearly that a change in relative prices does not just have a mode switching effect, but may instead lead to a reduction in total generation by, for example, the postponing of a trip until car is available. Although this does involve a proportional switch in mode usage via the generation effect the conventional approach disguises this by the assumption of an over-simple choice pattern.

Prospect of Model Evaluation
The following two chapters are devoted to the application of this basic leisure travel demand model to empirical evidence. Chapter 7 concentrates on the estimation of basic trip generation models of the types discussed in this chapter. In Chapter 8 certain implications arising out of these models are developed and the questions of attraction and accessibility are tackled in more detail in the context of a single urban area. We conclude this chapter with a brief preview of this evidence, setting the scene and explaining the approach adopted.

One warning which must be issued at the start is that the lack of an adequate complete data source has led to problems in maintaining a consistent treatment of the topic and, in some cases, in achieving a satisfactory formulation of the model to be tested. Two main data sources have been used, the 1965 National Travel Survey and the 1966 Oxford Transportation Study. The main implication here is that we cannot aim to achieve a definitive working model, the data requirements for which have been seen to be large and expensive particularly for a distribution model. A useful investigation has, however, been undertaken which highlights the areas requiring further study, and which does permit formulation of a more detailed proposal for a complete testing of the model, with supporting evidence.

The second major reservation is that the objective of this study was not to produce working forecasts of the demand for recreation, either in the aggregate or for any specific facility. The aim which runs through the empirical studies, as well as through the theoretical sections of this book, has been to establish a working hypothesis of recreational activity patterns and the associated mobility, consistent with economic behaviour, and to justify this empirically as evidence for the later development of more complete and satisfactory models for producing such specific forecasts.

A third proviso concerns the statistical techniques used in the course of the empirical work. It has been necessary to employ multivariate techniques on large samples of data to investigate most of the implications of the hypothesised model. These are expensive in terms of both labour time and computing time. Full testing of the models would require a careful examination of all alternative functional forms and alternative specifications of variables, all leading to a very large number of possible combinations. The criterion for judging relative performance is not clear. Conventionally the degree of fit, the value of R^2 in a regression equation, is taken as the basic measure but, as we have already seen, this is not necessarily the most satisfactory index. The structure of the equation in terms of significant coefficients (as tested by the t-statistic) is just as important and, for many of the purposes of this study, is superior in comparing the results for different data sets. For these reasons, and the problems of obtaining comparable equations, no attempt has been made to test all possible forms, nor necessarily to maximise R^2. The basic philosophy has been to test simple linear versions of a model wherever possible and only introduce non-linearity when this seemed desirable on *a priori* grounds. The coefficient values estimated should be regarded only as indicative of the direction and order of magnitude of the influence of particular variables and not as planning parameters. More specific statistical problems are discussed as they arise.

7. The Demand for Leisure Travel–Empirical Results

The previous chapter has established the basis for modelling the key variable of the analysis – travel. It has attempted to show why the more conventional transport models are inappropriate in the case of leisure travel, particularly when the output of the travel model is required as an input to an evaluation model. In this chapter some results from testing such a model, albeit in a preliminary form, can be outlined. After an introductory discussion of the data, the basic estimated models are presented, and the remainder of the chapter consists of detailed analysis of particular influences.

The Data

Nature and Organisation of the Data

It was essential for this analysis that a very representative set of data should be used, in particular data that was independent of specific locational influences. This rules out the data collected in most urban transportation studies which are implicitly biased by the urban areas in question. The instability of similar models estimated on different sets of data from different urban areas is evidence of this lack of spatial transferability. This study does have the advantage, not enjoyed by such transportation studies, of not having to produce specific forecasts in the context of an urban plan and can therefore concentrate on the underlying behaviour.

One set of data which does match up to this basic requirement is that collected in the course of the National Travel Surveys organised by the (then) Ministry of Transport from 1964 to 1966. The largest of these, for 1965, was the one chosen for this study since the sample had been designed to yield unbiased subsamples at the regional level as well as the national and this would permit some investigation of the spatial stability of the model used.[1] The information had been collected to provide information on a large scale on the patterns of travel and the trends in trip making in Great Britain, and not with any specific model-building exercises in mind. For this reason the data does not always

115

match up to the detailed requirements of our model; in the absence of a complete data collection exercise on a similar scale the National Travel Survey is by far the best source available.[2]

The information collected during the survey consists of a weekly travel diary for each person aged 3 years or over in each of the sampled households. These diaries were collected in twenty-six fortnightly phases spread over a twelve-month period to avoid seasonal or other such bias. Because of the lack of locational specificity no origin–destination information was collected, simply journey purpose, the mode of transport used on each stage of the journey and its money cost, and the length of each stage and the total journey.[3] As it was necessary to obtain mobility patterns for each individual the records for each journey were aggregated over each journey purpose to obtain a total number of journeys for each purpose by each mode for the week. No analysis was made in the modelling exercise of the use of different modes for the separate stages of journeys, multistage journeys were analysed according to the main mode used, as defined by stage length. The stage has been used as the main unit in the tabular presentations, however, based on the whole sample since this facilitates easy comparison between generation and modal split patterns. As well as total trip making, the total mileage covered by each person was calculated.

The detailed journey-purpose classification was grouped into six categories as shown below, of which we shall only be concerned with the first three in this study.

Recreation
Eating or drinking out
Sport (for spectators and amateur competitors)
Entertainment and public social activities

Social
Visits to friends and relations

Pleasure
Holidays
Pleasure trips other than for specific purposes cited above

Shopping
Convenience shopping
Goods shopping
Personal business

Work
Journeys to and from normal place of employment, except where the
    journey from work is for any purpose other than returning to the
    normal home residence

Other
Journeys in the course of work
Students' journeys to or from schools and colleges

This classification may be criticised on certain logical grounds, particularly the distinction drawn between recreation and pleasure purposes, but it does have the advantage of grouping together the more homogeneous journeys in terms of frequencies and journey lengths in terms of their relationships with certain key explanatory variables. It is in many ways a statistical grouping, based on the evidence of frequency distributions of the basic journey purposes, but this was necessary to ensure certain minimal variances in the dependent variables chosen and to cause the least possible interference with the identification of important influences.

Very detailed information was available on the mode of transport used, for example rail was classified by class of travel, bus by type of service (stage carriage, express, etc.) and car according to ownership and whether the journey was made as driver or passenger. Such detail was inappropriate for the individual-based modelling exercises envisaged because of the very heavy zero bias which would occur in the mode generation models. For this reason the main modes were grouped. Rail, stage carriage bus, car and van driver, car and van passenger and walking (only those stages over one mile were recorded in the Survey) were separately identified, all other means of transport being grouped together.[4] To reduce the number of separate equations and because of difficulties with non-car-owning households the two car/van modes (driver and passenger) were combined for the modelling exercise, and it was also found that the heavy zero bias and low variance in the use of rail for the purposes to be considered would lead to identification problems. For the mode generation models the comparison was restricted to bus and car, but since these two modes account for 61.4 per cent of all journey stages in non-car owning households and 78.4 per cent in car-owning households, this does cover the major part of the market. The total trips model does include journeys and stages by all possible means of inland transport, however.

Regional Variations in Mobility
As mentioned above it was decided to conduct the modelling exercise on the regional subsamples. The broad patterns of recreational mobility in the eleven planning regions are illustrated in Tables 7.1 and 7.2. A representative selection of six of these regions, Scotland, North-west, West Midlands, East Anglia, Greater London, and the rest of the South-east, was used for model estimation, and to avoid overburdening the analysis with too many similar equations, only an illustrative selection of the results is presented here.[5]

TABLE 7.1   Recreational and leisure travel patterns in Great Britain, 1965

Average no. journey stages per person per week

Region	Recreation	Social	Pleasure	All purposes
Scotland	1.6	2.0	0.6	12.3
Northern	1.7	1.7	0.6	11.4
Yorks and Humberside	1.5	1.8	0.9	12.0
North-west	1.5	2.0	0.6	12.5
Wales	1.3	1.4	0.7	9.9
West Midlands	1.8	1.9	0.7	12.9
East Midlands	2.1	1.7	0.8	13.2
East Anglia	1.5	1.8	0.6	12.8
Greater London	1.8	1.8	0.8	13.2
South-east	1.7	1.8	0.7	13.4
South-west	1.5	1.8	0.9	11.9
Great Britain	1.7	1.8	0.7	12.5

SOURCE   National Travel Survey 1965, unpublished tabulations.

TABLE 7.2   Recreational and leisure mileage in Great Britain, 1965

Average mileage per person per week

Region	Recreation	Social	Pleasure	All purposes
Scotland	6.2	12.6	12.3	67.1
Northern	5.6	11.4	12.4	63.4
Yorks and Humberside	5.6	9.9	17.3	66.0
North-west	4.6	12.2	12.2	63.0
Wales	5.6	10.0	11.4	62.8
West Midlands	7.0	11.7	14.1	71.0
East Midlands	8.2	11.6	13.1	71.9
East Anglia	5.6	13.7	15.0	77.3
Greater London	4.6	12.3	12.0	69.3
South-east	6.4	15.7	11.3	82.2
South-west	5.0	14.1	16.3	73.8
Great Britain	5.8	12.6	13.0	70.0

SOURCE   National Travel Survey 1965, unpublished tabulations.

The regional comparisons show that variations in total mobility between regions do not conform to any rigid pattern. In terms of numbers of trips, only the Northern region and Wales are notably below the average although the North-west can be added to these when mileage is considered. East Anglia and the South-east outside London have above-average rates, more pronounced in terms of mileage than for trips. The regional variations in leisure mobility are greater and of a different nature. For recreation, Wales is below average on trip rates but virtually up to the average on mileage, whilst Greater London produces a slightly above-average trip rate, but a mileage rate well below the average; such factors are obviously related to trip lengths and regional structure. It is the Midland regions, particularly the East Midlands, which display genuinely above-average recreational mobility in terms of both trips and mileage.

A different pattern emerges for social travel where Scotland and the North-west have higher trip rates but around-average mileages, Wales has both a lower trip rate and below-average mileage, whilst the average number of trips made in the South-east and Yorkshire and Humberside are made over much longer distances in the former and much shorter in the latter. Pleasure travel reveals yet another variation. No region deviates markedly downwards but Yorkshire and Humberside and the South-west do have slightly above-average figures for trips and these are confirmed by those for mileage.

This brief overview of the data does reveal the large variations present, confirming our hypothesis of a very complex underlying behavioural pattern. Such regional disparities could be due to differing social structures or to differing physical topology. By considering each region separately (rather than simply as a regional dummy variable in an aggregate model) part of the variation is standardised out and this should permit some clue as to the source of regional variations to be detected.

Regional Variations in Modal Split
As well as the differences in overall mobility, we expect to find substantial variations in mode usage between regions, again resulting both from demand-side factors (the socio-economic characteristics of the resident population) and from the supply side (the physical structure of the region and its transport networks affecting accessibility). Table 7.3 illustrates such regional variations with data for four contrasting English regions, and further breaks the data down to give comparative figures for each of the three leisure travel purposes.

The main features are the dominance of car in all leisure journeys, at the expense of public transport. The greater importance of family journeys for social and pleasure purposes is seen in the split between driver and passenger figures for car usage. One exception to the lesser importance of public transport is the use of bus in the course of social journeys which is at least as great as the overall figure for all purposes, rail usage also stands up well in this case. The abnormal figure for 'other modes' in East Anglia is largely represented by the use of bicycles, and the figure for East Midlands (not shown in the table) also shows this feature. For the pure pleasure journeys the use of local buses is much less in all the regions although rail is quite important because of its share of longer stages. It is also interesting that, with the exception of East Anglia, over one-fifth of all pleasure stages are made on foot, even when only counting walking stages exceeding one mile in length.

TABLE 7.3   Comparison of modal split on recreation and leisure trips – Selected regions, 1965

				% Journey stages by each mode			
Region and purpose	Rail	Bus	Car/Van driver	Car/Van passenger	Walking	Other	Total
North-west							
All purposes	1.8	40.3	20.9	15.3	10.8	10.9	100.0
Recreation	0.6	29.4	34.3	21.4	8.2	6.2	100.0
Social	1.8	40.3	18.3	24.0	9.4	6.2	100.0
Pleasure	2.6	14.5	16.3	32.2	21.1	13.3	100.0
West Midlands							
All purposes	0.8	31.2	24.8	17.5	13.0	12.7	100.0
Recreation	0.6	22.8	35.6	23.1	11.1	6.8	100.0
Social	0.5	32.5	22.3	26.4	10.7	7.6	100.0
Pleasure	1.5	9.8	18.1	35.1	21.8	13.7	100.0
East Anglia							
All purposes	1.5	11.9	26.3	19.6	8.1	32.6	100.0
Recreation	0.7	7.8	40.5	26.0	7.1	17.9	100.0
Social	1.6	12.0	23.5	34.6	6.8	21.5	100.0
Pleasure	1.3	5.3	26.6	43.0	9.6	24.2	100.0
South-east							
All purposes	4.0	18.7	28.0	19.9	11.3	18.1	100.0
Recreation	1.6	11.2	44.4	25.9	7.9	8.9	100.0
Social	3.0	19.2	26.2	30.3	9.5	11.7	100.0
Pleasure	1.5	7.3	19.9	37.1	22.4	11.9	100.0
Great Britain							
All purposes	3.8	31.0	23.2	16.9	12.1	13.0	100.0
Recreation	1.8	23.0	34.6	22.0	10.9	7.7	100.0
Social	2.9	32.3	20.6	25.8	10.4	8.0	100.0
Pleasure	2.6	10.4	16.8	34.4	23.7	12.1	100.0

SOURCE   National Travel Survey 1965, unpublished tabulations.

This brief overview of the modal split of leisure trips suggests that some pronounced differences will emerge in the mode generation equations, both between regions for each journey purpose and within each region for the different journey purposes.

Car-ownership
One of the factors which gave rise to some difficulty in the previous chapter is the question of car-ownership. The conclusion reached was that separate consideration of car-owning and non-car-owning groups would be necessary if useful answers were to be obtained, particularly for mode generation models. Table 7.4 summarises the trip and mileage generation rates and the modal split patterns for the two groups in the

country as a whole, confirming the pronounced differences in leisure mobility which are associated with the ownership of a car. For recreation and pleasure those in car-owning households make about twice as many journeys and travel up to three times as far as those from households without a car. Social journeys, which appear to be less likely to be postponed when a car is not available, reveal a lesser divergence in trip rates but the car-owners are still much more mobile in terms of mileage overall.

TABLE 7.4   Comparison of trip generation and modal split for car-owning and non-car-owning households, 1965

			% Journey stages by each mode						
	Rail	Bus	Car driver	Car passenger	Walking	Other	Total	Total Trips	Total Mileage
Car-owners									
Recreation	1.2	9.9	51.5	24.7	7.2	5.5	100.0	2.3	13.3
Social	2.0	12.9	37.2	34.9	6.9	6.1	100.0	2.2	18.9
Pleasure	1.1	3.5	26.9	43.3	17.1	8.1	100.0	1.0	19.3
Non-car-owners									
Recreation	3.1	48.6	1.7	16.8	17.9	11.9	100.0	1.1	4.2
Social	3.8	55.8	0.8	14.6	14.6	10.4	100.0	1.6	7.2
Pleasure	5.2	21.5	1.0	20.2	34.1	18.0	100.0	0.5	7.6

SOURCE   National Travel Survey 1965, unpublished tabulations.

As would be expected the non-car-owners make a much greater proportional use of public transport, and also a very much greater use of their own feet in satisfying their demands for leisure activities, although given the difference in total mobility, differences in the absolute propensity to use each mode by the two groups are much reduced, those in walk stages being virtually removed. What is additionally noticeable is that a substantial proportion (over 20 per cent in the case of pleasure travel) of all stages by non-car-owners are made by car. As many pleasure stages are made by car as are made by bus by those without a household car available.

This completes our overview of the data to be used in the model-building exercise. Very diverse patterns of leisure mobility have been identified between the data subgroups defined by region and car-ownership, and the inter-group patterns differ by journey purpose and by the mode in question. In such a complex situation the prospects for obtaining a model with a high level of explanation are not great. What we shall concentrate on in the discussion of the results to follow is variations in the structures of the equations identified.

The Regression Model
It will be recalled that the model developed in Chapter 6 hypothesised
that trips are dependent on a vector of socio-economic characteristics,
S, and a vector of supply prices of the relevant activities. The latter will
depend broadly on the spatial potential, P, of the area in which a person
is resident for the activity in question, and the likely accessibility, A,
along an available transport network.

Expressed in the form of a linear equation the model to be estimated
is given as

$$T_r^{kp} = \alpha + \sum_1^m \beta_i S_i^p + \sum_1^n \gamma_i P_i + \sum_1^s \delta_i A_i$$

where T_r^{kp} refers to the number of trips by person p for purpose k in
region r. The linear form was used as the simplest to interpret and
some preliminary testing on non-linear forms of certain variables
suggested that no general improvement in the overall performance or
definition of the equations was to be obtained although better fits could
be obtained for individual subgroups of data. However, in order that
the equations and the estimated coefficients should be kept comparable
for all the subgroups, the linear formulation was retained for all cases.

Selection of Independent Variables
The remaining task is the selection of appropriate variables to represent
the S, P and A vectors in the model. The use of data not collected
specifically with this model in view has, of course, presented some
constraints, particularly with regard to the potential and accessibility
factors. The variables used in the regression estimation are summarised
in Table 7.5.

The socio-economic influences are fairly well defined. Personal
characteristics of income, age, sex and socio-economic group,[6] the
conventional 'generalised income' influences of most economic demand
studies at an individual level and which have been shown in
Chapter 5 to have an important influence on leisure activity patterns,
were all identified. In addition it was necessary to introduce certain
household factors which, as external influences, could affect the
behavioural pattern of the individual. Three variables were used,
measuring household income, household size and the individual's status
within the household. Aggregate household income was introduced for
two reasons. Firstly, it was necessary to have an income variable
relevant for non-earners in the household and, secondly, even for
earners it expresses the additional dimension of the household's
aggregate economic size. This latter point of economic size was felt to
outweigh the purer income effect which would have required a
standardised income per head variable. In practice it was also found that

TABLE 7.5 Summary of independent variables

S_1	Personal income (£)
S_2	Age (years)
S_3	Sex – Male = 1
S_4	S.E.G. – Professional and Managerial = 1
S_5	S.E.G. – Non-manual = 1
S_6	S.E.G. – Supervisory and Skilled manual = 1
S_7	S.E.G. – Unoccupied = 1
S_8	Household income (£)
S_9	Household size (No. of persons)
S_{10}	Status – Head or housewife = 1
P_1	Urban area – Conurbation = 1
P_2	Urban area – 250,000 to 1 million population = 1
P_3	Urban area – 100,000 to 250,000 population = 1
P_4	Urban area – 50,000 to 100,000 population = 1
P_5	Urban area – 25,000 to 50,000 population = 1
P_6	Rural area – Under 3000 population = 1
P_7	Population density (persons/acre)
P_8	Distance to central area (miles)
A_1	Number of cars owned
A_2	Full driving licence = 1

there was virtually no correlation between this household income variable and household size in terms of number of persons and thus no multicollinearity bias from the inclusion of both variables. As well as indicating likely external effects in terms of economies or incentives to vary the activity pattern, household size reflects the cost of family travel and the likelihood of problems arising in scheduling joint family activities. The status variable (a dummy variable indicating whether a person is the household head or housewife rather than just a member of the household) indicates a further dimension of household structure.

The other variables which could be constructed from the data cannot be assigned easily to the P and A vectors hypothesised in the basic model. These are mainly variables describing characteristics of the area of residence of the household such as the size of the urban area (in terms of population), the population density of the ward of residence (the second stage-sampling unit) and the distance from the nearest defined central area. It can be seen that all of these aggregate indices incorporate elements of both P and A factors since both the density of opportunities and the density of the transport network which governs accessibility are related to these measures of urban structure.

Two more specific aspects of the A vector with respect to car travel could be incorporated, the number of cars owned by car-owning households (or available to members of the household),[7] and whether the individual held a full driving licence. These two variables indicate the likely availability of a household car to the individual, although ideally a more sophisticated index of availability is required.

Interpretation of Results

We must finally establish a set of criteria for the assessment of the equations estimated. Least-squares estimates of multiple-regression equations generate two types of statistics – the regression coefficients and correlation coefficients. It has been customary to measure performance in terms of the latter, the objective being maximisation of R^2 (the square of the correlation coefficient) which measures the proportion of total variance in the dependent variable attributable to the estimated equation. This has, however, all too often been achieved at the expense of relevance, in terms of the underlying behavioural model, and at the expense of a well determined equation in terms of its regression coefficients. This can mean that an equation with good fit need not have good predictive power. Zonally aggregated models have been particularly bad in this respect, the reduced variance of the dependent variable leaving less to be explained by the equation whilst most of this is, in any case, attributable to variables which are essentially scale factors, such as population. Since no behavioural factors are identified the equation performs badly as a means of forecasting anything but naive changes in the system.

For predictive purposes it is better to have an equation which is well defined in terms of the significance of its regression coefficients. Disaggregated models usually enable better definition because of the greater degrees of freedom available.

Some comment is necessary concerning the validity of the least-squares technique in these circumstances. There is always a danger of bias in a situation of limited value dependent variables because of the non-normality of the distribution of values of such variables.[8] The likely error from this, in this case, is not thought to be great enough to justify the necessary correction procedures,[9] although this remains an area where some care will be necessary in interpretation of results and future development of techniques will be profitable.

As was expected the explanatory power of the estimated equations was not great but, on the whole, fairly well defined equations were identified. The estimation procedure used rejected variables not significant at the 10 per cent level so an initial comparison can be made simply in terms of the pattern of significant determinants. Levels of explanation tended typically to be in the range of 5 to 12 per cent, and none higher than 20 per cent was recorded, although given the large numbers of observations and the correspondingly large number of degrees of freedom these were nearly all significant (in terms of the F-ratio) at the 1 per cent level (and the majority of these at the 0.1 per cent level). The basic patterns of the equations is presented in outline form in Table 7.6 for non-car-owners and Table 7.7 for car-owners. These tables identify the significant coefficients for the total trip

TABLE 7.6 Equation structures for non-car-owners – Selected regions

	Recreation trips				Social trips				Pleasure trips			
	Scotland	North-west	East Anglia	Greater London	Scotland	North-west	East Anglia	Greater London	Scotland	North-west	East Anglia	Greater London
S_1 Income	−				−			−	−			
S_2 Age	+	−			−	−			+			
S_3 Male			+		−	−		−	+			+
S_4 Professional/Managerial	+			+						+		
S_5 Non-manual	+	−		+	+	+	+				+	
S_6 Skilled manual		+		+	−			+			+	+
S_7 Unoccupied	−	−						−			−	
S_8 Household income	+	−		+	+	−	+	+	+			
S_9 Household size	−		−	−	−	+		−				
S_{10} Status	+	+		−	+	+		−	−			
P_1 Conurbation										+		
P_2 City												
P_3 Large urban												
P_4 Medium urban												
P_5 Small urban												
P_6 Rural				−					+			
P_7 Density	−	−			−					+		
P_8 Distance	+	−			−					−		
A_1 Cars		+										
A_2 Licence												

TABLE 7.7 Equation structures for car-owners – Selected regions

		Recreation trips				Social trips				Pleasure trips		
		Scotland	North-west	East Anglia	Greater London	Scotland	North-west	East Anglia	Greater London	Scotland	North-west	East Anglia	Greater London
S_1	Income	−				−	−	−					
S_2	Age							−		−			
S_3	Male		+	+	+	+							
S_4	Professional/Managerial	+	+		+	+			−		+		
S_5	Non-manual		+	+	+	+	−						
S_6	Skilled manual		−					+					
S_7	Unoccupied	−											
S_8	Household income	+			+	+		+		+			−
S_9	Household size					−			−				
S_{10}	Status	−	−	−	−		−		−			−	
P_1	Conurbation		−			−	+	+					
P_2	City	−	+										
P_3	Large urban							+		+			
P_4	Medium urban									+			
P_5	Small urban									+			
P_6	Rural	−	−				+	+		+			
P_7	Density		−			−	−				−		
P_8	Distance					−	−	+	−				
A_1	Cars	+	+		+	+	+		+	+		+	
A_2	Licence	+	+			+			+			+	+

equations in a selection of regions, indicating the direction of influence. The diversity of equation structure between regions and between journey purposes within any one region will be immediately obvious. Additionally, a comparison of the two tables highlights some basic differences between car-owning and non-car-owning groups.

Attempting a three-way comparison is not an easy task and only a fairly synoptic analysis will be given here. Three broad findings do emerge:

1 The model is slightly more satisfactory for car-owners than for non-car owners.
2 There is a marked deterioration in performance as the journey purpose becomes less specific, the equations for social travel are slightly worse than those for recreation, and those for pleasure very much worse.
3 There is a very strong regional factor, and those regions with the more diverse structure produce better defined equations. Scotland and the North-west are consistently superior in this respect. It may have been expected that the most homogeneous region, Greater London, would yield the best results, given the very crude locational variables used. Furthermore, although there are differences in the socio-economic determinants between the regions the greatest contrasts are in respect of the locational factors.

In the following section of this chapter a closer look at the relative importance of the main determinants of variation in leisure travel patterns will be taken.

Analysis of the Determinants
Separate consideration of the effect of individual variables on trip making, mileage generated, and mode usage is deferred until later in the chapter. In this section we aim to look, in a little more detail, at the relative importance of the main determinants and also to make some comparisons between the initial overall trip models and the alternative mileage and mode generation models. The illustrative examples are taken mainly from one of the regions studied, the North-west, since it is one of the more balanced regions in terms of regional structure and variety of types of area. The conclusions are, however, based on the whole spectrum of results for the four areas summarised in Tables 7.6 and 7.7.

First of all we shall restrict the analysis to consideration of trips for recreation since this is the easiest of the three purposes for which to construct a meaningful model. Tables 7.8 and 7.9 present the results for this model in comparative form for the two car-ownership groups in the North-west region.

TABLE 7.8   Recreation travel in the North-west – Non-car-owners

		Total trips	Mileage	Car trips	Bus trips
S_1	Income		+0.20(2.86)	+0.01(3.12)	
S_2	Age	−0.01(1.85)			−0.004(1.76)
S_3	Male				
S_4	Professional/ Managerial			+0.36(2.20)	−0.54(1.97)
S_5	Non-manual		+3.02(2.26)	+0.18(2.96)	
S_6	Skilled manual		+4.02(2.81)		
S_7	Unoccupied	−0.55(5.34)			−0.36(5.06)
S_8	Household income	+0.02(3.65)			+0.01(2.83)
S_9	Household size	−0.10(2.92)			−0.06(2.27)
S_{10}	Status	−0.47(3.36)	−3.27(3.49)		−0.31(3.18)
P_1(L)	Merseyside	+0.26(1.65)			+0.21(1.82)
P_1(M)	Greater Manchester	+0.54(3.89)	+1.80(2.08)	+0.10(2.40)	+0.34(3.47)
P_3	Large urban				
P_4	Medium urban				
P_6	Rural				
P_7	Density	−0.02(4.67)		−0.004(3.88)	−0.01(3.68)
P_8	Distance	−0.06(2.39)			−0.04(2.49)
A_1	Cars				
A_2	Licence	+0.34(1.68)			
Constant		1.65	2.34	0.09	1.06
R		0.300	0.184	0.206	0.256
F		12.30	8.75	11.07	8.72

The two most important social influences on the recreation travel pattern emerge as household status and not being occupied in gainful employment. Both have strong downward influences on the level of trip generation, mileage generated and the number of trips by individual modes. This suggests that recreation away from the home is more the province of the younger, but employed members of families, and for this reason age does not figure strongly in this linear formulation. Sex is not such an important independent determinant.

Income does not appear to exert any strong influence independently of the other factors. Occupation, however, does seem to be important, professional, non-manual and skilled manual groups all having above-average trip rates and mileage.

Household size is negatively related to trip rates, occurring more frequently as a determinant in the case of non-car-owners, but with a rather pronounced effect on the car-owning group as well in the North-west region. The cost factor may be expected to dominate in non-car-owning households, in the car-owners' case this may be an indicator of demand pressure on the family car.

TABLE 7.9   Recreation travel in the North-west – Car-owners

		Total trips	Mileage	Car trips	Bus trips
S_1	Income			+0.02(2.22)	
S_2	Age				
S_3	Male				
S_4	Professional/ Managerial	+0.87(2.41)			
S_5	Non-manual	+0.87(3.33)		+0.66(3.75)	
S_6	Skilled manual	+0.78(2.88)	+2.92(1.93)	+0.31(1.65)	
S_7	Unoccupied	−0.42(1.84)	−4.66(3.71)		−0.29(4.32)
S_8	Household income				
S_9	Household size	−0.20(3.86)	−0.85(2.39)	−0.12(2.94)	
S_{10}	Status	−1.12(6.36)	−7.16(5.97)	−0.43(3.02)	−0.34(5.30)
P_1 (L)	Merseyside				+0.32(2.27)
P_1 (M)	Greater Manchester	+0.46(2.80)	+2.90(2.81)	+0.44(3.52)	+0.29(3.39)
P_3	Large urban	+0.42(1.74)			+0.68(4.92)
P_4	Medium urban				+0.44(3.09)
P_6	Rural	−1.15(2.92)	−4.63(1.78)		
P_7	Density	−0.02(2.93)		−0.01(1.78)	
P_8	Distance				+0.05(3.43)
A_1	Cars	+0.42(2.33)	+3.33(2.75)		
A_2	Licence	+0.43(2.17)	+5.73(4.44)	+0.84(4.95)	−0.36(5.01)
Constant		1.99	8.78	0.79	0.19
R		0.340	0.309	0.339	0.285
F		11.88	14.45	17.77	12.10

Locational factors do not show easily identified consistent patterns because of the widely differing structures between the regions. Table 7.8 shows clearly the very different effects of the two conurbations of Merseyside and Greater Manchester on trip patterns and the other conurbations considered, Greater Glasgow and the West Midlands, have patterns different again. For this reason it is not likely that the other area variables will produce consistent results. There is some evidence, however, that the larger urban areas do have some scale influence on recreational trip making and the smaller urban areas a rather lesser influence. Population density does show a fairly widespread and consistently negative influence. Taken with the size of urban area variables this may suggest that recreational opportunities are not centrally located but are more suburban phenomena, a point we shall consider in more detail in the following chapter. Central area distance is not, however, identified so consistently. For recreation it tends to be negative so that although the less densely inhabited areas are those with greater recreational generation there is also a definite urban effect on recreation with increasing distance from a central area reducing the level of mobility. For pleasure trips it may be noted that this effect is reversed, suggesting that those more remote from urban recreation facilities may substitute less specific pleasure activities.

The car availability variables are important, driving licence possession particularly so, the number of cars being of rather less widespread importance.

We have so far concentrated on the overall mobility equations. If we disaggregate to the mode level the influence of particular variables can be assessed rather more precisely by classifying these as pure generation, mode switching and mode differential factors. This illustrates the importance of using this mode generation method, pure generation and mode switching variables would perform adequately in a conventional trip generation–mode split analysis whereas variables which act differentially on different modes will not.[10]

The classification is achieved in terms of the relative coefficient sizes, a pure generation variable should have an equal proportional effect on each mode whereas a variable causing mode switching should leave total generation unchanged and have coefficients equal in size with opposite signs for the two modes. In fact, examination of Tables 7.8 and 7.9 shows that it is differential action, i.e. unrelated coefficients, which dominates. The lack of specific modal characteristics of cost and time meant that little in the way of pure mode switching effects could be identified. Pure trip generation influences were restricted to the small group of income, sex and household status variables, those which essentially determined the level of recreational activity. Other socio-economic factors such as age and occupation, and more particularly the locational variables, display a differential effect.

The variables measuring size and type of urban area give a broad indication of likely public transport availability, and accordingly these have generally positive coefficients for bus travel and negative co-efficients for car travel. The influence is not linear, the greatest public transport effect seems to be in the urban areas of 100,000 to 250,000 population. Examination of the conurbation coefficients in the North-west shows that there is a strong generation effect, from recreational potential, which acts differently on the two modes. This is an accessibility effect and presumably reflects the differing levels of access given to different sorts of destination by different modes with public transport serving city centre destinations well but suburban destinations relatively poorly.

Of the socio-economic variables it may be noted for example that the higher occupational group variables have a particular effect on car travel in non-car-owning households and that personal income does increase car usage significantly. Most interesting is the household size variable which was noted above to have a deflationary impact on trip generation. The results of the separate mode models show that this is most pronounced for car usage in car-owning households, suggesting some evidence of pressure of demand.

We have concentrated so far on recreation travel, with some reference to the less well defined pleasure trips, for which, in general, the results are rather poor in the absence of attraction and accessibility variables more precise than the generalised proxies used here. The results for social travel, again given its rather more loosely defined likely destinations, are also weaker than for recreation, but some distinctive variations in structure can be noted.

The locational influences, as expected, are rather more unstable, particularly as far as the smaller urban areas and rural areas are concerned. Amongst the socio-economic factors, age is much more important as an independent influence on social travel and sex is also important, women having the greater propensity for social travel in contrast to the result for recreation. Since the unoccupied status variable also takes a negative coefficient this is not just the dominance of non-working housewives. Social travel seems to be most important amongst the younger working women, possibly part-time workers, since the personal income effect is also negative. It can also be noted that amongst car-owning households, the number of cars owned, and possession of a driving licence are strong positive influences. Social travel may be less of a family activity than at first thought. It may also be seen that increasing household size reduces social travel although, more so than other leisure activities, it seems to be undertaken by the more senior members of the household as evidenced by the effect of household status.

The main conclusions to be drawn from this analysis are:

1 The detailed pattern of influences is diverse and unstable between regions and journey purposes.

2 Of the socio-economic influences, the social (i.e. demographic and occupational factors) are more perceptive discriminators than the economic at disaggregated levels, although age and sex are apparently less important than other indicators of family structure.

3 No single locational factor is identified, but a pattern can be built up through cross-classifying areas according to the three variables used, size and type of urban area, population density and central area distance. The variety of regional structures, in terms of these three variables, is the source of much of the coefficient instability since the observed patterns are being measured against varying regional norms.

In order that these influences can be placed in a clearer perspective the remainder of this chapter considers a selection of these important variables in turn to illustrate the results found. The tabular analysis used is much less precise than the multiple-regression analysis because it is not possible to show the effects of simultaneous influences. However, it does enable us to show the different actual levels of trip making by different classifications of the population. To avoid complicating these tabulations too much no regional breakdowns have been given, although some tables have been split according to car-ownership when this was particularly appropriate.[11]

Economic Factors
The statistical analysis has suggested that the pure economic factors, essentially income, do not provide a particularly perceptive indicator of variations in leisure mobility, independently of all other factors. Nevertheless, the interrelationship of income with occupational, age and other social indices means that a classification of the population by income can provide a good indicator of likely leisure trip generation.

Table 7.10 depicts clearly the stronger association of recreation trip generation, with variations in income and although this trip effect is less in the cases of the other two journey purposes there is nevertheless a strong positive relationship between income and mileage.

If we consider household income so that the zero income effect of non-earners is excluded a fairly smooth relationship in all non-work trip generation is identified (Table 7.11). The elasticity of trip making with respect to household income is of the order of $+0.5$ at the means for leisure travel purposes, not a very pronounced income effect. Again the more rapid increase in mileage with rising income is the result of a positive relationship between income and the average length of stages made. The modal split of these stages is also strongly associated with income – the car becomes increasingly dominant whilst bus and foot are less important for satisfying leisure travel needs (Table 7.12).

Social Factors
The trip generation pattern for the occupational groupings used in the statistical analysis is shown in Table 7.13. This conforms to the expected pattern, consistent with expected earnings except that non-manual groups do seem to be somewhat more mobile than equivalent manual worker groups and unoccupied persons have a rate of trip generation around the average of all groups. No very definite pattern emerges from analysis of the modes of transport used except that the car is more important for the more mobile groups. The only groups with a very different pattern from the average are the non-manual workers who have a much higher propensity to use public transport, particularly rail, than the equivalent manual groups.

TABLE 7.10 Personal income and leisure mobility, Great Britain, 1965

| | Gross weekly personal income | | | | | | | | |
	Less than £8	£8–12	£13–17	£18–22	£23–27	£28–37	£38 and over	No earned income	Average
Recreation									
Weekly stages	1.6	2.0	2.2	2.7	3.3	3.6	3.9	1.1	1.8
Weekly mileage	8.7	10.6	11.3	14.6	18.8	21.6	24.9	12.4	9.3
Social									
Weekly stages	2.0	2.2	1.9	2.1	2.2	2.1	1.8	1.9	2.0
Weekly mileage	11.8	14.1	13.6	16.4	19.7	21.1	21.5	12.4	13.7
Pleasure									
Weekly stages	0.7	0.7	0.6	0.8	0.9	1.0	1.0	0.7	0.7
Weekly mileage	14.2	12.6	12.4	16.2	15.7	20.9	17.2	11.8	13.2
Distribution of persons (%)	14.1	12.3	13.2	8.7	3.8	2.5	1.8	43.6	100.0

SOURCE National Travel Survey 1965, unpublished tabulations.

TABLE 7.11 Household income and non-work mobility,* Great Britain, 1965

| | Gross weekly household income | | | | | | | | | |
	Less than £8	£8–12	£13–17	£18–22	£23–27	£28–32	£33–37	£38–47	£48 and over	Average
Weekly stages	5.0	5.2	5.8	6.2	7.0	7.8	8.5	9.1	9.9	6.7
Weekly mileage	23.8	28.6	33.0	40.1	45.4	53.8	64.0	62.6	79.5	42.8
Distribution of persons (%)	7.1	9.8	19.2	21.5	15.6	10.6	6.0	5.8	4.6	100.0

* Includes shopping as well as leisure travel.
SOURCE National Travel Survey 1965, unpublished tabulations.

TABLE 7.12   Household income and modal choice for non-work travel,* Great Britain, 1965

Stages by each mode (%)

Gross weekly household income	Rail and Underground	Local bus	Car/Van driver	Car/Van passenger	Walking (over 1 mile)	Other modes	Total
Less than £8	2.1	45.8	4.8	13.0	22.1	12.2	100.0
£8–£12	2.0	44.9	9.4	15.7	19.2	8.8	100.0
£13–£17	2.2	36.4	15.2	19.4	17.4	9.4	100.0
£18–£22	2.1	31.1	20.2	22.5	14.7	9.4	100.0
£23–£27	1.8	26.5	25.2	24.4	13.8	8.3	100.0
£28–£32	1.9	23.6	29.1	25.1	10.9	9.4	100.0
£33–£37	2.7	20.0	31.2	26.4	11.0	8.7	100.0
£38–£47	2.4	18.1	33.7	27.2	11.6	7.0	100.0
£48 and over	4.4	11.6	42.7	28.4	8.0	4.9	100.0

* Includes shopping as well as leisure travel.
SOURCE   National Travel Survey 1965, unpublished tabulations.

TABLE 7.13   Occupational status and non-work mobility,* Great Britain, 1965

	Professional and managerial	Non-manual	Supervisory and skilled manual	Other manual	Unoccupied
Stages	9.0	8.1	7.6	5.6	7.5

* Includes shopping travel.
SOURCE   National Travel Survey 1965, unpublished tabulations.

It was noted in the regression analysis that the important demo-graphic factors were not so much the conventional ones of age and sex, but more those of family structure. Table 7.14 confirms the rather indirect effect of age, with a pronounced non-linearity but of rather different form for each journey purpose and for the two sexes. This evidence is based on vehicle stages only, which may underestimate total mobility by younger age groups and women but does not substantially affect the pattern of the results. Peak mobility occurs in the 16–20 age group for females for all leisure purposes, and for males only for the pure pleasure journeys. In the case of recreation, males reach peak mobility slightly later – in the 21–29 age group – although their generation of trips at age 16–20 is about one-third higher than for corresponding females. For social trips too the peak age for men is 21–29, although in this case, this is the only age at which their mobility exceeds that of comparable women. One other interesting feature, although not unexpected, is the rates of trip generation amongst children for social, and more particularly pleasure, trips which are comparable with those for adult women. This tends to suggest that children as such do not lead to a drastic curtailing of leisure mobility.

TABLE 7.14   Age and sex and leisure mobility (Vehicle stages only), Great Britain, 1965

		Recreation		Social		Pleasure	
		Stages	*Miles*	*Stages*	*Miles*	*Stages*	*Miles*
Children	3–4	0.7	3.1	1.3	9.2	0.5	10.3
	5–10	0.6	2.9	1.0	7.4	0.5	10.6
	11–15	1.2	5.4	1.1	7.5	0.5	11.0
Males	16–20	2.7	15.6	2.0	12.6	0.6	13.2
	21–29	3.1	19.5	2.6	21.2	0.5	12.9
	30–64	2.1	11.4	1.4	12.6	0.5	12.5
	65 and over	0.7	3.1	1.0	7.6	0.1	6.6
Females	16–20	2.0	11.4	2.3	15.1	0.6	14.9
	21–29	1.4	8.8	2.3	17.1	0.5	13.2
	30–59	1.1	6.2	1.6	13.3	0.5	13.1
	60 and over	0.4	2.0	1.2	8.9	0.3	6.7
All		1.3	7.6	1.6	11.8	0.5	11.5

SOURCE   National Travel Survey 1965, unpublished tabulations.

Comparable modal split figures were not available, but data on modal split over journeys for all purposes for the various age and sex groups reveals the much greater dominance of the car in the journeys made by adult males than for comparable women. Young children also have an above-average rate of car usage, presumably reflecting the importance of the car for family journeys. The minor modes, bicycle and motor cycle, account for high proportions of journeys by teenage groups. Relatively low usage of car was identified for retired groups. This is possibly a feature which will be reduced in importance through time as a greater proportion of the population has become used to the availability of a car during working life and retains it into retirement.

Locational Factors
The interrelationships existing amongst the social and economic variables, which lead to the need for multidimensional cross-classification if meaningful independent influences are to be identified, are also found, both within the group of locational variables and between these variables and economic factors. The tabular relationships presented in this section are thus even more tentative than those in the two preceding. The likely impact of an area's potential and accessibility on mobility can only be assessed when defined, in terms of the variables available here, by the nature of the surrounding area, urban, rural, conurbation, etc., the distance to the nearest appropriate central area, and the population density of the immediate area. Thus we would expect two areas of comparable density and at equal distances from

the centres of London, Edinburgh and Norwich (for example) to have very different mobility patterns. Similarly, areas of comparable density at differing distances from the centre of the same city would also reveal different patterns.

However, some broad patterns can be identified from a simple examination of the information on type of area and population density. Table 7.15 outlines the different mobilities of residents in four types of area: London, the main conurbations, other urban areas, and rural areas. Whilst no very clear pattern of variations in trip generation

TABLE 7.15   General type of area and leisure mobility, Great Britain, 1965

	Greater London	Other conurbations	Other urban areas	Rural areas
Recreation				
Stages	1.8	1.5	1.6	1.6
Mileage	4.6	7.6	8.7	9.7
Social				
Stages	1.8	2.2	1.8	1.9
Mileage	12.3	11.5	12.6	15.3
Pleasure				
Stages	0.8	0.6	0.7	0.8
Mileage	12.0	12.3	13.8	9.3

SOURCE   National Travel Survey 1965, unpublished tabulations.

emerges, the mileage figures do exhibit a stronger relationship with area type. For recreation and social trips average mileage is least in the conurbations and greatest in rural areas, whilst for pleasure trips the rural area mileage is much less, from the same number of trips, than in the conurbations or other urban areas.

This consideration of generalised types of area does mask some interesting variations occurring between more detailed specifications of the areas. Whilst these variations (see Table 7.16) are on the whole not large they do demonstrate that, for example, each major conurbation has a reasonably unique structure. This suggestion is amplified by the mode usage patterns in these areas (Table 7.17). These results illustrate the reason why there is instability in model estimation for different urban areas, instability which can only be overcome by more precise measures of urban structure.[12] A recent assessment of public transport usage in British towns and cities has also revealed great instability between areas, particularly as far as use for off-peak purposes is concerned.[13]

Population density emerges as much more a measure of mode availability and accessibility. The effect on total trip generation is not very pronounced. For car-owners there is a peak in total trip generation

TABLE 7.16 Detailed type of area and non-work mobility,* Great Britain, 1965

	Conurbations					Urban areas of population				Rural areas
	London	Birmingham	Manchester	Liverpool	Glasgow	$\frac{1}{4}$–1m	100–250th	50–100th	25–50th	3–25th	Rural areas
Stages	8.1	8.0	8.3	6.9	8.0	7.9	8.1	7.9	7.9	7.8	7.0

* Includes shopping travel.
SOURCE National Travel Survey 1965, unpublished tabulations.

TABLE 7.17   Detailed type of area and mode usage (All stages), Great Britain, 1965

% Stages by each mode

Type of area	Rail and Underground	Local bus	Car/Van driver	Car/Van passenger	Walking (over 1 mile)	Other modes	Total
London	14.1	30.1	21.4	13.5	13.0	7.9	100.0
Birmingham	0.8	39.0	20.9	14.9	14.1	10.3	100.0
Manchester	1.7	44.2	19.8	14.3	11.0	9.0	100.0
Glasgow	5.7	60.8	9.8	8.0	10.1	5.6	100.0
Liverpool	1.8	55.2	13.6	12.0	8.5	8.9	100.0
Urban							
250th–1m	1.2	44.6	20.3	14.4	11.6	7.9	100.0
100th–250th	1.6	32.7	22.6	16.1	11.5	15.5	100.0
50th–100th	2.2	33.8	21.1	15.5	13.6	13.8	100.0
25th–50th	2.1	26.2	22.7	18.4	13.6	17.0	100.0
3th–25th	2.2	19.2	28.3	21.0	11.9	17.4	100.0
Rural	1.1	18.5	31.7	24.6	9.2	14.9	100.0

SOURCE   National Travel Survey 1965, unpublished tabulations.

at a density of 7.50 to 9.99 persons per acre, with a fairly symmetric distribution about this modal value. Total trip generation by non-car-owners appears to bear no relation at all to the population density, the distribution being very irregular. Mode usage, however, is strongly associated with this variable (Table 7.18). A steady transfer in importance from car to public transport occurs with increasing density.

Table 7.18   Population density and mode usage (All stages), Great Britain, 1965

Gross population density Persons/Acre	*% Stages by each mode*						Distribution of households (%)
	Rail	Bus	Car	Walk	Other	Total	
0.01–0.49	1.3	13.2	59.5	6.6	19.4	100.0	9.7
0.50–0.99	3.2	17.6	55.7	7.5	16.0	100.0	4.7
1.00–2.49	1.9	21.3	50.7	12.5	13.6	100.0	8.3
2.50–4.99	2.4	22.8	45.9	12.0	16.9	100.0	9.3
5.00–7.49	3.1	27.0	45.5	11.4	13.0	100.0	8.4
7.50–9.99	3.7	27.6	44.2	12.5	12.0	100.0	8.4
10.00–14.99	3.0	31.1	40.4	13.2	12.3	100.0	13.9
15.00–19.99	3.4	33.6	38.7	11.2	13.1	100.0	11.0
20.00–29.99	4.0	36.2	34.3	13.5	12.0	100.0	11.3
30.00–49.99	8.2	41.0	29.7	12.7	8.4	100.0	9.6
50.00–74.99	7.3	40.2	26.3	12.3	13.9	100.0	3.8
75.00 and over	17.1	40.9	22.1	15.1	4.8	100.0	1.7
							100.0

SOURCE   National Travel Survey 1965, unpublished tabulations.

To some extent the figures in the table are biased by the probability of car-ownership in the different density bands. As expected this probability is much greater in the very sparsely populated areas (well over 50 per cent of households own cars) than in the densest areas (only some 40 per cent own cars). Nevertheless, examination of the mode usage patterns for the separate groups shows the same pattern of transfer between modes, albeit at different degrees of intensity. The proportion of stages made by car by car-owners falls from over 70 per cent in the sparsest areas, to under 60 per cent in the more densely populated, whilst for non-car owners the proportion of stages made by public transport increases from under 40 per cent to around 65 per cent for comparable density bands.

One additional effect it was possible to test directly from the tabular data was that of public transport accessibility on bus and rail trip generation. Since this data was only available for part of the sample it has not been possible to incorporate it into the regression models.

Tables 7.19 and 7.20 summarise the survey findings of the distribution of the sample with respect to public transport facilities. The populations of Scotland and Greater London appear to be best served by rail, over 20 per cent in the other English regions and nearly 30 per cent in Wales are more than a 26-minute journey away from a station by public transport. Everywhere, except the London region, only some 20 per cent of people or less live within a comfortable 15-minute walk of rail transport. People without cars tend to live marginally closer to rail but there is very little difference between the groups.

Turning to bus accessibility we can note that some 25 per cent of the population are within a 2-minute walk of a bus stop, though this is not necessarily an appropriate stop for the journeys they may wish to undertake. It is interesting that Londoners tend to have marginally worse accessibility to bus than those living in other areas. Again the

TABLE 7.19 Accessibility of rail transport

	% Persons at a given distance by usual mode from nearest rail station					
	Less than 7 min walk	*7–13 min walk*	*Over 13 min walk*	*4–13 min by public transport*	*14–26 min by public transport*	*Over 26 min by public transport*
Scotland	12.3	9.8	6.2	27.1	29.3	15.1
Wales	5.2	2.6	0.7	26.9	35.6	29.0
Greater London	28.2	25.5	11.1	15.9	15.2	4.2
Other English regions	11.0	9.0	11.8	22.4	23.9	21.5
Total sample	10.8	9.3	10.6	23.1	25.0	21.3
All non-car-owners	11.1	9.1	8.8	25.7	25.9	19.5

SOURCE National Travel Survey 1965, unpublished tabulations.

TABLE 7.20   Accessibility of bus transport

	% Persons at given distance from nearest bus stop				
	Less than 2 min walk	2–3 min walk	4–6 min walk	7–13 min walk	Over 13 min walk
Scotland	23.9	30.3	30.8	10.5	4.6
Wales	19.0	32.5	28.2	10.3	9.9
Greater London	15.9	28.6	33.8	17.9	3.7
Other English regions	26.1	30.2	27.7	11.9	4.1
Total sample	25.5	30.3	28.0	11.7	4.4
All non-car-owners	26.0	31.2	29.2	10.5	3.1

SOURCE   National Travel Survey 1965, unpublished tabulations.

distribution of non-car-owners shows only a slight tendency for them to live nearer to bus facilities.

The influence of accessibility on usage of these modes of transport (for all journey purposes) is shown in Tables 7.21 and 7.22, for the same groups. The expected decline in mode usage with worsening accessibility is identified. With the exception of the London area where rail trip generation is maintained at a relatively high level regardless of accessibility, presumably because of differing network characteristics, relative speed, frequency, possibility of interchanges etc. in this region, only those living within a 15-minute walk of a rail station make any significant use of rail as a regular means of transport. Even the non-car-owners have no particular propensity to use rail.

For bus, where there are not such large differences in network characteristics between areas, a much smoother relationship between accessibility to the mode and mode trip generation can be identified. Scotland and London again have higher rates of bus usage but this is related to the urban bias in both samples, and in the case of Scotland,

TABLE 7.21   Accessibility of rail and rail trip generation

	Average no. rail stages by persons at given distance from rail station					
	Less than 7 min walk	7–13 min walk	Over 13 min walk	4–13 min by public transport	14–26 min by public transport	Over 26 min by public transport
Scotland	1.5	1.2	0.4	0.4	0.2	0.1
Wales	0.9	0.8	0.0	0.4	0.1	0.1
Greater London	2.1	3.2	1.7	2.3	2.1	1.9
Other English regions	1.3	1.9	0.6	0.4	0.4	0.2
Total sample	1.4	1.8	0.6	0.4	0.4	0.2
All non-car-owners	1.5	1.6	0.6	0.5	0.3	0.2

SOURCE   National Travel Survey 1965, unpublished tabulations.

TABLE 7.22   Accessibility of bus and bus trip generation

Average no. bus stages by persons at given distance from bus stop

	Less than 2 min walk	2–3 min walk	4–6 min walk	7–13 min walk	Over 13 min walk
Scotland	7.9	6.8	5.6	3.5	1.3
Wales	4.5	4.1	3.2	2.4	0.4
Greater London	6.1	4.5	4.9	4.4	2.5
Other English regions	4.6	4.1	3.7	3.2	1.4
Total sample	4.9	4.4	3.9	3.2	1.3
All non-car-owners	6.8	6.0	5.2	4.6	2.2

SOURCE   National Travel Survey 1965, unpublished tabulations.

car-ownership. As for rail, bus usage in London does not decline as far with increasing inaccessibility as in other areas. A much greater contrast is noted in the pattern for non-car-owners – consistently much higher generation and slightly less decay with increasing distance.

The question of accessibility also raises the concept of the distance decay function for the journey itself since this will reflect the relative ease with which demands are met at different distances from the home. Table 7.23 presents this information for the three leisure purposes and, for comparison, for the work and shopping journeys where the required facilities are more easily defined.

TABLE 7.23   Stage-length distributions for journey purposes

% Stages of given length

	Less than 2 miles	2 miles and less than 4 miles	4 miles and less than 10 miles	10 miles and less than 30 miles	30 miles and over	Total
Recreation	48.2	15.4	24.1	10.0	2.2	100.0
Social	40.1	16.3	16.2	12.5	4.3	100.0
Pleasure	32.3	8.8	16.8	23.6	18.5	100.0
Shopping	58.4	15.2	18.9	6.2	1.1	100.0
Work	48.8	16.7	24.8	8.5	1.1	100.0

SOURCE   National Travel Survey 1965, unpublished tabulations.

From this table it can be seen that, with the expected exception of pleasure journeys, there is a fairly standard pattern of stage-length distributions, a very high proportion of stages for all purposes being very short, less than 2 miles. Slightly higher proportions of stages are over 10 miles in length for the leisure journeys than for shopping or work. Nevertheless, it would seem that the bulk of leisure journeys conform in range and destination to the patterns set by the work and shopping journey.

Not directly an accessibility factor, but nevertheless related because of the varying standards of mode availability, both public and private, and availability of facilities, is the breakdown of journeys by the day of the week on which they are undertaken (Table 7.24). Whilst Saturday and Sunday are by far the most important single days for leisure, a very high proportion of leisure journeys are undertaken on weekdays. Although separate weekdays are not shown in the table, Wednesdays and Fridays are very popular for sport and entertainment respectively, but no other single day approaches the level of the weekend days.

TABLE 7.24   Leisure mobility by day of week

	% Stages/mileage made on		
	Monday–Friday	Saturday	Sunday
Recreation			
Stages	62.5	23.6	13.9
Mileage	53.1	28.9	18.1
Social			
Stages	56.5	19.5	24.0
Mileage	47.4	21.3	31.3
Pleasure			
Stages	50.6	17.6	31.8
Mileage	45.7	21.1	33.2

SOURCE   National Travel Survey 1965, unpublished tabulations.

Some Conclusions

The analysis of this comprehensive survey data has identified a very complex multivariate structure. The major relationships have been analysed by the use of multiple-regression analysis on a large number of subsets of the data as defined by planning region and car-ownership. The aim has not been to derive a definitive planning model from the analysis but rather to identify the major influences on variations in leisure mobility and place these in a consistent conceptual framework.

The mode generation approach adopted has been shown to have important advantages over the conventional hierarchical trip generation–modal split model because of its more precise identification of the important supply price factors. Location, in the various ways measured here, does have an important impact on the mobility pattern and this is highlighted when the varying levels of accessibility implied by different modes are considered.

Transportation models have always suffered from being unstable through space, significantly different coefficients being estimated for data from different locations. The equations for the different planning regions estimated here illustrate this feature. However, there is also evidence that this instability is related to structural differences between regions and the associated socio-economic distributions. More precise specification of the supply prices of activities should permit both the achievement of spatially stable and transferrable models and improvements in the performance of those models.

We have concentrated on models based on individual units of observation although the explanatory performance could have been improved by aggregation. Such aggregation would not have materially increased our understanding of the workings of the demand side of the market, however.

One final word of warning is necessary before we turn to consider the supply–demand relationships in more detail. The models have been described as demand models because they aim to show the level of consumption given certain parameters, broadly income and supply price. It must, however, be remembered that they have been estimated on the available cross-sectional data for actual consumption. No account has been taken of frustrated demand, individuals with the willingness and ability to pay for a particular activity who are prevented by, for example, the lack of adequate transport or of the facility itself. It is this feature which distinguishes any such analysis of consumption in a spatial dimension. However, in this analysis, taken from a nation-wide sample rather than a specific urban area as has been normal, the wide range of supply situations and consequent range of supply prices encountered will mean that this is a nearer approach to a true demand model than is usual.[14] The tabular analysis, however, in no way presents data on demand, only on actual levels of consumption; the former can only be inferred.

What is required, however, is a more complete analysis of the working of a specific leisure market in which both demand and supply can be considered. The following chapter performs this task for a single urban area.

8. The Leisure Sector in an Urban Area

The main purpose of this chapter is to undertake a closer investigation of the relationship between the supply of leisure facilities and mobility. The precise indices of attraction and accessibility suggested in Chapter 6 could not be derived for the models tested in Chapter 7, but by confining our attention to a single urban area some tentative estimates of this interaction can be made.

The area chosen for this analysis was Oxford since this met the basic requirements of a free-standing city of manageable size, for which basic trip data could be obtained.[1]

There are three parts to the discussion. In the first two parts of the chapter we shall be examining aspects of the spatial distribution of leisure facilities, looking at the economics of location and the actual distribution found. In the third section, we shall be considering in more detail the impact of variation in the distribution of such facilities on the mobility patterns of different groups of residents.

The Economics of Location of Leisure Facilities
This is not an appropriate place for the detailed development of a theory of location. Nevertheless it is useful to begin the discussion by setting it in the context of the general principles of location economics.[2] The process to be discussed here is where free, independent facilities will locate in a given urban structure with known demands and costs. The further question of where they *should* locate to obtain the most efficient functioning of the area is deferred until the planning considerations of the following chapter. Hence we are considering the economic behaviour of entrepreneurs intent solely on maximising their own welfare (profit), regardless of the actual ownership of the facilities in question.

Location
The location decision is essentially one of trading-off between the inputs to the particular enterprise (i.e. the components of cost) and the market

144

(i.e. the components of revenue) once the assumption of a non-spatial economy has been dropped. The 'producer' is thus faced with two decisions, one of determining where the necessary inputs and markets are located, and, assuming the unlikely event of them being entirely contained within the same location not to apply, then of introducing the costs ('transfer costs') of moving either or both through space.

The transfer cost is an addition to the unit cost, or price of the output. In the case of services where the output is consumed at the point of production the transfer cost of the output is borne not by the producer but by the consumer. Even in the case of normal goods an element of transfer cost is borne by the consumer in a visit to a retail establishment. The incidence of the transfer cost does not affect the profile of the total transfer-cost curve, the sum of all such costs regardless of who bears them. The key function in the planning context is the total transfer cost and a likely objective of recreational policy is the minimising of transfer costs. In considering the independent facility, only the producer's transfer costs will feature in the cost structure. However, consumers' transfer costs may well affect demand, so that for the consumer they are perceived as a higher supply price and for the producer a reduction in revenue potential.

A number of simplifying assumptions can reasonably be made in the case of the location of recreational facilities. Firstly, it can be assumed that the location of such facilities will not affect the residential location of the majority of customers; household equilibrium location is usually established with respect to other activities, workplace, educational establishments and possibly shops. Secondly, we can assume that land rents are determined independently of the demands of activities in this sector since, whilst the land requirements for recreation may be quite high relative to other activities, the density of development of that land and associated turnover will be relatively low. This would tend to mean that the bid-price curves of recreation activities in no place lie above those for equal satisfaction (profit) of competing activities and hence will not determine the rent gradient for the area. The bid-price is a key concept in the theory of location referring to that price which a potential user of land is prepared to pay at a given location and which will leave him indifferent between that location and the most desirable location (for which the price is known).[3] This uses the assumption that net returns on activities will be equalised throughout an area and that land prices will be the adjusting factor. Plotting the maximum bid prices at each location against distance from the most desired location (the city centre) yields a true price–location relationship called the rent gradient. The outcome of this will be that recreational activities developing at a low density will either have to pay a premium on rents above the *ex ante* bid rent to use accessible sites, and suffer higher costs and lower profits, or use more peripheral sites at which revenue will be lower because of their location.

If we examine a simple economic explanation of this problem, we can illustrate the choices of location and the density of development for a developer in the recreational sector. For the moment we make the simplifying assumption that the revenue potential for all activities is greatest at the city centre and declines outwards, the city being assumed to be on a featureless flat plain.[4] Therefore we can assume that the curve for average revenue per unit area will fall away from the area of highest potential as shown by the *AR* curve in Figure 8.1. It is necessary to standardise for area to obtain a meaningful relationship, although in this case it is not essential to introduce the abstract concept of space units used by Evans (1973, pp. 21–5); the nature of the site will be

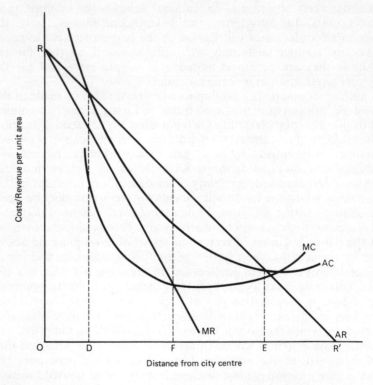

FIG. 8.1

largely determined by the activity in question. Given the rent gradient the average cost per unit area will fall away from the city centre but at a declining rate, and since increasing input transfer costs may be incurred (rising labour costs through the need to pay a premium on wages to attract labour to a less accessible location, for example), average costs per unit area may reach a minimum at a certain distance and then start to rise again (*AC* in Figure 8.1).

It can easily be seen from the diagram that the developer will choose a site within the ring at least *OD* miles from the centre but no greater than *OE* miles. Any point nearer to the centre than *D*, will have average costs greater than average revenue because of land rents; any further away than *E* the revenue potential of the site is too low and average revenue falls below average costs. The optimum site is at *F* since this maximises the profit per unit area, that point where the marginal-cost saving of moving slightly further out is just offset by the revenue loss incurred.

If the cost structure is assumed invariate for different activities then their actual siting will depend on the slope of the average revenue curve (Figure 8.2). An activity which is centre-oriented, such as that given by AR_1 in Figure 8.2 is presumably one which is patronised by groups

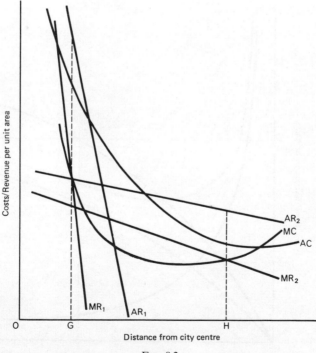

FIG. 8.2

from the whole population, particularly those using public transport (since revenue potential will be affected by accessibility). AR_1, which locates at G, close to the centre, may thus represent an activity such as a cinema. Activity 2 represented by AR_2 has only a relatively slow revenue decay, it is essentially a suburban activity, not so affected by accessibility. This locates at H and may represent an activity such as golf.

Density of development
So far we have been rather unrealistic in that we have not considered the density of development. A 2000-person cinema, possibly showing three different films at the same time, can occupy a relatively small ground space, but even if total floor area is taken the likelihood is of a high revenue per unit area. On the other hand a golf course is estimated to require 1/6 acre for each person,[5] such that revenue per unit area is bound to be low. It is obviously unrealistic to make comparisons across this range, but consideration of more comparable developments can be interesting. In Figure 8.3, OD represents the cost of developing at different densities on a site at a given location at which

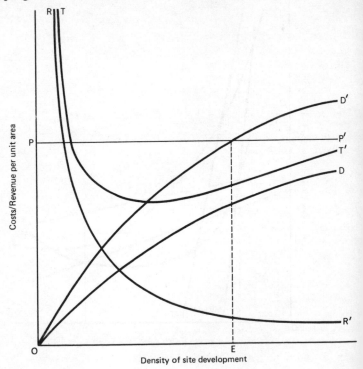

Fig. 8.3

the ground rent is given. The shape of *OD* is taken from the empirical evidence on building costs compiled by Stone (1959) that development costs increase at a decreasing rate as the density of site development increases. Consequently *OD'* represents the marginal cost of increasing the site density and lies above *OD*. The given ground rent for the site is shown by the rectangular hyperbole, *RR'*, this showing that, as density increases, the cost is spread over a larger effective floor area, hence cost per unit area falls. Total costs will thus be given by *TT'*, the vertical sum of *OD* and *RR'*.

Since the site location is known the revenue per unit area is given, as *PP'* in Figure 8.3. We assume for simplicity that revenue is independent of density although this is unlikely. In these circumstances the optimal density of the development is at density *OE* where marginal revenue equals marginal cost. Since revenue depends on location the optimal density will vary with location and hence we can combine the information of Figures 8.1 and 8.3 to obtain a trade-off of optimal developments between location and density. If revenue also varies with density, *PP'* would need appropriate modification and the construction of an appropriate marginal-revenue curve leading to a three-dimensional trade-off.

In Figure 8.4, quadrant A gives the average revenue curve which defines the necessary minimum average revenue for a development to break even at different locations with given cost structures. Quadrant B defines the optimal density of development at each revenue level. Projection of these density levels through the 45° line of quadrant C enables us to derive a relationship between density and location in quadrant D. This function, sloping downwards to the right with developments near to the city centre being at a higher density than those further away, is exactly that which would be expected on *a priori* grounds.

To translate from our rather arbitrary consideration of homogeneous 'recreational developments' into specific recreational facilities will require the introduction of production technologies; these will effectively constrain the feasible density ranges for particular activities. Hence if golf cannot be developed at a density higher than *G* in Figure 8.4 then golf courses will not be economic propositions within a radius of *OF* miles of the city centre. Similarly if to break even, a project such as a cinema requires an average revenue of *OR* it must be built within *OS* miles of the centre and therefore at a density of at least *CT* on the given site.

Location under Competition
We have thus far considered the average-revenue curve as given, defined by total potential of the urban area and the distribution of that potential

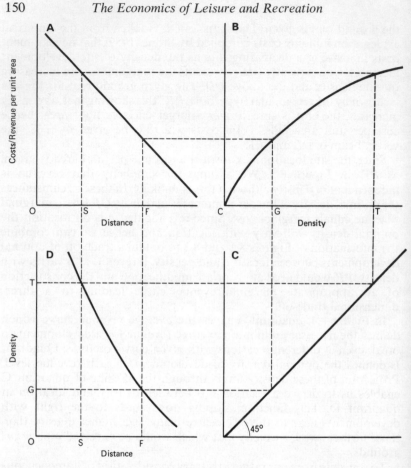

FIG. 8.4

in the area. This is the *market* average-revenue curve, however; that facing the *individual* recreational facility will depend on the structure of the market and the spatial distribution determined. If, for example, there is a market average-revenue curve of RR' (Figure 8.5) but this must be shared between two firms, then if they obtain equal shares each faces an average-revenue curve of SR'. If the cost curve is given by CC' then the optimal range is reduced from the ring DE to the narrower ring GH, i.e. the inner band DG is now too expensive for the smaller firm and the outer band HE produces too little revenue. Competition for sites within the narrower band may of course tend to bid up rents and hence CC'.

We must now consider what the dynamic response to this situation

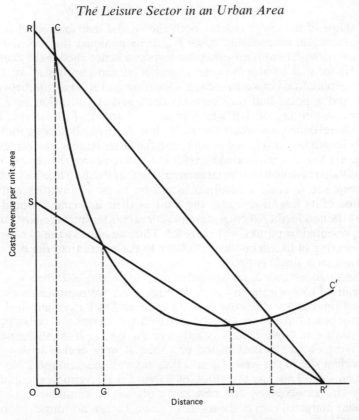

FIG. 8.5

is: will firms cluster or separate? At first, it appears advantageous for the firms to move apart, but once there are two firms anywhere within the defined market OR' neither obtain the full market average revenue at any location. In Hotelling's (1929) famous example of ice-cream sellers on a linear beach with evenly distributed demand the most profitable location for each was alongside the other, and they would settle into a stable equilibrium when they were both at the centre of the beach. In our model of the city the revenue potential is not distributed uniformly, because of decreasing density of population and worsening accessibility as we move away from the centre. If an existing firm (A) is optimally located, at F in Figure 8.1, any new firm (B) entering the market cannot achieve the full market average-revenue curve for any location between F and R'. The market average-revenue curve represents the total revenue potential from the demand of consumers throughout the market area of which the cross-section OR' is one radial.

The shape of the curve reflects both the spatial distribution of those consumers and accessibility costs. It can be assumed that consumers will always wish to minimise transfer costs and hence choose the nearest site. Hence if B locates between F and R' it can capture all of that revenue potential between its chosen location and R' and that between itself and a point half-way between itself and A's location at F. It cannot obtain any of that which remains nearer to F, however. The average-revenue curve must therefore shift downwards throughout its whole length for both B and A, although the latter retains a larger share of the market. B is motivated therefore to locate nearer the centre than F to obtain revenue from the larger market at the existing firm's expense. A's response to such a situation would be to move inwards with B because of its loss of revenue; the limit of their movement would be where the new facility average-revenue curve cuts the average-cost curve as represented by point G in Figure 8.5. Thus we observe the likelihood of clustering of like firms slightly closer to the centre than the optimal location for a single supplier.

The analysis based on consideration of a single radial can be generalised to a whole city area. In Figure 8.6 we represent a cross-section right across the city. Assuming the city to be symmetrical the revenue potential and cost functions are mirror images and the optimal location for a single facility is either at F_W or F_E. If A, the existing site, is at F_E in the east of the city then B may decide to use the equivalent site in the west, F_W and thus take all the demand from the western side. This has the effect of halving the revenue potential at every site as given by the new curve $R'_W SR'_E$. Examination of the relevant marginal curves shows that F_E and F_W are no longer optimal under this regime. Both facilities have the incentive to move towards the centre to enlarge their market at the expense of the other, and new optimal positions will develop at G_E and G_W. Profit levels are lower but we may expect that consumers will benefit from, on average, lower transfer costs. The conclusion of this initial extension is, therefore, that like establishments will tend to locate at sites in similar positions on each radial and that these sites once again will be nearer to the centre than found optimal for a single facility.

We must further consider the generalisation to a three-dimensional area. Whilst demand may be evenly distributed across the area, accessibility will not – those locations on the main radial routes will thus have greater potential than those off such routes. Thus instead of forming a ring of equally spaced sites, competing facilities are likely to cluster at nodes on main radial routes.

Thus far we have considered only a given *ex ante* demand and revenue situation, and recreation as a unitary concept. It seems reasonable to assume, following the evidence of Chapter 5, that recreational activities

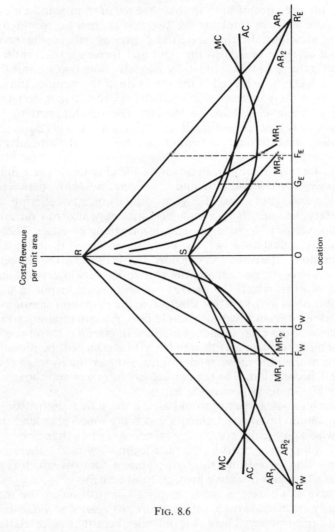

FIG. 8.6

are fairly close substitutes for one another and therefore will need to compete for similar locations. A person, for example, indifferent between swimming and squash rackets, would choose the most convenient in the absence of different prices; hence the existence of one in a location will affect the revenue potential of the other. However, it may also be true that there are strong complementarities involved producing significant external economies of clustering. Whilst the consumer may be indifferent at a given time between swimming and squash, the presence of both in the same location may induce him to make more visits in total for the two sports than he would to two separate locations. In this way, the clustering moves the revenue-potential curve outwards to the right and increases the profitability of both ventures. In this context, we may also note that if some degree of jointness can be achieved in the provision of the facilities the saving in total costs may increase this profitability even further, moving the average-cost curve inwards to the left. The development of multi-purpose sports centres would fall into this category. This more simply internalises the externality; in either case there is a definite advantage in clustering.

Hence we have demonstrated that, in the absence of price differentiation, we would expect to find clustering, not only between like establishments, but also between establishments offering complementary facilities. This complementarity may also run outside the recreation sector to include, for example, retailing premises. There will be limits to clustering set by both economic and technological considerations. The economic consideration is the relationship between the total size of the market and the cost structure which will limit the number of firms which the market can sustain, or to put in a more relevant context for our future discussion, the minimum size of market necessary for the survival of a single firm. As this minimum market size increases, the corresponding increase in essential travel costs will become more relevant and the tendency to cluster will be diminished. In terms of the illustrative model of this chapter the average-revenue curve will become flatter as the market size increases and the influence of more high-potential centres is felt.

The technological barrier would arise if the activity in question had large minimum input requirements, especially concerning land inputs, which would physically prevent the existence of more than one supplier in a given locality. Added to the pure technology factor there is also the imposition of restraint through planning controls which is again likely to affect land-intensive projects most acutely.

We have so far abstracted from price competition in the market. Obviously a firm could trade-off location costs against revenue through an active price policy. There is a difficulty here that price elasticities may be quite high given that the product of many recreational facilities may not be strongly differentiable; the greater product homogeneity the less scope for price competition. It is also possible that quality competition is regarded as more important, particularly in the cases where the 'product' is not sold in measurable units but on a club basis where higher prices may be regarded as synonymous with quality, status or prestige.[6] Empirical evidence would be needed before the importance or unimportance of the price effect could be assessed adequately. It would seem reasonable, however, to take as a working hypothesis that price competition will not be a dominant factor, but that price in conjunction with quality may be used as a means of sustaining firms in non-optimal locations.

The Spatial Supply of Leisure Facilities

In the preceding section, we have discussed some basic principles concerning the location of leisure facilities under the assumption that they are provided by independent, profit-maximising enterprises. The advantage of this approach is that it establishes a basis for our further investigations. In this section, we shall examine the empirical evidence on location; in the following chapter we shall be taking a more realistic stance, concerning ourselves with the more normative issues in the planning of the leisure sector.

The empirical investigation of location is under two broad headings: the actual locations chosen within the market area, and the degree of clustering at those locations both within a certain activity and with other activities. The hypotheses about these issues deduced from the theoretical considerations are that (i) optimal location will occur within an intermediate band between the centre and the periphery of a defined market area, (ii) that the denisty of development will increase as the centre is approached, and (iii) that regardless of the chosen location there will be a pronounced clustering of both like and unlike enterprises at that location.

Empirical Evidence on Location

The simplest way to collect data on the location of non-residential establishments in an urban area is through the telephone directory. This has the advantages of being convenient and up to date and since all businesses and professions are entitled to one free entry in the classified section, it provides an unbiased selection.[7] It does, however, mean that the investigation must be limited to organised facilities, such facilities as public parks and recreation grounds could not be thus covered. These are, of course, more readily observable on large-scale maps of an area but were not included in this study of location exercise for two main reasons. Firstly, as public facilities they are not located on any financial criterion, and consideration must be left to the following chapter, and secondly their locations are likely to be influenced by physical features more than any other facility. Essentially they are developed on land not suitable for other development such as alongside a river or alternatively as a deliberate part of an overall plan for area development. Golf courses are likely to fall into the same category, but in any case tend not to be a significant part of an urban scene left to market forces.[8]

Location was described in terms of the zonal structure of the study area designed for the Oxford Transportation Study. The main advantage of this was its facilitation of cross-referencing between the data sources. Ideally for the location study a random zoning system e.g. of grid squares, should have been used since the purposive zoning of the study, intended to identify homogeneous areas, would tend to cluster certain types of establishment. However, since the zoning design was based on residential criteria rather than on the establishments in which we are interested, this bias is not felt to outweigh the advantages of using the same structure. The zones vary in overall size but this reduces the spread of population sizes and since this is a crucial factor in determining the revenue potential of each zone this may be an advantage.[9]

The zones were grouped into eight sectors, one representing the central area and the remaining seven radial sectors. Within each sector the zones were grouped according to road distance from the city centre. The central area (Sector 0) was split into two, the city centre and the outer centre, the latter being identifiable separate areas from the city centre but within Sector 0. The remaining sectors were each grouped into four sub-sections. This classification yielded a total of six bands, the boundaries between these bands being at roughly $\frac{1}{2}$ mile (0.8 km), 1 mile (1.6 km), $1\frac{1}{2}$ miles (2.4 km), $2\frac{1}{2}$ miles (4 km) and $3\frac{1}{2}$ miles (5.6 km) distance from the city centre. There was some variation in these distances between sectors but the differences in networks meant that the corresponding accessibility to the centre was roughly constant for all sectors.

Only three groups of facility could be identified with a reasonable distribution of establishments: clubs (political, social and sports),[10] cinemas and theatres, and restaurants and public houses. Unfortunately all other facilities are so sparse in an urban area of this size that no distribution could be identified so the analysis had to be restricted to these. Table 8.1 summarises the distribution of locations for these three groups. The unequal width of the bands distorts the picture slightly; a more accurate representation is given for bands standardised for width in Table 8.2. It was felt that the width of each band and consequently distance to the centre was a more relevant factor than the area of the band (which would increase proportionally to the square of the width and the inner radius). In a monocentric urban area it was felt that the linear representation used in the earlier part of this chapter would be a better description of the spatial market than a full adjustment in terms of area. The actual locational pattern expected is not of equal areal distribution within each band but of clusters along the main linear radial routes. Consideration of locational profiles for each sector in the empirical evidence does yield similar patterns to that for the city as a

TABLE 8.1 Distribution of recreation facilities, Oxford

No. of establishments*

Approximate distance from centre	Clubs	Cinema/Theatre	Restaurants, etc.
½ mile	10 (20)	5 (62.5)	62 (31.1)
½ mile to 1 mile	3 (6)	0 (0)	37 (19.2)
1 mile to 1½ miles	17 (34)	1 (12.5)	27 (14.0)
1½ miles to 2½ miles	11 (22)	1 (12.5)	34 (17.6)
2½ miles to 3½ miles	6 (12)	0 (0)	19 (9.8)
Over 3½ miles	3 (6)	1 (12.5)	14 (7.3)

*Per cent of total is given in parentheses.

TABLE 8.2 Standardised distribution of recreation facilities, Oxford

% of establishments (standardised)

Approximate distance from centre	Clubs	Cinema/Theatre	Restaurants, etc.
Less than ½ mile	25.3	73.5	39.4
½ mile to 1 mile	7.6	0.0	23.5
1 mile to 1½ miles	43.0	14.7	17.2
1½ miles to 2½ miles	13.9	7.4	10.8
2½ miles to 3½ miles	7.6	0.0	6.0
Over 3½ miles	2.5	4.4	3.0

whole. The spatial economics of the urban area tends to take place along these radii rather than round particular rings. Table 8.2 can, therefore, be taken as a representative distribution of establishments.

It can be seen from the three types of establishment considered that the more commercial facilities do have a stronger tendency to be located in the central area where potential is highest and a steadily declining propensity as one moves away from the centre. For clubs, however, the peak location occurs in the intermediate range.

A Statistical Theory of Location
Statistical distribution theory can be useful here since if the observed distribution is tested against various theoretical distributions satisfying the same parameters and that which gives the closest fit is identified, a simple model of location can be derived. The probability generating function of the best-fit distribution tests the hypothesis concerning the process by which establishments locate relative to one another. Such a model of location is necessary if forecasts of future levels of facility provision in the private sector are to be made.

Two basic hypotheses have been proposed concerning the location of retail establishments, and these were tested against both retail data for the Oxford area for comparative purposes and two of the three groups of recreational facility. The small number of cinemas and theatres made it impossible to derive a distribution for this group. Artle (1965, pp. 133–8) examined retail clusters in Stockholm in terms of the Poisson distribution. This implies randomness in location since the probability of a certain event occurring K times in a given period (or of K establishments being found in a given zone) is given by

$$P(K) = \frac{e^{-\lambda}\lambda^K}{K!}$$

where λ is the parameter of the observed distribution (λ = mean = variance of the theoretical Poisson distribution).[11] Artle measured clustering or repulsion (where the presence of an establishment reduces the likelihood of another locating in that area) by the ratio of the standard deviation of the observed distribution to that of the theoretical Poisson distribution ($= \lambda^{\frac{1}{2}}$). Hence an index value of unity would imply random locations, a value greater than one implying non-random clustering because the spread of the observed data is greater than that of the random process, and conversely, a value of less than one suggesting mutual repulsion.

An alternative hypothesis, which builds in a more sophisticated probability generation function, and gives greater precision in identifying a correct location hypothesis, has been suggested by Rogers (1965). Rogers used more generalised distributions of the type of which the Poisson is a special case. The one which fitted the case best was the negative binomial distribution.[12] The argument is that if establishments tend to cluster into groups but these groups are of different sizes (varying means), and the groups are themselves located randomly in the study area then the establishments will be distributed between the zones as negative binomial. The probability density function is here defined in terms of the number of 'failures' (k) encountered prior to the rth 'success' in finding a zone with an establishment. Thus

$$P(k) = (-1)^k \binom{-r}{k} p^r q^k = \binom{r+k-1}{k} p^r q^k$$

where q/p = mean and q/p^2 = variance of the observed data.[13]

One problem encountered was that the estimated parameters of the distributions were biased by the extreme values for the central area in the case of the retail establishments and also of restaurants etc. In order that a more accurate picture of the distribution in non-central areas could be assessed, alternative sets of distributions were calculated on parameters estimated after exclusion of central area information. Comparative distributions are shown for professional services, convenience goods, general household goods and clothing, footwear, furnishing etc., together with those for clubs and restaurants etc. in Figure 8.7. The

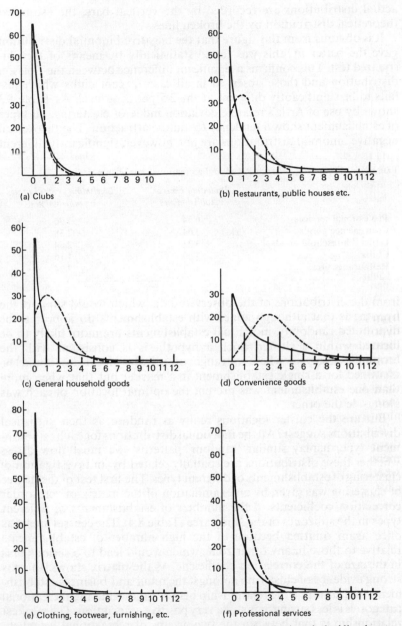

(a) Clubs

(b) Restaurants, public houses etc.

(c) General household goods

(d) Convenience goods

(e) Clothing, footwear, furnishing, etc.

(f) Professional services

FIG. 8.7. Solid line denotes estimated negative binomial distribution, dashed line denotes Poisson distribution. Vertical bars denote observed distribution.

actual distributions are recorded by the vertical bars, the estimated theoretical distribution by the broken lines.

It is obvious from this figure that the negative binomial distribution gave the better fit; this was tested statistically by means of the chi-squared test. This confirms a significant difference between the Poisson distribution and those observed in all cases except clubs which just fails to be significantly different at the 2.5 per cent level. As Table 8.3 shows by use of Artle's relative deviation index of clustering, all types of establishment show a tendency to mutual attraction. The theoretical negative binomial distributions are not, however, significantly different

TABLE 8.3   Clustering indices – Retail and recreational establishments

	Including central establishments	Excluding central area establishments
Professional services	6.54	1.96
Convenience goods	3.64	2.58
General household goods	3.22	2.64
Clubs	1.69	1.15
Restaurants, etc.	4.72	2.24

from the distributions of the observed data, which would support the hypothesis that although zones with establishments do appear to be distributed randomly, individual establishments are more likely to be located within a cluster. Such a hypothesis is consistent with the economic analysis where a range of possible locations could be identified for a single establishment in a market but that when more than one establishment was present the optimal location of each was alongside the other.

But are the cluster locations really as random as their statistical distributions suggest? All the individual distributions for each establishment type display similar 'random' patterns – we must now assess whether these distributions are spatially related by an investigation of clustering of establishments of different types. The first test of the degree of clustering was given by an examination of the matrix of zero-order correlation coefficients of the numbers of establishments of different types in the subzones of the study area (Table 8.4). The central area was once again omitted because of the high number of establishments relative to those in any other zone, which would lead to a serious bias in the size of the correlation coefficient. As the matrix shows, there is strong evidence of clustering amongst the retail and business establishments and although the relationship between these and the recreational categories is less strong, it is still a very positive association. The weakest relationship is that between the two groups of recreational establishment.

TABLE 8.4 Zero-order correlation matrix for zonal location of establishments

	1	2	3	4	5
1 Professional services	1.000	0.814	0.831	0.690	0.632
2 Convenience goods		1.000	0.828	0.692	0.647
3 General household goods			1.000	0.814	0.505
4 Clubs				1.000	0.316
5 Restaurants, etc.					1.000

Any conclusion drawn from this must be fairly tentative and no direct causality between the locations of different types of establishment is being tested. The evidence does suggest, however, that recreational establishments do tend to locate in similar areas to retail and business establishments presumably because of the spillover effects[14] but that the nature of this clustering differs for different recreational establishments such that these establishments are less likely to cluster. Our original hypothesis may require some amendment here. Complementarity is strongest with non-recreational activities and although the relationship between different recreational establishments is of mutual attraction this is much weaker.

A Deterministic Model of Location
A second method of testing the randomness of location was to build a simple location model in terms of the characteristics of the immediate area of the establishment. Three explanatory variables were used: distance from the central area (D), zonal population (P) and average zonal income (Y). The first of these is a proxy for the likely revenue potential and location costs in the uniform city of the abstract model, the second two variables introduce the more realistic assumption of variations in revenue potential, independent of distance from the centre because of non-uniform density gradients and distributions of economic potential. The equation estimated by multiple regression was, therefore

$$N_i = \alpha + \beta_1 \log D_i + \beta_2 P_i + \beta_3 Y_i$$

The logarithm of distance was used, as this non-linear formulation is both more reasonable and in preliminary testing gave a better fit than did a direct linear formulation.

The result for the location of clubs in a zone was

$$N_i(\text{Clubs}) = 1.512 - 0.309 \log D_i + 0.0001 P_i - 0.001 Y_i \quad R = 0.353$$
$$\phantom{N_i(\text{Clubs}) = 1.512 - 0} (1.61) (1.07) (2.91)$$

and for restaurants etc.

$$N_i(\text{Restaurants}) = 3.333 - 1.736 \log D_i + 0.001 P_i - 0.001 Y_i \quad R = 0.402$$
$$\phantom{N_i(\text{Restaurants}) = 3.333 -} (2.91) (2.29) (2.91)$$

These results were consistent with comparative equations for retail and business establishments, the coefficients of $\log D_i$ and P_i were rather larger in all other cases than for clubs but the signs were consistent. The signs of the coefficients of the distance and population variables were as expected; an increase in distance reduces potential and therefore the likelihood of location but local peaks in potential (because of pockets of higher density) counteract this tendency. The income coefficient appears to have the wrong sign in terms of potential but this variable may be taken alternatively as an index of social class of an area and hence of possible land costs. None of the coefficients is highly significant, however, in terms of the t-statistic and the overall performance of the model is also poor. This would suggest that there remains a large element of randomness in the location of establishments.

Conclusions

The inconclusive performance of a simple deterministic model taken together with the implication of statistical distribution theory that location is not significantly different from a random process suggests that facility provision in the private sector cannot be modelled accurately. This would also suggest that the market for recreational facilities is not in a stable spatial equilibrium. Such a situation means that we may expect greater variations in the supply price of recreation to the consumer than in the supply prices of other goods and services and therefore be able to identify a price determined demand function. The remainder of this chapter concentrates on this problem.

Although we have not produced a completely satisfactory model of location in the sense of being able to make predictions with any acceptable level of confidence, it may be noted that empirical investigation has borne out the three basic hypotheses deduced from the theoretical considerations: (i) site locations are concentrated in an intermediate band for clubs and to a lesser extent for the more commercial activities, (ii) the facilities which are developed at a greater density, cinemas and restaurants, are clustered more strongly in the central area, and (iii) there are considerable complementary clusters.

Spatial Supply and Mobility

The model of demand for recreational travel developed in Chapter 6 was based on the hypothesis that variations in the supply price of recreational facilities would affect the level of recreational mobility. The data used for the individual-based model estimated in Chapter 7 did not permit the use of specific indices of supply, but the aggregate indices used did indicate the likely importance of such factors in determining the pattern of travel for leisure purposes. By taking this single urban area it was hoped that the significance of some of the more specific indicators of attraction discussed in Chapter 6 could be assessed.[15]

The first estimates of a conventional multiple-regression equation based on zonal data and including such factors amongst the list of independent variables suggested that most of the variance in trip making could be explained by socio-economic factors. However, the equations proved to be very unstable with regard to both the respecification of the list of independent variables and the introduction of additional observations. This was evidence of multicollinearity inducing bias. What was required was an objective means of reducing the list of possible influences (some thirty variables in all could be defined) to a more easily managed number. Multivariate techniques such as factor analysis allow this to be done without the need to predetermine the structure of the interrelationships.[16]

Such techniques have been used frequently in social area analysis as a means of classifying zones through the use of derived factor scores.[17] In this case the objective was simply to identify key surrogate variables for each of the uncorrelated factors. It was possible to produce a solution for this structure for seven factors which could be interpreted to represent, respectively, aggregate zonal attraction, level of transport service, economic status, recreational attraction, total accessibility, age and family structure, and occupation–social status. Re-estimation of the model on variables representing these seven factors produced not only more stable equations but also revealed the importance of the indices of attraction and accessibility relative to the socio-economic factors.

An explanation of this result is that it is to be expected that location decisions of households will depend on their socio-economic status and their propensity for mobility. Hence, in the short run they may be expected to be in equilibrium, and consequently a cross-sectional analysis will not reveal any independent effect of locational factors. However, a change in supply price will upset this equilibrium and it is therefore necessary to analyse the urban structure more deeply in this way.

Such analysis of aggregate mobility patterns in a specific urban area has revealed that there is a strong link between the supply price of facilities and the amount, and nature, of leisure mobility, albeit an indirect one in many cases through the residential location decision. Forecasts of the likely *ex post* demand for a recreational facility may be seriously mis-estimated if variations in this price are not allowed for.

The implications of this result are important. Any change in supply price arising either from the facility location or the accessibility components of that price will affect mobility and hence the revealed demand for facilities. The location model has suggested that such a change in revenue potential, by shifting the average-revenue curve of the supplier may induce relocation by altering the optimal position. This in turn leads to readjustments. Hence there is a complex chain of interactions and feedback which adequate planning models must aim to represent.

We must turn in the next chapter to a rather more normative situation, considering planning with an objective function representing collective economic welfare rather than the interaction between independent consumers and producers each aiming to maximise individual welfare functions.

9. Economic Planning of Recreation Facilities

The previous chapter has considered only a small part of the recreation sector, but has found that, independently of other influences, variations in the amount of recreational activity are linked with variations in supply prices. This finding suggests that the market is not in equilibrium since a correctly functioning market should result either in the elimination of price variations or a situation in which those variations exactly matched some other socio-economic influence leading to variations in the demand for recreation. If price were less important for one group of people than for others the variation in demand would be a function of that factor, not of price at a given moment of time. The failure of a market to achieve equilibrium is usually the result of imperfections. Initially, therefore, we could regard planning simply as a means of overcoming such imperfections, for example influencing location through the application of town and country planning controls.

In the case of recreation, however, this is unsatisfactory since we are dealing not just with market imperfections, but with complete market breakdown in the provision of certain recreational facilities which have a greater degree of 'publicness'. Using the taxonomy discussed in Chapter 3 these will be those which, at levels of demand below capacity, can be consisdered non-rival in consumption, and where price exclusion is difficult or unjustifiable.[1] In these cases a market system may even fail to provide any supply, and hence the public sector will need to develop the entire system.

There is a third aspect to planning when considering recreation, the merit–want aspect. This arises when the social valuation of recreation exceeds the private valuation at the margin. In this case the authorities wish to increase the level of consumption above that which would obtain without any interference, and therefore will finance the provision of activities in excess of the supply which would be forthcoming in a free market in the hope of reducing supply price and stimulating demand.

Hence the concern of this chapter is with defining an optimum level

165

of recreation provision in terms of both the total supply of recreation facilities, their composition in terms of the specific activities involved, and their spatial distribution. Secondly, we must establish guidelines and standards for the planning of an optimal system and of individual projects. Much of the discussion will be restricted to urban recreation, but most of this can be generalised to the regional or national level.

Considerations in Recreation Planning

Planning Standards
It seems appropriate to start the discussion by considering the *status quo*. Thinking on recreational provision has been dominated by a 1925 recommendation of the National Playing Fields Association that 6 acres of playing space, and at least 1 acre of parks and public gardens, should be provided for each thousand persons. This standard was confirmed in a document of the (then) Ministry of Housing and Local Government (1956) as a basic guideline, but there is evidence that this has been accepted as the target by many planning authorities.[2]

This target was not, however, the outcome of any careful assessment of the actual demand for such recreational services. As Evans has remarked in the Forbes study, it is 'largely the result of unsubstantiated armchair theorising' (1974, p. 250). The 'demand' figure is derived firstly by taking the proportion of the population in the age groups which are assumed to provide most recreation demand, 10–40 years (some 50 per cent of the population in 1925). Assuming that of this group 30 per cent had no desire for recreation and a further 30 per cent would be at institutions (mainly schools and colleges) with their own recreational provision, the remaining 40 per cent (20 per cent of the total population or 200 per thousand) would be active seekers of recreation. This is the arbitrary demand figure. The reduction in the proportion of the population in the 10–40 age range over the years has not been allowed for because of the assumed extension of recreational age beyond 40, and the assumption that improved recreational facilities in schools will increase the proportion of active recreation seekers amongst adults. On these grounds this basic demand propensity of 200 per thousand has been left unchanged.

The supply figure of 6 acres of active recreational space is essentially a technological one since 6 acres can just accommodate a senior and junior football pitch, a cricket square, a three-rink bowling green, two tennis courts, a small children's playground and a pavilion. If these are taken to be the basic facilities required by an average community then the basic space necessary is determined.

More recent studies have suggested that this is a gross overestimate of the necessary provision *per capita*. Winterbottom (1967), in a study of open space use in Chelmsford, found that a maximum of only some 5 or 6 persons per thousand would be actively demanding space at any one time. This introduces an important point, that the number of individuals requiring recreational space must also be placed in a temporal context and, further, that given the varying activities which will be demanded within a given area, the available technology will affect the precise land requirements.[3] Accordingly, Winterbottom's conclusion was that $2\frac{1}{2}$ acres per thousand population was a more realistic target, to which he added the arbitrary amounts of $\frac{1}{2}$ acre per thousand for a formal park and a further $\frac{1}{2}$ acre for play areas giving a grand total of $3\frac{1}{2}$ acres, exactly one-half the total of 7 acres suggested earlier by the N.P.F.A.

A more rigorous assessment is that produced by the Sports Council (1968) utilising information on open-space provision in new towns. The figure derived from this study is one of about 2.4 acres per thousand population.

Such assessments are very arbitrary in terms of their assumptions regarding location however. Larger sites will have larger catchment areas and generate economies of scale in the provision of recreational services. The best interests of the community may still be met by a network of smaller local sites. Work of the G.L.C. (1968 and 1969) into open-space provision in London has suggested that there is a hierarchy of public open spaces defined by a relationship between size and catchment area. At the top of the scale comes the large metropolitan park of 150 acres or greater, located on average at between 2 and 5 miles from home. Below this is the district park of 50 to 150 acres at about $\frac{3}{4}$ mile from the average home, and at the bottom of the scale is the local park of 5 acres or so at about $\frac{1}{4}$ mile average distance. There may also be smaller sites at more frequent intervals in some cases. Closely related to this size–distance interaction is the frequency of visits, and this also raises the further questions of the presumed mode of transport for access and the consequent needs for car-parking provision, etc.

Even if reasonably tenable aggregate relationships between land availability and public recreation requirements can be established and placed in a stylised spatial environment in the manner discussed above, this is still a long way from solving our basic problem of defining an optimal urban recreation system. The basic assumptions remaining are of the composite recreational commodity used in the previous chapter which has the property of providing equal satisfaction per unit at a particular level of consumption regardless of which activity we are considering, and that we can assume consumers to be distributed spatially at a constant density. The following sections consider the relaxation of these assumptions in turn.

Planning for a variety of recreational activities

In the discussion on planning standards above we have dealt entirely with open spaces and outdoor recreation. There are two reasons for this: firstly this is the sector which has traditionally been within the public domain and has therefore received more attention, secondly the greater land requirements for a given 'output' of recreational services make it a more obvious target for planning in the land-use sense. In this section we shall aim to right this imbalance.

The model of location in the free market of Chapter 8 identified the likely relationship between the density of a development and its location. It was suggested that there would be technological factors limiting the extent of the substitution possible. This means that there is a dual causality present. The optimal density of development, and therefore the possible uses to which a given site can be put, will be determined for a site in a given location. Conversely, a developer wishing to develop a site for a specific activity will be limited in the feasible range of choices of site location.

The same problem faces a planning authority which, on the basis of its simple macro-calculation of requirements as outlined above, has to locate a range of defined facilities with due regard to development costs, land costs, etc. On the other hand the authority may also face the first problem of having a virgin site designated for recreation in a structure plan and thus have to take a decision on the best possible usage.

Implicit in any decision is a production function concept. Each activity has certain requirements of land and capital equipment which can be represented, for two contrasting cases, as the rays OA and OB in Figure 9.1, which define possible land/capital ratios. If we were to consider a single commodity the curves $R_1 R'_1$ and $R_2 R'_2$ would be conventional isoquants. Since in the case of recreation OA and OB represent discrete activities, the isoquants have to be considered as activity levels which produce equal satisfaction. Thus Figure 9.1 indicates that to produce equal satisfaction on the part of the recreationists (and this is a subject to which we shall return later in this chapter) we can either develop activity A to a level involving L_1 acres of land and K_1 units of capital equipment, or activity B to a level involving only L_2 acres of land but K_2 units of capital. Obviously the choice depends on the relative costs of land and capital. If, given the size of the budget available, the relative prices are as given by the slope of the line $P_L P_K$ in Figure 9.1 then activity B is preferred to activity A because it is more economical of the relatively more expensive factor, land. If we assume that the price of capital equipment is independent of location, which is certainly reasonable in an urban context, although would be less so because of delivery costs if we were to consider the broader regional or national planning of recreation, with development

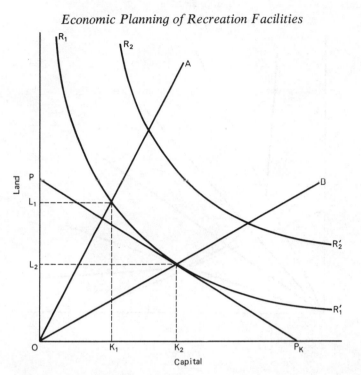

FIG. 9.1

in relatively remote areas, then the price ratio will be determined by variations in the price of land which is dependent on location.

A smooth isoquant is a very unrealistic assumption in this example, but if we replace it by a figure such as that shown in Figure 9.2 by $RR_A R_C R_D R_B R'$ the analysis is not changed, except that we may note that much larger variations in the relative prices of the factor inputs can be tolerated before there is an incentive to switch from one activity to another.

Hence the solution is no different from the free-market one once the level of satisfaction to be derived, and the total expenditure level, have been given. Optimal development will depend on relative prices and therefore on location. A very similar distribution of activities will be expected to develop in the planned environment as in the free market with the large land-users towards the outskirts of a city and the more intensive developments closer to the centre. However, a public authority does have certain differences from the private developer, one of these being the ability to influence the price ratio so that decisions are taken on the basis of optimal shadow prices rather than prevailing market prices.

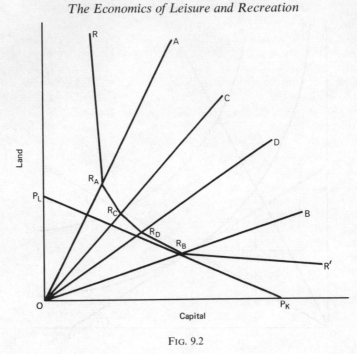

FIG. 9.2

The shadow price is likely to differ from the market price most in the case of land. The bid-price, as seen in Chapter 8, is the price which the purchaser (or in the case of rented land the rent which the renter) is prepared to pay for a site of a given size at a given location which keeps him at the same level of satisfaction as would that site in the best possible location. The bid price of recreation is likely to be below the market price at most locations, with the possible exception of certain peripheral sites or sites with particular physical characteristics making them unsuitable for residential, commercial or industrial development.

However, such an opportunity cost of lost income approach is based purely on financial considerations, and ignores for example the psychic income to the community of the existence of recreational open-space facilities. More generally it ignores the degree of publicness present in recreation, and therefore we should not expect the market to provide an optimal or efficient solution. When the market for the final product has broken down we cannot expect to seek a simple market solution to the factor allocation problem. Any general economic solution must attempt to account for this by an appropriate modification to the prices used to overcome market distortions.

Option Values

It is not only the classic criteria of the public good, non-rivalness and non-excludability, which distinguish recreation from normal goods but also the temporal incidence of demand. Recreation ranks as only a small part of an average consumer budget, the purchase of recreation, and particularly the purchase of a visit to a specific site, is a relatively infrequent occurrence. The difficulty with infrequent consumption is that the revealed preferences in terms of actual visits or actual revenues accruing are not an adequate reflection of potential preferences. Failure to provide a facility may thus lead to a greater loss of potential welfare in the future than a crude assessment of consumer's surplus would indicate.

Such a situation has been characterised as involving an 'option value', a willingness to pay for the possibility of consumption in the future, even if that possibility is, in fact, never exercised.[4] Option demand becomes important only in a situation where there is the possibility of the removal of supply in the future, for example, failure to preserve a natural environment or the commercial development of an open space by building. In general terms it occurs when there are large costs involved in the re-expansion of curtailed output of the goods or services in question, and hence current supply enters positively into the utility functions of prospective future users. The presence of identifiable option values in addition to conventional consumer's surplus depends on there being uncertainty about the future.[5] It is essentially a risk-aversion premium, the difference between the maximum option price people would be prepared to pay and the expected consumer's surplus from the option.[6]

There is a further aspect of the social opportunity cost of development which must be considered – the extent to which any developmental investment is reversible. In the case of urban recreation a decision to develop a site for recreation is clearly a reversible one particularly for outdoor recreation; at any stage in the future it is possible to redevelop for commercial, industrial or residential purposes – the more so the less capital-intensive the original development. If the converse decision has been taken, to develop for purposes other than recreation, then it may still be possible at some future date to reverse this, but it would be unlikely to be the costless decision of the former case where less fixed-capital investment was involved. If an investment decision is costlessly reversible then the only loss of taking what proves to be the wrong decision is any difference in rent the site could command under different uses.

If, however, we consider a natural-resource-based recreational facility then development of any kind will be irreversible in the sense that there is no costless way of restoring the site to its original form once development has taken place. A good example of this situation is the case of water resources where an undeveloped area of natural beauty can either be left for individual recreation, as a 'wilderness area' in the American terminology, or developed as a reservoir or hydro-electric scheme, together with organised recreational services. The problem arises because the unorganised demand for wilderness recreation is likely to have a higher option value. If this is true then the time path of the benefits of non-development will show an upward trend. On the other hand it has been argued that the time path of benefits from developments of this kind will usually be on a downward trend, essentially because of technical progress.[7] The optimal time for any major development appraised by cost–benefit analysis tends to be immediately because of the rate at which future benefits are discounted, uncertainty and general myopia.

We have considered briefly above some of the problems faced by a public authority in assessing the costs and returns of following alternative development policies. We shall return later in this chapter to a statement of some decision rules for this policy, but we must now take a more detailed look at variations in the demand surface which can also affect decisions on recreation policy.

Planning with variations in the demand surface
It has been a convenient assumption so far that there exists a uniform density of demand surface. We know that the expected average revenue declines as we move away from an urban centre because of increasing distance and a lower population density. There is no reason to suppose that this decline will be as smooth as assumed, or that it will display similar patterns in all directions of movement. Cities do not show the regular structure it has been convenient to assume, divisions may be more sectoral than concentric rings and so forth.[8] Nevertheless, the direct relationship assumed between distance and density on the one hand and revenue potential on the other can be retained with appropriate modification. However, we have also assumed that each unit of the population has equal revenue potential, it is this assumption which we must now relax.

It has been shown in the preceding analyses that the revealed demand for recreation is not determinable on a straight *per capita* basis. It varies substantially in association with factors which are themselves strongly associated with the location decision and the variation in social structure within urban areas. Any weighting of the potential demand by the propensity for each group to undertake recreational activities will lead to a more irregular surface. The free market would tend to result in locations biased towards areas with a population with a greater propensity for recreation, thus minimising impedance costs for the more certain markets and hence guaranteeing the revenue potential. This tendency may of course be encountered to some extent, as seen in Chapter 8, by associated variations in land costs, but nevertheless the mix of recreational facilities in space is usually market-determined.

For the planning authority this is, on the surface, an efficient solution to the extent that total travel costs of consumers are minimised. The formal solution is a straightforward programming problem, selecting sites to minimise the sum of these transfer costs and other input costs which vary with location. Since the transfer costs will depend on the transport network there is an important linkage here between the transport and land-use planning processes.

However, the solution is only based on the revealed preferences of consumers, and as we have already seen the apparent demand curve may not be a true reflection of real preferences because of both frustrated and option demands. If these are ignored there is a real danger of distributional problems arising.

The distribution problem in the case of option demand is essentially an inter-temporal one, any losses incurred because the taking-up of options is denied will only be felt in the future. For this reason they will be difficult to assess adequately. Moreover, because they are only options it will be very difficult to identify those groups wishing to hold such options given that there is no market mechanism dealing in futures in this instance. Reliance would need to be placed on attitude surveys which may be inaccurate, and increasingly so with an extension of the time period in question. The difficulty here may be seen as a bias in response towards an expected answer if the future option is available as a free good.[9] There is a particular problem where recreational projects are viewed essentially in a conservation role as against an alternative use as in the case of water-resource projects either for water supply or electricity generation which also have employment- or income-creating effects.

If the industrial project also has a developed recreational spillover, for water-based recreation, there is a distributional question within the recreation sector and the two sets of options require comparison. A further point related to the question of options also provides a bridge to the question of frustrated demand. How can options be assessed in the case of alternatives which are new to an area, i.e. where demand has previously been frustrated by lack of supply? The above examples of wilderness- and water-based recreation could be a case in point if there existed no immediately available alternative for the water-based activities, and thus no demand had developed in the *ex ante* situation. The values placed on this option would therefore have no real meaning since the option could not have previously figured amongst the choices available.[10] It has already been seen that individual preferences are extending to a wider range of choices in the field of recreation, and thus it may be expected that stated preferences will increasingly include options which are incorrectly valued.

The specific question of frustrated demand is a more immediate problem, and one which affects the inter-personal distribution of benefits. If no attempt is made to assess the options which individuals would wish to have available then groups which are unable to reveal their preferences will be discriminated against. This inability may be due to either physical reasons such as the absence of feasible transport services, or to economic reasons such as the high cost of reaching the facilities provided or the maintenance of a high price for use of facilities by a severe restriction of supply (through exclusive club organisations) in the private sector. Variations in revealed demand associated with car-ownership or socio-economic factors may thus not be inherent differences in demand between the various groups but simply reflections of the way in which the existing supply discriminates between groups, particularly in terms of location.

This is a classic case of an identification problem with observed demand being supply-determined. Without an independently determined demand curve there is no chance of an unbiased estimate of the true benefits being derived for a particular project. Whilst a truly independent curve may not be a readily estimable proposition, this factor may be at least partly taken into account by use of what has been termed 'merit weighting'.[11] The objective here is to assess the relative social benefits of alternative projects, not in terms of their precise monetary valuations to the different groups involved but in terms of more arbitrary scaling of the merit of the project's benefits. Thus the provision of a swimming-pool in a socially deprived area may be weighted, say, twice as heavily as one in an area of higher income and social status, where the number of people benefiting is the same. Such a procedure could also be used to compare different types of recreational project.

Obviously the solution obtained will differ from the optimal, but it is likely to be superior to that suggested by a purely market consideration because of its explicit recognition of the distributional issue. The solution is based on a known treatment of the distributional impact.

Pricing and Investment Policy for Recreation

So far in this chapter, we have been concerned with raising the problems encountered in the planning of a recreational system, pointing out the ways in which the results of the sort of empirical analysis set out in earlier chapters have to be modified in the final assessment and suggesting some alternative approaches. In the following pages, we shall show how these factors are to be pulled together into a coherent economic policy for recreation.

The objective of economic policy is, as stated at the beginning of this chapter, to attain an optimum level of recreational provision. Optimum in this context is not just the definition of an appropriate market-clearing solution but a solution consistent with the best interests of consumers, the availability of resources, and the community as a whole. This solution is one which includes recognition of both the external effects of a particular policy and its impact through time.

The important point to be made at the outset is that we cannot treat recreation on a project by project basis because of the degree of substitution between sites and activities which we have identified. The evaluation procedure must, therefore, assess the change in benefits which is derived from the entire recreation system.[12] The problems for the planning authority are first, to determine the capacity of the recreational system; secondly, the location of the individual supply sites; and thirdly, to devise a pricing policy which ensures not only an overall balance between demand and supply for the sector as a whole, but also avoids overloading particular parts of the system.

Determination of Capacity

The concept of capacity is a difficult one in this context. In the conventional micro-economics of the firm, we can distinguish between technical capacity in the sense of the maximum physical output level of a plant, and optimal capacity – the point at which short-run average costs are at a minimum. Capacity is thus determined essentially by technology, although the choice of output level will also require consideration of demand factors and the firm's growth policy.

Capacity of a recreation system may also be thought of in a purely technical sense, the maximum number of persons which can be accommodated by a facility at a point in time. This has been referred to as 'the ecologist's carrying capacity...the maximum number of individuals of a species that can be supported by a given habitat under conditions of maximum stress'.[13] This is clearly analogous to technical capacity in the case of industrial plant, but an equivalent concept of optimal capacity is harder to define. The main difference would seem to be that in the case of recreation the consumer is aware of the capacity and the degree to which it is being used, whereas in other cases the characteristics of the good itself do not change with the level of output, this being only indirectly reflected through price. The change in the characteristics may be more than just the onset of congestion as capacity is approached, leading to rises in both private and social marginal costs. There may be differing views on the quality of the product at non-congestion levels of usage, such as assessed by Fisher and Krutilla (1972, p. 120), in their study of wilderness capacity, in terms of the probability of encountering other people during the recreational experience.

In Figure 9.3 we represent a normal situation of a free good with no congestion until the physical carrying capacity is reached at level of

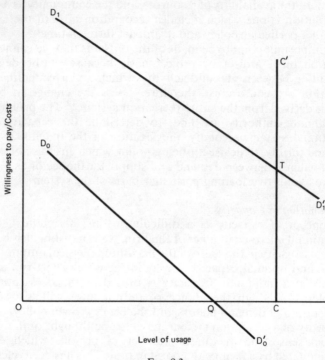

Fig. 9.3

usage OC. From this we can see that if the demand curve is as given by $D_0 D_0'$ then there is excess capacity. If however, it is as given by $D_1 D_1'$, demand is in excess of capacity at the zero price and consequently queuing or some other physical allocation system will develop. Alternatively demand can be restricted to the available capacity by rationing or through price using a toll of amount CT.

If increasing congestion costs are incurred at less than capacity then the situation will be as in Figure 9.4. In this case the marginal private costs are represented by PG, showing rising costs up to the physical capacity limit CC'. If the quantity is expressed as a flow variable then any attempt to increase usage beyond C may result in a fall in the effective quantity consumed but with costs still rising along the continuation of the marginal private cost curve *PGP'*. Marginal social costs, because of the external consequences of the increasing congestion costs, will lie above private costs over the relevant range up to capacity *C*, as given by the curve *SS'*. Equilibrium in this case is not established at Q_0 where the willingness to pay just equals marginal private costs because of the excess of social costs at this point. Imposition of a user

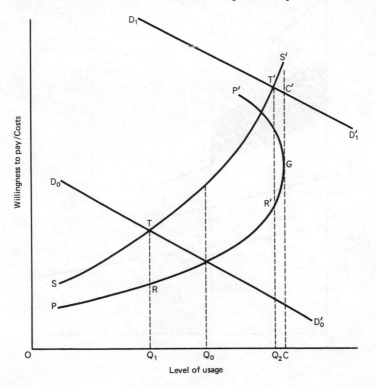

FIG. 9.4

tax will allow a social equilibrium to be established at Q_1 where willingness to pay just covers marginal social costs, the optimal tax being *RT*. If the demand curve moves outwards to a position beyond the optimal carrying capacity, say to $D_1 D'_1$ in Figure 9.4, then a tax of *R'T'* will be necessary to constrain demand to a level of OQ_2 within that capacity. This imposition of a user tax therefore constrains demand to within physical capacity of the system, ensures an optimal distribution of available capacity according to the costs of the system and provides rigorous grounds for assessing the need for an expansion of capacity.

When private costs do not exist in this sense but the congestion effect is felt more as a loss of benefit or willingness to pay, this cost-based analysis is inappropriate. The situation is more as depicted in Figure 9.5, with a series of demand curves, each representing the willingness-to-pay

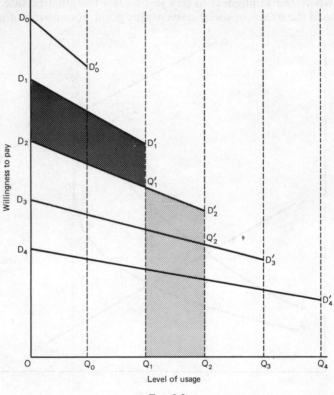

Fig. 9.5

function within a particular range of expected usage or, in other words, at perceived levels of congestion. It is assumed that congestion effects are viewed as discrete jumps in the level of usage, e.g. from Q_0 to Q_1. Costs are, for the moment, assumed constant and unaffected by the level of usage. The relevant variable derived from this analysis is the total benefit, that is the area under the demand curve, for any expected level of usage. Thus if the expected level of usage is OQ_1 the total gross benefit derived is the area under the demand curve $D_1 D'_1$, i.e. $OD_1 D'_1 Q_1$. If there is an expected increase in usage of $Q_1 Q_2$ then the loss of benefit felt by existing users will be reflected in a downwards shift in the demand curve from $D_1 D'_1$ to $D_2 D'_2$ and a consequent loss of benefit as represented by the area $D_1 D'_1 Q'_1 D_2$. This loss of benefit must be balanced against the benefit derived by the $Q_1 Q_2$ new participants who, assuming that they have similar willingness-to-pay perceptions as existing users and thus follow the same demand function, will obtain $Q_1 Q'_1 D'_2 Q_2$ in additional benefits. Up to the point where the loss in benefit from each increase in usage is just equal to the gain in benefit by new participants it is worth while to expand capacity. In Figure 9.6 this is represented by the marginal-benefits curve, MB_0, the optimum level being Q_n where marginal benefits become zero.

The feasible capacity is therefore set by perceptions of the quality of the product. Figure 9.6 also illustrates how the feasible capacity can be increased if the marginal-benefits curve can be moved outwards to the right. One possible way in which this could be done is by better

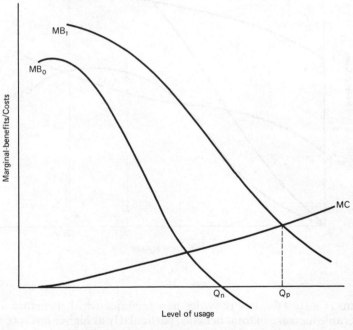

Fig. 9.6

management procedures to reduce the perception of congestion, better timetabling, measures to reduce encounters between competing groups and so forth, depending on the nature of the recreation activity in question. If the marginal cost of these management procedures is given by MC and it succeeds in moving the marginal-benefits curve to MB_1, then the capacity can be increased from Q_n to Q_p.

Of course, the scale of operations remains to be determined in the usual way. Variations in the fixed-cost elements such as capital expenditure can lead to the optimising intersection occurring at a higher level of usage since this will shift both the marginal costs of operation curve, and the marginal-benefits curve to the right. This is best seen by reference to the associated total curves for costs and benefits in Figure 9.7. An investment of $K_0 K_1$ will shift up the total-cost curve

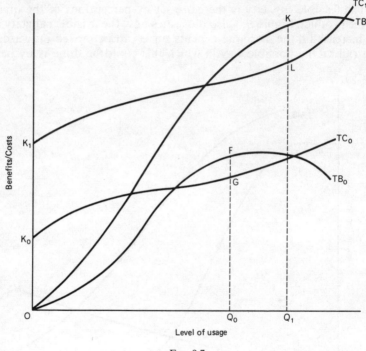

FIG. 9.7

from TC_0 to TC_1, but provides new facilities which generate a considerable increase in total benefits, particularly at higher levels of usage because of the increase in potential capacity and hence reduction in probability of congestion. This new level of total benefits is shown as TB_1. The marginal-cost curve will still rise to the right at higher levels of usage because of the need for greater management of the facilities. The relevant optimal levels of usage occur where the cost and benefit curves are tangential in each case (marginal cost equals marginal benefit) and hence investment has resulted in an increase of optimal usage from OQ_0 to OQ_1. This expansion is only worth while if the increase in total benefits is greater than the increase in costs which has been incurred, that is if the difference between benefits and costs at Q_1, KL, is greater than that at Q_0, FG.

Measuring Benefits
The willingness-to-pay concept as an indicator of consumer benefits which has been used in the above discussion for simplicity must now be looked at more carefully. The problems associated with alternative definitions and means of measuring consumer benefits in recreation have been discussed in detail in Chapter 3. A particular difficulty arises in the case where the product is not marketed, and willingness to pay is not revealed by actual behaviour.[14] Some researchers have attempted to use interview techniques to assess this value and since stated willingness to pay can be very suspect, willingness to pay to avoid exclusion has been used with some success.[15] Nevertheless, what a person will pay to avoid exclusion does not necessarily measure benefit in the same way as willingness to pay. This is partly because of the distinction between compensating and equivalent variations and partly because of the possible presence of an option value which should be identified separately from current consumer's surplus benefits.

How then should consumer benefits be assessed in the recreational planning context? We have seen that there are three possible approaches to supplement the direct willingness-to-pay assessment. Firstly, we can establish a quasi-market in recreation by observing the trade-offs between recreation and marketable goods and services with a direct money value. Secondly, we can use simulation techniques to place consumers in a more realistic situation than the blunt willingness-to-pay question, a situation in which they must make real money-valued choices. Thirdly, in the longer term and in the macro planning context, we can observe collective choice in action through the political process. None of these individually can supplant the direct technique but taken together may give greater grounds for confidence in any valuations adopted.

Site Planning
Thus far we have only discussed the way in which an optimal capacity of the system may be defined, purely in terms of the likely benefits and costs. The second stage of the procedure is to identify the best distribution of that capacity, both between activities and in space. The spatial distribution of capacity will affect both the price of inputs and hence the costs of making capacity available and the access costs of the consumer. Again a crucial feature of this spatial distribution in

recreation is the proportion of variations in costs which will be borne directly by the consumer; this will be much higher than in most activities.[16] Wrong decisions on location and organisation will thus again affect the benefits side of the equation rather than the costs. Specific problems concerning site location have already been discussed in detail above. Here we shall introduce one further issue concerning the relation between the specific site and the system in a dynamic context.

From a given situation the desirability of an increase in the capacity of the system, as depicted in Figure 9.7, can be assessed. It is to be expected that there will be a number of alternatives open, each with calculable costs and benefits. That project making the best contribution to the system as a whole will be the one with the highest incremental benefit/cost ratio, given that all distributional and other factors have been accounted for in the estimates entering the analysis. However, each of these alternatives changes the system in a unique way and may affect the feasibility of subsequent modifications. Using a simple diagram such as Figure 9.8, we can see that starting from situation 0 there may be four openings available in period I, listed as IA, IB, IC

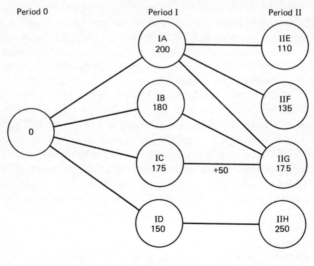

Fig. 9.8

and ID, each with its associated increase in net benefits to the system discounted back to its value in the period of introduction. Long-term planning reveals other possible projects for period II, viz. IIE, IIF, IIG and IIH. However, the benefits estimated for these will depend on what has been done in period I for two main reasons. Firstly, they may by physically interdependent, either as complementary developments or as alternative uses of a single site. Secondly, the change in consumer habits occasioned by the development in period I may then render different valuations of period II projects, again either positively or negatively.

The links shown between projects in Figure 9.8 indicate the possible paths of investment which yield the appropriate valuations, any other time path would either be impossible or would have a negative effect on the valuations. The + 50 indicated on the path via IC and IIG identifies a complementarity which raises the valuation of project G to 225. The valuations are net present values at period zero of projects undertaken in the period given, assuming that a project is completed and operational within the period in which it is undertaken.

Consideration of projects in period I by themselves would rank projects in the order A, B, C, D, but the introduction of reference to period II shows that higher total net present values come from the combination of C + G or equally from D + H (where D is the lowest-ranked project in period I but the only one campatible with G, the highest-ranked project of all). There may still be a case for adopting project A however because of its greater compatibility with future developments, particularly where there is a large element of uncertainty present.

The difficulty arises because of the irreversibility of projects; any mistakes cannot be easily rectified. This renders the path to a solution much more difficult as has been shown in recent work dealing with the general issue of non-reversible investment decisions.[17] However, the solution which emerges will still be the equivalent one of equating the marginal costs and benefits, suitably discounted; the possible development path matching this criterion will be the optimal one.

Hence we may conclude thus far by reiterating the general decision rule that optimality in planning for recreation is achieved by equating the marginal benefits from any investment with the marginal costs incurred, whatever restrictions are placed on the assumptions of the analysis. These restrictions, however, which have been the main subject-matter of this chapter, will complicate the procedure by which this point of equality is identified by altering the effective costs or benefits or the rate at which these need to be discounted. The effective outcome of this would be to optimise the allocation of demand to individual sites at the point where the marginal social opportunity costs of each site were equal to each other as well as to marginal system benefits.

Pricing Policy and Finance
We have thus far only considered part of the problem by concentrating

on the determination of capacity without explicit reference to the prices at which the recreational services will be marketed. Explicit prices are not necessary as long as the analysis is restricted, as above, to a comparison of costs and benefits to the community as a whole. Having worked out this equilibrium situation for the recreation sector it is necessary to ensure that a pricing mechanism allows the attainment of this equilibrium without further distortion.

If the recreational service were to be offered at a price, for example lower than a given person's stated willingness to pay, it can be seen that he will derive a consumer's surplus from this situation and that also he may be induced to use the facility more than at an equilibrium price. Thus whilst the consumer may derive an increase in benefit, the resulting increase in demand may upset the sectoral equilibrium. Conversely if the price is too high the individual will lose benefit and the facilities available will be used at below-optimal capacity. Hence our first conclusion would be that the optimal price was that which just equalled both the marginal-benefit and the marginal social opportunity cost of the facility, a classic marginal cost pricing situation.[18]

However, at this stage we must recall that we imposed certain social externality criteria on the recreational system such that we might deem it desirable for the amount of recreation to be in excess of that consumers are willing to pay for at marginal social cost. We can meet this by appropriate modification to the marginal-cost curve.

The benefits to society can be regarded as a subtraction from the full social opportunity costs which would be incurred in the absence of those benefits. In this way the basic pricing principle can be retained, ensuring an optimal solution in the recreation sector.

Within the sector, the pricing structure is also important in its allocation of the demand to specific facilities. Again marginal-cost equalisation is the basic criterion, although recognition of the spatial dimension introduces a distortion. Some adjustment of the benefit function to allow for the transport costs incurred by the consumer becomes necessary if the desired optimum is to be achieved. This is particularly important in that benefit perception and consumer response to price changes will be different with regard to travel costs than they are to on-site charges, as was noted in the critique of the Clawson method.

We should also add a proviso relating to the implications of the pricing policy outside the sector. The argument for a second-best solution, where the conditions for a full optimum first-best solution with price equal to marginal cost are not met in other sectors of the economy, rests on the distortions in allocation which may arise if a non-conforming marginal cost pricing policy is enforced.[19] If, by pricing recreation at its marginal social opportunity cost, recreational services are being sold cheaper relative to their opportunity (resource) costs than other goods and services, then there will be a tendency to inflate demand in the recreation sector at the expense of non-recreation, thus causing a reallocation of resources.[20] The appropriate deviation from marginal cost pricing which should be followed as a result of this will depend on the degree of substitution or complementarity with those goods or services in other sectors of the economy which are not priced at their marginal costs.[21] Only if recreation is strongly complementary to the output of other sectors which price above marginal costs should the price of recreation be set below its marginal costs, and by an amount which just outweighs the existing distortion.[22] The implied correction in the joint demand for recreation and its complements is that the induced excess demand for recreation boosts the demand for its complements and results in a nearer-to-ideal output for the combined demand of the two goods. It would seem reasonable to adopt this attitude in the case of recreation since the only real substitute to be considered is work. The consumption of most other goods can be seen as complementary, either because of their direct involvement in the recreational activity, such as vehicles, sports equipment, television sets etc., or their permissive effects on recreation through the ownership of household durables such as refrigerators, electric lawnmowers etc. which release consumers from committed leisure time for recreation. On these grounds therefore, there does exist a case for pricing recreation at below its marginal cost in the interests of allocational efficiency. However, the amount by which this is done would depend on a very careful assessment, both of the degree of complementarity involved in each case, and the consequent careful weighting of each price/marginal-cost ratio in the rest of the economy. We must also allow for the very different relative importances of recreation and the complementary goods in consumers' budgets, this will certainly affect the cross-price elasticities in question. Further we must remember that such Pareto-type conditions depend on very restrictive assumptions, and in particular that the given distribution of income is taken to be optimal.

Even without pricing at less than marginal cost it is likely that recreational facilities will face severe financial problems because of the likelihood of constant or falling average costs. In this classic deficit situation of public enterprises some form of subsidy intervention is likely to be necessary unless price discrimination can be applied, which introduces rivalness and may have very regressive characteristics.[23] The subsidy issue is well documented with regard to the nationalised industries but is less well formalised in the case of urban services, except for the special case of urban transport.[24]

The case of recreation does not seem to introduce any major new considerations – the most likely justification is the provision of capacity in excess of that which the free market would provide and which is deemed to be socially desirable. The problem with subsidies in recreation, as with the Arts, would seem to be the likelihood of the reduction in the range of facilities offered if, as would be expected, the subsidies are concentrated on certain key facilities, for example an urban sports centre replacing many separate sites. The distribution of subsidies is thus an important and difficult problem.[25] Whilst there are strong social arguments for a subsidised expansion of recreational facilities, care must be taken with the income distributional effects implied in the raising of finance, particularly from non-users. To some extent the monopoly profit made on suboptimal levels of output of complementary goods provides a tax base, although there is no reason why the accounting profits and subsidies should match the necessary economic requirements.[26]

One way of ensuring that the burden of finance was borne by recreationists, while still enabling redistribution from more to less viable activities, would be through a recreation tax, in addition to standard indirect taxes such as that on value-added. The concept of a special tourist tax is more relevant to resource-based activities, particularly those used by non-local residents where there is a need to maintain an infrastructure larger than that which the local community can reasonably bear. The problem is often that of the correct balance between the beneficial (multiplier) effects of tourist expenditure and the wish to minimise the costly externalities. The danger of taxes on tourist expenditure is that they may reduce income potential, as visitors avoid spending on food, accommodation, car parks etc., but not the volume of visitors and external costs.[27]

Conclusions – Recreation and Urban Planning
In this chapter, we have considered a wider aspect of recreation planning, that of the sector as a whole within a defined spatial area. This has been seen as the key to recreation policy since because of the interrelationships between sites and activities explored earlier, project planning cannot be carried out independently of an overall sectoral plan.

Such an approach increases the complexity of recreational planning and introduces severe practical problems. The inability to produce accurate estimates of social opportunity costs and even more so of benefits can make the definition of an optimal situation an impractical proposition. Nevertheless the framework is important both as an indicator of desired objectives and, at a more practical level, as a blueprint for the sort of additional information required.

Pricing policy and its financial implications will depend on the size of cross-elasticities between recreation and other goods and services and the basic price–cost relationship in these other markets. Subsidies and the determination of optimal capacity levels imply a notion of socially desirable levels of recreational activity which is a much broader dimension involving other social science disciplines. Dynamic considerations show the need to be aware of the implications of current decisions for potential future ones and consequently the danger of myopic investment decision rules.

There is a broader issue too – the place of recreation in overall urban planning. Again there is more than one dimension. On a purely economic basis we can consider the implications on the efficiency of the whole urban economy of alternative policies for recreation. In this light we can examine the issues of competitive uses for land, the efficiency of a given transport network in servicing the needs of industry, commerce and residents, and the role of recreation in maintaining human capital and the efficiency of the economy's labour inputs. On the other hand we may have to set against efficiency criteria the requirements of land-use planning in a non-economic sense, the aesthetic and social considerations of different urban structures. It is these considerations which can lead us to modify the valuations in our overall efficiency criterion by providing weights for the various components of cost and benefit involved, to make it a true criterion of social efficiency.

10. Conclusions and Prognosis

In this final chapter the main conclusions of the various parts of this study will be drawn together. The most satisfactory way of approaching this is through an imaginary case study of planning a project such as a multipurpose urban sports centre since this highlights the most important problems and places them in the proper perspective. The chapter is concluded with a brief outline of directions for further research which emerge from the attempt to operationalise the procedures.

A Case Study

Establishing the Need for Recreational Investment
The starting point of any analysis is assessment of the existing situation. In the context of recreation an inventory of the nature and location of existing facilities provides the first task. From this information supply-price indices of recreation can be established incorporating information on the quality of the sites available, accessibility on different transport networks. This implies careful definition of the area in question. If the project in question is already defined, as will often be the case, then the relevant catchment area can be defined from knowledge of trip-length distributions for the activity and any close substitutes. If the task is to ascertain the project with the highest return out of a list of several alternatives, or the more basic structural planning task of determining whether any development of the sector is required at all, then the definition of the planning area is less straightforward. Often the area will be that of the planning authority in question but recreational demands do not always respect such divisions.

A useful disaggregation could be the separation of the sector into smaller markets on the basis of known substitution characteristics of activities or on population characteristics. A typical example of the latter could be separate consideration of car-based recreationists from those reliant on public transport. These more discrete parts of the sector may be easier to define and handle.

A parallel exercise is the assessment of the recreational needs of the area not just by the application of crude *per capita* space requirements but by careful consideration of the composition of the population and the levels of potential demand for recreation implied by activity models. Activity models should be based on regional or national data and imported for specific studies. This avoids the need for specific modelling which in itself has the dangers of being biased by the existing levels of facility provision.

Imbalance between needs and provision constitutes a *prima facie* case for planning action. There is a further, and possibly more important disequilibrium, that between needs (potential demand) and actual consumption (revealed demand) which arises because of such factors as wrong locations leading to high supply prices. Such imbalance would be indicated by larger-than-average trip lengths or higher-than-average access costs and hence lower-than-average trip frequencies. Of course it is possible that this type of imbalance can be corrected by improvements to the transport network rather than investment in recreation facilities themselves and such a possibility should be considered, particularly where there is spare capacity at existing facilities.

If these various provisional studies establish the need for an expansion of capacity in the recreation sector the second stage is to determine the nature and size of the expansion. Any final decision will normally be dependent on the subsequent stages of evaluation but this stage is crucial in that the preparation of short lists on rule of thumb procedures may well beg important questions whilst on the other hand some short-listing is essential if the scale of the exercise is to be kept manageable.[1] The majority of urban recreation planning exercises will be limited in the possible solutions by the dictates of structure plans and available financial provisions. If technical considerations are also introduced the possible range of scales of development may be very limited. Finally, the long-term implications of development policies require assessment.

The sort of situation which might arise from this examination of the current position is that major deficiencies are identified in the provision of swimming and indoor sports facilities – squash, badminton, gymnastics – whilst there are large variations in the provision of outdoor sports facilities for football, cricket, tennis etc. from area to area. In addition planned urban development and rising land prices may be placing pressure on these existing facilities both from increased demand and the increasing opportunity cost. What is needed is increased capacity on a smaller land area, that is an increased density of recreational development. A solution is provided by a multipurpose sports centre which can serve several needs simultaneously and even more during the course of a week by having flexible design together with careful management. Each separate activity can gain benefits from a common infrastructure and overheads such as changing facilities, booking arrangements, car parking.

Let us assume a choice of project sizes and sites is available. For each of these possible projects the same evaluation procedure will be followed as outlined below.

The Generation Effect

The first modelling prerequisite is a model of mobility for the appropriate market incorporating specific price effects. Ideally this need not require special data collection and estimation but spatially transferable models have not as yet been estimated with any degree of confidence and more general regional and national models fail to identify specific supply prices. In the immediate future a model-building exercise will, therefore, be necessary following the guidelines laid down in Chapter 6. The main points to be reiterated are the importance of the attraction–accessibility variables, and the desirability of an individual- or household-based model. Any aggregation into person types or zones can be performed as necessary, but aggregated generation models cannot then be disaggregated.

Once a satisfactory model of existing mobility levels has been achieved (including the subsequent distribution aspects which we shall consider below) the effect of the new facility can be introduced. This will alter the aggregate supply price of recreation in the appropriate market to each observation in the trip generation model. Applying these new values and the estimated coefficients yields a forecast level of total generation. This is, of course, only an estimate and hence the confidence interval about the forecast is important such that sensitivity testing of the resultant benefits can be carried out to give a range of overall evaluations of the project.

Redistribution of Recreational Activity

As mentioned above, the existing situation also needs to be modelled in terms of the allocation of total demand to specific facilities requiring a further behavioural model. Again in Chapter 6 the implications of different modelling approaches were discussed. It was found that some aggregation would normally be necessary at this stage both by person type to reduce the number of non-zero observations and by geographical zones to reduce the number of flow observations on which the model is calibrated to a manageable level. Modal split could be estimated simultaneously with distribution but preferences have been expressed for either a separate modal market-share model link by link after distribution or defining the original generation model markets mode by mode. Ideally a comparison of results from alternative approaches should be made.

The preferred distribution model is a singly (production) constrained interaction model with attraction based on the same weights used in the generation price effect and the deterrence function based on generalised costs rather than simple distance. This allocates the given generation of traffic amongst the available destinations on the basis of their attraction and accessibility. Further constraints, in the form of cost penalties, can be added if congestion is likely to develop at any site, and the effect on distribution assessed.

On the introduction of the new site a new destination is added or an existing destination gains an increased weight. Any alteration to the transport network will also necessitate revision of the appropriate generalised cost. The model can then be used to allocate the new level of trips amongst the destinations on the basis of the calibrated parameters of the model.

The resulting number of trips allocated to the new facility gives the estimated demand for that site comprising both newly generated recreation trips and those reallocated from existing sites. This of course only estimates likely demand on strict *ceteris paribus* assumptions. Trends in various influencing variables can be introduced to produce likely demand levels over a period of time, such as movements in income, travel costs, educational levels, but estimation of trends in the parameters controlling the influence of these variables on both total trip production and their allocation will require the building-up of time series of data on a comparable basis.

One final aspect which deserves specific mention is that of charges to be made for site usage. These form part of the supply price and are implicit in the attraction factor applied to each site. In order that the correct weighting is given to this charge some background work on the price elasticity of demand may be necessary. It is important that consumer response to variations in travel costs or total costs is not taken as indicative of response to variations in site costs. At this stage some experimentation with the effects of alternative pricing structures is envisaged in an attempt to ensure reasonably optimal levels of usage of all facilities in the sector.

Benefit Assessment

Having obtained an estimate of the likely number of users of the proposed facility this has to be translated into a measure of the benefits enjoyed by the community as a result of its existence. Since the definition of consumer's surplus along the length of the demand curve raises particular problems of the size of benefits at low levels of usage, and since the demand curve itself is only defined at two known points, the before and after situation, this is normally reduced to an estimate of the change in benefits. Accurate identification of these changes involves separate consideration of the different classes of beneficiary. Failure to effect this division into existing demand, newly generated demand and external effects on non-users can result in a biased estimate of benefits.[2]

Existing Users. Those individuals taking part in the market prior to the new facility can be considered in two parts – those who divert demand to the new facility and those who do not. The distribution model reallocates demand to the new facility if the total cost is lower than that incurred in the old situation. The reduction in cost may be the result of increased attraction of the new site or lower access costs. Our preferred definition of supply price was a generalised cost so that site charges could be greater at the new site but improved facilities result in a lower overall perceived price. In other words the consumer's willingness-to-pay function shifts upwards by an amount just equal to an exactly compensating fall in price. However, even if the site supply price is perceived greater than in the old situation, lower access costs can easily lead to diversion.

Existing users may also be induced to increase their demand, but in this case they will be identified by the model, and logically, as new users since their extra demand is generated by the change in the situation.

Existing demand which does not divert may also incur a change in surplus since the reduction in levels of demand at existing sites may well lead to a reassessment of willingness to pay. This would normally be upwards because of reduced congestion on site as illustrated in Figure 9.5.

New Users. Newly created demand does not of course benefit from a change in user cost but from the opportunity to participate because user cost has fallen below the willingness-to-pay function. This is a much more difficult class of benefits to assess as shown by the classic diagram (Figure 10.1) in which it involves estimating the area of triangle *RST*, the rectangle *PQRS* being the increase in benefit to existing demand.

Non-users. This category of benefits, or more often costs, illustrates the importance of not considering the particular recreation market in isolation from the rest of the sector and the rest of the urban economy. New facilities may have implications for non-participants through the effects on transport networks, noise, car parking and ultimately through the diversion of resources from elsewhere in the economy.

We have reviewed above the main sources of benefit, but this still leaves the actual valuation of the benefit in question. What must be

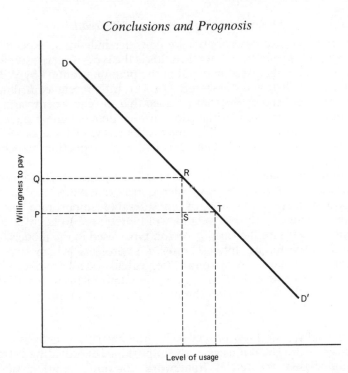

Fig. 10.1

remembered is that the prices and costs used have been carefully specified as generalised costs, they include assumed consumer perceptions of attraction and time spent in the activity or in travelling as well as actual monetary outlays. The values placed on such factors as these are implicit in consumer behaviour but for the crucial modelling phases, the trip generation and distribution models, the relevant cost functions have to be engineered from external data. The ultimate solution is thus critically dependent on these values and the interpretation placed on observed trade-offs.

It is for this reason that the basic model of consumer behaviour was stressed in Chapter 4 since this highlights the relevance of consumer response to particular values. Accurate evaluation of benefits will necessitate careful consideration of all the behavioural parameters in the light of the structure of the basic utility model.

At this point we can link back to an important theoretical issue. In Chapter 3 it was pointed out that consumer's surplus defined as the area under a normal Marshallian demand curve is only one of a series of such measures and that more realistic measures of welfare change necessitate the use of Hicks-type demand curves compensated for the implicit income charge. If we consider individual expenditure functions and expenditure flows then this is the type of curve estimated. These have been discussed in detail in the planning context by Wilson and Kirwan (1969) and Neuberger (1971a). In a recent contribution Foster and Neuberger (1974) have argued that the equivalent variation is the more correct basis for the compensated demand curve since this involves the sum of money which makes the individual just as well off as he becomes as a result of the effective price reduction associated with the new project.

Beyond this point of just what is implied by the benefits measure derived there are further issues which require explicit mention. Income distribution factors may be of considerable importance in the recreation context such that weights will be required to aggregate the identified benefits for the various person types used in the models. The choice of appropriate interest rates for projects which are not productive, but may feature strong option values and alternatives which are not costlessly reversible, will again present problems which must be solved explicitly even if rule of thumb solutions are adopted.

An Overview

The above discussion has provided the framework for analysis of the sports-centre project. It illustrates the importance of providing a strong behaviour-based theoretical framework for interpretation of the statistical results. We have also seen the advantage of treating the modelling of trip generation and flows separately from the evaluation of the benefits. That this procedure needs to be carried out for each potential project shows the complexity of an adequate model-based planning process. Nevertheless this procedure does provide a rigorous basis for the appraisal of investments.

We have concentrated on the public planning arena using implicitly a social welfare function as the objective function. This is implied in the nature of the cost functions, the criteria for site selection and the assessment of non-user costs and benefits. With suitable modification of this objective function to a private (profit) function the basic analysis is applicable to the single site of the independent entrepreneur. Pricing for the profit-maximiser can be derived by the appropriate modification to the criterion for optimal capacity usage with the known cost and demand functions, the former of these again referring solely to private costs rather than the social opportunity costs used in this analysis.

Planning Implications

It remains for us to summarise the main implications for the recreation planner and modeller.

The essential feature of the planning process outlined in this study has been the incorporation of interaction and feedback. The critical areas will be the identification of the market to be analysed and the external linkages of that market with the rest of the urban economy. This means that we must move towards a more general equilibrium approach to the whole of urban planning. Piecemeal optimising will always lead to wrong results unless the rest of the economy is already in equilibrium. However, any change in one sector such as this can upset that equilibrium if it exists.

Secondly, within a sector or a submarket of that sector, we cannot hope to achieve correct results on a project by project basis. Correct evaluation of each individual project depends on an overall consideration of the recreation system.

Thirdly that system is not only important as a means of analysing the market at a given moment of time, the interdependence of sites within the market, but also the development of the market through time, the interdependence of current and future projects.

Modelling Implications
The model is the tool of the planner and not his master, the implications for model development therefore derive from those for planning. Essentially we have seen that techniques derived from conventional transport modelling procedures, however sophisticated, will be inadequate in the recreation context because of their non-accordance with the behavioural logic of a theoretical model. The main conclusions have been the need for an elastic trip generation model, influenced by the supply prices of the purpose for which the trip in question is made and a distribution model which is dependent on exogenously produced attraction factors.

A great deal of the analysis has, as a result, been concerned with defining and specifying these price and attraction factors and the appropriate ways of incorporating these into a deterministic model.

This comprehensive model structure has been seen to be superior to many of the techniques used in recreational modelling to date. Such techniques as the Clawson method and others based solely on the trip distribution model may have the advantage of greater simplicity but much less confidence can be placed in their results.

The model structure required goes beyond these purely travel aspects, however. There is the need for an activities model both as a basic means of estimating total demand potentials activity by activity and as a means of interpreting the parameters of the transport models for evaluation purposes. It is this area where the biggest implications for future research lie.

Research Priorities

Much of this study has been of the nature of a preliminary investigation, identifying the critical areas of the planning and modelling process. Putting the procedure summarised in the urban sports-centre example into practice implies a considerable research effort at all stages. There seem to be three major, separable tasks.

1 Further investigation of recreation markets concentrating on elasticities of substitution and the nature of price response is necessary to identify the correct dimensions for disaggregation.
2 Correct interpretation of the main results has been shown to hinge on the activities model. It has been stressed in the study that complete activity modelling using full time-budget information is unlikely to be necessary for every planning exercise but more basic research into empirical activity models is required.
3 The interface between the trip generation and trip distribution model remains unsatisfactory. This is a more general issue than the case of recreation but the interface is particularly critical here. More research is required into the nature of the crucial cost functions and their roles in the two models. The basic objective is to isolate the variables which are planning parameters and make them truly exogenous whilst avoiding the need for the imposition of values, such as of time, for variables which have implicit behavioural values in the model structure.

Concluding Remarks

It is not easy to distil the wide-ranging findings of this study into neat conclusions, especially when the conclusions themselves read more like a preface for all those areas in which work remains to be done. As we stated at the beginning, this study is intended as an exploratory one providing a rigorous analysis of what has been achieved and what needs to be achieved in a growing and important area of research. It is encouraging that so much analysis of the problems has been possible on existing data, and that augurs well for the future as any means of economising on the expensive task of data collection and analysis may lead to the more widespread adoption of rigorous analytical techniques. To this end any moves towards the building of models which have stable parameter values when moved through space represent a critical area of research.

We conclude by reiterating the remarks of Chapter 1. This has been a study based on the analytical framework of economics since in the last resort decisions are implied which can only be taken on the basis of rigorous economic appraisal. Leisure and recreation is an area which has attracted the attention of many disciplines, however, all of which have an equal role to play in designing a policy for recreation planning which meets the best needs of the community. Above all it is an area of considerable and growing importance in which new problems will continue to present themselves. Already we are seeing the growth in recreational expectations coming into conflict with resource problems, particularly through the rising costs of fuel. Any of these or future problems can only be tackled if we have a basic understanding of consumer behaviour and powerful means of analysing choices and taking rational decisions.

Appendix A
Leisure Activities Survey

The analysis of Chatper 5 is based on a mail questionnaire survey of individuals in just over 3000 households in Oxford. Respondents were asked for details of leisure activities outside the home for a week in April 1971 and certain other relevant information on socio-economic status, family structure, residence etc.

Survey Size
This was largely determined by the available resources, financial and manpower. The basic sample size of some 3000 households which might be expected to yield a total response of up to 1200 households was reasonable. The existing survey framework and the original zone structure of the Oxford Transportation Study Area was used to enable the derivation of zonal figures for comparison. Forty zones with original sample sizes of 45 households or more were used and these yielded a total sample size of 3043 households.

The Sample
The lists of sample addresses in each zone used in the original survey, which were provided by the Oxford City Engineer's Department, had been generated from a random-walk procedure selecting every eighth dwelling (due allowance having been made for multiple occupation, flats etc.).

Within the households sampled, data was collected for individuals over the age of 15. This cut-off point was selected for two reasons. Firstly, it was desirable not to include children in a self-administered questionnaire because of their level of understanding or appreciation of its purpose, and also there may be greater doubts about any rational allocation decisions being made because of their particular non-earning status.

The Questionnaire
The questionnaire forms collected information in four parts. Part I of the questionnaire was concerned with eliciting information on employ-

ment and time availability, part II with use of time during the survey week, and part III with personal details. Part IV covered information on length of residence, structure of household, relations in the area etc.

The questions concerning the leisure activities referred to a whole week. To keep the questionnaire as short as possible, full details of times and modes of travel etc. were not asked for the leisure activities, but frequency of participation and whether this was more or less than the normal level were asked.

Response Rates

The usable response was just under 15 per cent, a little lower than hoped for, but not surprising considering the complexity of the questionnaire and the proximity to the 1971 Census. Personal contact would have been necessary to raise the response any higher.

The final coded response gave details on 858 individuals from 436 households. This was compared with the earlier data for the same area for bias. Some bias towards the higher socio-economic groups was found, but this is quite common in mail surveys. The age distribution was, however, fairly accurate.

Analysis

The data was coded and stored, in individual observations. Tabulations were prepared by using the University of Sussex survey analysis program by courtesy of David Hitchin. Further statistical analysis was enabled by the preparation of cross-product matrices used as the input to a regression-analysis program. This method shortened the time necessary for each subsequent analysis as a full input of the data was not needed.

Appendix B
The National Travel Survey–
Sources and Definitions

Survey Design
The Survey was designed to study the travelling patterns of a nationally representative sample of households on a continuous basis throughout 1965. The sample was to be such that separate quarterly analyses could be performed on national data and that separate analyses could also be carried out on individual planning regions. Information was collected on all journeys made by all individuals in each household sampled over a seven-day period, these periods being staggered so that equal numbers started on each day of the week, in each of 26 fortnightly phases, throughout the survey year.

The Sample
A multistage stratified random sample was designed. The three stages used were:

1 Primary units – local authority administrative areas.
2 Intermediate units – wards or parishes or combinations of these within selected local authority areas.
3 Final stage – random sample of addresses from electoral register.

Two stratifications were then defined, firstly by planning region for England and Wales and by four divisions of Scotland, and secondly, within these, into three types of area; conurbation, other urban areas (including high-density rural) and rural areas. To provide a sufficient sample in all planning regions for separate analysis without over-sampling in some regions, certain regions were given a weighting factor of two, and then the sample distributed between the regions in proportion to the weighted 1961 population. Within each stratum the primary sampling units were selected with a probability proportional to their population sizes, and these distributed over the 26 phases.

The intermediate units were also selected with a probability proportional to size, these being allocated to different phases. Twenty one addresses were selected with equal probability from each of these zones, and three of these allocated to each of the seven starting days in that phase.

In all some 12,500 households were sampled covering 36,000 persons aged 3 and over.

Data Collected

Four basic types of data were collected:

1 Household Information – relating to general household information, family structure, income, and location and area of residence.
2 Vehicle Information – relating to any vehicles in the household's possession, and their use during the survey week.
3 Individual Information – relating to the personal and economic characteristics of the individual.
4 Travel Data – details of each journey made by each member of the household during the survey week: purpose, mode, cost etc.

Definition of Travel

The Survey covers all travel by land, water, and air modes between points within Great Britain and adjacent islands; journeys extending outside these limits are only included as far as the relevant port or airport of departure. The only travel within this definition which is excluded is short walks of less than one mile, and travel integral to a job, e.g. by bus or lorry drivers, or persons on foot-patrol duties. This only applies to travel in the course of work where there is no purpose at the end of the journey so that travel by commercial travellers is included.

Definition of Journeys

Travel is structured on a two-level basis. The first-order unit is the journey – defined as a *one-way* course of travel with one single main purpose, although it may have other subsidiary purposes or be undertaken by any combination of different types of transport. The end of a journey is signified when a main purpose is fulfilled. A main purpose is distinguished from a subsidiary purpose by the criterion that a separate journey would be made to fulfil a main purpose. If two main purposes are the reason for a continuous course of travel, stopping at each in turn, these will be recorded as two journeys unless both are at the same destination. Outward and return legs of a return trip count as two journeys, and round trips also constitute two journeys split at the geographically furthest point from the origin.

The second-order unit is the stage – a separate stage is identified either by a different form of transport or by requiring to purchase a separate ticket.

Car-ownership
A car-owning household is a household with, in its possession, a three- or four-wheeled vehicle used or usable for the conveyance of any household member during the seven-day recording period whether such vehicle is owned by a household member, by an employer, by any other person, or hired for the whole period, availability rather than ownership being the main criterion.

Recording Period
Data was collected for each individual for a continuous period of seven days, these periods being spread over a whole year with equal representations of each day in the week as a starting day. The number of stages recorded and all the generation rates used in the analysis thus refer to journeys made on average by the sample in a representative week.

Data Handling and Analysis
The Department of the Environment had prepared a large number of two- and three-way tables from edited data tapes. These ten volumes of tabulations held by the Department provided the basis for the analysis of Chapter 7. The tabulations in Chapter 7 are extracts from certain of these, or are composed from a number of the basic data tabulations.

For further statistical analysis, copies of the edited data tapes were purchased from the Department. At this stage the data was still in its original form of household, individual, and journey records. This had then to be reformed into individual observations, each containing the independent variables necessary for the regression analysis plus matrices of trips and mileage, by mode and journey purpose, derived from the journey records for each individual. Finally, numerically coded information was turned into actual values, or series of dummy variables.

The final stage of data handling was the preparation of cross-product matrices which formed the basic input to the successive regression runs.

This procedure was the most convenient way of handling the large numbers involved – each data set had between 250 and 2000 observations, the majority being in the range 1000 to 1200. It did limit the possibility of respecifying equations, however, to the variable structure already selected. Complete reanalysis of the data would have been prohibitively expensive.

Notes

Chapter 2

1 Examples are Veblen (1899) and Bukharin (1919).
2 This is often evidenced by the problem faced in retirement, particularly as people retire at younger ages.
3 Two classic expositions are Robbins (1930) and Mincer (1963).
4 Linder (1970, p. 14) refers to this as 'consumption time' when it involves the use of consumption goods, or 'culture time' when goods are less relevant.
5 Ibid., p. 15.
6 See Owen (1969b).
7 This may appear a little awkward at first, but it is assumed that people use organised holidays for convenience (the externalities involved), whereas recreation is normally organised as of necessity, in the nature of the product.
8 See Becker (1965) and the more detailed discussion in Chapter 4.
9 The justification for this is given in greater detail in Chapter 4, p. 64.
10 This point is developed further, with evidence, in Vickerman and Collings (1974).
11 There is a direct relationship between the two measures so that in a single-route study, or a study where the trip-length distribution is very highly peaked (as in many journey-to-work cases) the measurement of journeys is an adequate measure of passenger mileage.
12 This concept of the standardised mile is due to B. T. Bayliss, see Bayliss and Hebden (1970), where it is argued that it may be more relevant in the goods sector since the actual route mileage differences may be much greater.
13 See Quandt and Baumol (1966).
14 See National Board for Prices and Incomes, Report No. 112 (1969).
15 For further discussions of quality change, see Bayliss and Hebden (1970) and Deakin and Seward (1969), Chapter 2 and Statistical Appendix F.2.
16 See, for example, Harrison and Quarmby (1969) and Mansfield (1971a).
17 T. L. Burton (1971) Table 1, pp. 42–3.
18 Patmore (1970), p. 1.
19 This is not to suggest that all now enjoy the privileges of the leisure classes identified by the early Marxists (p. 5, above). Modern society raises other problems, beyond the scope of this study, but see, for example, the excellent discussion of this in Parker (1971).
20 See, for example, Handy (1968).
21 See Alden (1971).
22 Bogan and Hamel (1964).
23 See articles in *The Times* on 28 and 29 December 1970 and 2 January 1971 and resulting correspondence on 11 January, 1971.

24 Useful surveys of this question are those of Jefferys (1952), Myrdal and Klein (1956) and Hunt (1968).

25 Sillitoe (1969), Table 7.

26 See *Trade and Industry*, 19 August 1971. Watson (1974) reports that by the end of 1972 there were 88 such sites providing a total of 224 cinemas.

27 Sillitoe (1969), Tables A.45 and A.46.

28 Some evidence on the distribution of golf courses is given in Patmore (1970), pp. 76–80.

29 For a review of the impact on selected sites and some suggested solutions, see Rubinstein and Speakman (1969).

30 See Clawson and Knetsch (1966), pp. 70–1. The estimated equation for this relationship for one park was

$$\log(V + 0.80) = 3.82462 - 2.39287 \log C.$$

where V = visits per 1000 home-zone population and C = travel cost estimate at standard cost per mile based on distance.

31 This replaced the much narrower area of interest of the National Parks Commission under the Countryside Act, 1968. The statutory requirements of the Commissioners are to 'keep under review all matters relating to the provision and improvement of facilities for enjoyment of the countryside in England and Wales; the conservation and enhancement of its natural beauty and amenity; and the need to secure public access for open-air recreation'.

32 Of these, twenty-seven are controlled by the National Trust and an eighth is the Royal Estate at Sandringham.

33 See comments in 'Cars v Country: An alternative', in *Drive*, AA Motorists Magazine, Autumn 1972. As many as 15 per cent of visitors felt that their visit to Stack Rocks in the Pembrokeshire Coast National Park was made worse by the provision of a free minibus service from a distant car park, instead of allowing free access to the cliff top by car. In addition about 25 per cent of cars approaching the area turned away when they found their access barred. Similar experiments were carried out at White Horse Hill in Wiltshire and Pen-y-Pas in Snowdonia. At White Horse Hill, 51 per cent insisted on their right to drive to the top, and 13 per cent turned away, although only 9 per cent of those co-operating felt their day had been made worse. The Snowdonia scheme was not comparable as it was a supplement of a congested car park at the top of the pass. These results are based on small samples of 100 or so taken on single days only and so cannot be taken as accurate estimates. The figures are, however, of considerable illustrative interest.

34 A comprehensive treatment of the existing distribution of outdoor recreation facilities and current activity levels is contained in Patmore (1970), Chapters 3–7.

35 For evidence of this, see Vickerman (1972a), Tables 6 and 7.

36 See Vickerman (1972a) for a summary of this and more complete details; also Chapter 7.

37 See Frankenberg (1965) and Goldthorpe *et al.* (1969) for discussion of some background material to this issue.

38 The terms 'compensatory' and 'spillover' were coined by Engels in his study of the working classes in the nineteenth century.
39 On the general impact of broadcasting from the social historian's standpoint, see A. Briggs, 'BBC's 50-year cultural revolution', the *Observer*, 19 November, 1972.
40 The basic equation was

$$L = 85.99 + 0.182W' - 0.042P(R)', \ R = 0.964$$

where L = leisure time, W' = adjusted wage rate and $P(R)'$ = estimated price of recreation. Note the positive relation between L and W' through time, suggesting a backward-bending supply curve of labour; see Owen (1971).
41 Much of the work of the Countryside Commission does not strictly result in this reduction in supply price as it involves a formalising of existing access areas, and to the extent that conservation is an aim the reverse may be true. However, the provision of ancillary facilities, and the element of advertising introduced, may have equivalent effects on demand.
42 See the discussion in Chapter 3 for further analysis of this point.

Chapter 3
1 This view is more fully developed in Chapter 9; see also Vickerman and Collings (1974).
2 Excellent reviews of the state of the art are given in two recent textbooks by Mishan (1971b) and Dasgupta and Pearce (1972).
3 See, for example, the case of the Third London Airport; assessments in Mishan (1970) and Dasgupta and Pearce (1972, Chapter 9); and for useful general reviews, Harrison and Quarmby (1969) and Lassiere and Bowers (1972).
4 See Weisbrod (1968); and for an application of equity considerations to the Airport case, Nwaneri (1970).
5 For example, the research by S.C.P.R. into time and environmental evaluation using the 'black box'; see Hoinville (1971).
6 It is immaterial whether the commodity is such that it is many people each purchasing one unit, or some people purchasing one or more units, or one person purchasing all the units sold – that is a question of the distribution of the benefit, not of its existence.
7 This was first noted by Henderson (1941); and see also Hicks (1943).
8 Changes in land values, the profits of adjacent businesses e.g. petrol stations, and so forth induced by a road improvement project leading to diversion of traffic fall into this category; see Walters (1968) for a comprehensive review of this problem.
9 These problems are well handled in two recent survey articles, Musgrave, (1969) and Mishan (1971a).
10 See Turvey (1963).
11 A classic example of this is congestion. Here every individual's presence has an effect on every other individual in terms of delaying, frustrating etc. The private cost to the individual is only that of his own delay in terms of time lost, extra fuel etc. and does not include the element that he contributes to each other person's delay. Thus the sum of the individual private costs will be

less than the true social cost; it is the latter which is more relevant for cost assessment. This topic is well treated by Walters (1968).

12 After Bergson (1938); see also Mishan (1971b), Chapters 45–7 and Dasgupta and Pearce (1972), Chapter 3.

13 See Arrow (1963).

14 This is an approximate measure which is convenient for graphical representation; there are of course problems in defining the marginal-cost curve at a zero output (i.e. extending it back to the vertical axis). This representation does avoid the need to complicate the diagram with average-cost curves which would provide an exact measure.

15 This method has been used in the case of angling, by Lewis and Whitby (1972).

16 These could be public funds, national or local, or alternative market sources, e.g. the use of earnings from other aspects of the activity such as advertising.

17 See Peston (1972) for an exposition of this taxonomy of goods in terms of excludability (a production characteristic of the good) and rivalness (a consumption characteristic). Private goods are rival and excludable, pure public goods are non-rival and non-excludable.

18 For an exposition of this view in terms of charging for cultural activities, see Robbins (1971) pp. 5–8. The capacity question has also been tackled by Peston (1972), who argues that when there is excess capacity at a zero price the good becomes non-rival (marginal cost of additional consumption is zero) but excludable since the marginal cost of producing an additional unit is non-zero. The problem of defining capacity in the case of recreation is deferred until Chapter 9.

19 In practice the situation may be akin to that of education with public-sector provision available free, but the simultaneous development of a more exclusive private sector of clubs.

20 Already, physical controls on access to some of the more vulnerable spots have had to be employed in an attempt to safeguard these resources; see Countryside Commission (1971, para. 3.28; 1972, paras. 2.6 and 8.20); and for more detail, Miles (1972).

21 An interesting example of the relationship between project appraisal and planning strategies is given in Commission on the Third London Airport (1971), Chapter 6.

22 Figures from the 1966 Sample Census show that out of the total labour force (in and out of employment) 4.03 per cent was assigned to those sectors which can be ascribed solely to leisure and entertainment industries (M.L.H. 881–4, covering Cinemas etc., Sport, Betting and Catering). These employed 558,680 females and 399,130 males and also showed a rather higher rate of unemployment than average.

23 Many farms develop farm shops or let rooms as a means of boosting incomes.

24 The total (direct plus indirect employment creation) multipliers based on M.L.H. 884 (Catering) were 0.000483 for tourism and 0.000239 generally, i.e. 4.83 jobs per £10,000 direct visitor spending; see Archer (1973).

25 For example, Smith and Kavanagh (1969), Smith (1971), Lewis and Whitby (1972) and Quarmby (1969).

26 The role of central government is in many cases that of rubber-stamping

proposals or of dealing with cases of conflict on appeal, but there is a procedure for 'calling in' planning proposals regarded as being of great importance as, for example, was done with regard to hypermarkets in 1972 (cf. Department of the Environment and Welsh Office, *Out of Town Shops and Shopping Centres*, Development Control Policy Note 13, 1972).

27 See Royal Commission on Local Government in England, Vol. 2, *Memorandum of Dissent by Mr D. Senior*, Cmnd. 4040–I, (1969).

28 Buchanan and Stubblebine's (1962) oft-quoted exemplars are neighbours arguing over a fence, and not over a public swimming-pool or international airport.

29 See Paul (1971) and Mishan (1967), Chapters 5 and 6.

30 A useful summary of the procedures used by the Roskill Commission is given in Flowerdew (1972); see also Commission on the Third London Airport (1970 and 1971). For critical reviews of these and various other methods of valuation suggested by witnesses to the Commission, see Paul (1971) and Mishan (1970).

31 A more detailed discussion of the Clawson method is contained in the following Chapter; see also Vickerman (1974c).

Chapter 4

1 Shift workers or habitual nightworkers would thus have a different conception of their time budget than a person working the same total hours but during the normal working day.

2 This approach was first discussed by Becker (1965).

3 See Lancaster (1966).

4 This may depend on whether any special equipment such as walking boots are purchased specially for this activity.

5 A more complete discussion of the case of shopping is given in Robinson, Hebden and Vickerman (1974).

6 This could be regarded as being measured in standardised time units (as discussed in Chapter 2 above) for which a standard cost per unit can be assessed.

7 This will need adjustment later to allow for the differing unit costs of transport between routes and modes, but for simplification all travel is here regarded as heterogeneous.

8 De Serpa (1973), p. 402.

9 Compare this with the theory of consumer demand for goods in terms of their intrinsic characteristics; see Lancaster (1966).

10 It must be recognised that this is essentially a short-run consideration. In the long run, when residential location can be changed, some explicit choices concerning transport must enter into the preference function; nevertheless, spatial structure will present a technical constraint, and some trading-off between, for example, work and leisure travel.

11 This bias was seen to be an upward bias, usually as an empirical fact rather than as a logical development of a theoretical model; see, for example, Wingo (1961) and Moses and Williamson (1963).

12 See Becker (1965), De Serpa (1971) and Evans (1972).

13 See Johnson (1966), Oort (1969), Owen (1969a) and Watson (1971) for the main contributions.
14 See Henderson and Quandt (1958) for a basic exposition.
15 See Johnson (1966), p. 138.
16 Oort (1969) refers to this as the marginal net benefit of labour, a composite of the income-earning potential of labour, balanced by the disutility of the time spent working.
17 Johnson (1966), p. 140.
18 This difference is normally assumed to be downwards on the basis that the marginal utility of work is negative, but if $\partial U/\partial W$ were to be positive the valuation of leisure time would be greater than the wage rate, cf. Chiswick (1967). Oort (1969, pp. 282–4) develops the model to show that rigidities in the working week may lead to this result being an inequality; those who work more than they wish to, value time more highly at the margin, i.e. more than the marginal net benefit of labour.
19 The Lagrangean expression is now:

$$V = U(X_i, L_i) + \lambda\left(Y - \sum_i p_i X_i\right) + \mu\left(H - \sum_i L_i\right) + \sum_i K_i(L_i - a_i X_i)$$

($K_i \geqslant 0$), the K_i being additional shadow variables, one for each activity.
20 For both K_i and $(L_i - a_i X_i)$ to be zero simultaneously is not precluded, but this does not affect the conclusion to be drawn.
21 De Donnea (1972), p. 363. De Serpa (1973) criticises this formulation as not yielding a useful measurable quantity, whilst being essentially the same.
22 See Quarmby (1967) for an example of this procedure.
23 These are a little-studied sector of data in such studies despite the emphasis given by the early study, Beesley (1965).
24 See, for example, the evidence in the survey of studies by Harrison and Quarmby (1969).
25 People's movement for all activities can be recorded by travel surveys and trends monitored through origin and destination studies–these should give superior coverage to any attempt to measure demand at sites, especially when these themselves may be undefined.
26 The price of time in an activity is strictly the value of time savings from that activity; in a solution of a model of the form of equations (10) to (12), and (23), the time price will be in terms of the parameter of the consumption constraint, a_i.
27 The method is clearly described by Smith (1971) in an empirical study of visits to a reservoir.
28 Other examples of use in the U.K. are those by Mansfield (1971b) and Lewis and Whitby (1972).
29 This has been argued in more detail in Vickerman (1974b and 1974c).
30 The problem of perceived costs has been well discussed by Neuberger (1971b).

Chapter 5
1 The survey was financed by the Department of the Environment as part of its time research programme; full responsibility for organisation of the survey and interpretation of the findings rests with the author, however.

2 Full details of the organisation and method, together with a critical appraisal and details of questionnaires, response etc. are contained in Vickerman (1972b). A summary is given in Appendix A.

3 For example, see the recent collection of sociological articles in Smith, Parker and Smith (1973).

4 See, for example, Gavron (1966), Jefferys (1952), Myrdal and Klein (1956) and Hunt (1968).

5 Compare, for example, Willmot (1966) and Abrams (1959) with Townsend (1961) or Tunstall (1966).

6 For a comprehensive source on such data for the U.K., see B.B.C. (1965).

7 The literature on this topic is large; the more important studies which break new ground are Clarke (1956), Wilensky (1961), Geistl (1961), Parker (1965) and Adams and Butler (1966–7).

8 A useful survey of community structures and influences is contained in Frankenberg (1966).

9 Some analysis of this factor has been made in Goldthorpe *et al.* (1969).

10 This case is discussed in Goldberger (1964), pp. 248–55.

11 If $\theta_i = \Pr(Y_i = 1)$ where Y_i can take only the values 0 and 1, then $Y_i^2 = Y_i$ and hence $\text{var}(Y_i) = \theta_i(1 - \theta_i)$ which means that the variance is not the constant σ^2 required by the least-squares procedure. Furthermore the estimates may lead to violation of the constraint that $0 \leqslant \theta_i \leqslant 1$.

12 The function for the variance of Y_i, $\theta_i(1 - \theta_i)$ changes little within the range $0.2 \leqslant \theta_i \leqslant 0.8$, viz. AA' is the true logistic formulation of θ_i (which is $\Pr(Y_i = 1)$), with respect to the value of a given X_j; BB' is the linear estimator. This problem is excellently handled in Cox (1970), Chapter 2.

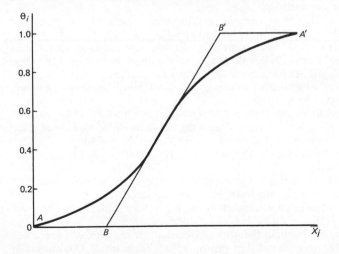

13 Goldberger (1964) has suggested a two-stage solution to the limited value dependent variable problem when there is a strong zero bias. He suggests the estimation of a binary (zero–non-zero) model and then a separate model for all

non-zero values. Such correction procedures are costly and usually lead only to small improvements in the model.

14 There is no simultaneous-equations bias from including Y_1 and Y_3 as explanatory variables; as the direction of causality is clear the structure is recursive.

15 This could be either the unpaid overtime of executives or the result of industrial overtime being mainly undertaken by the more skilled and supervisory workers.

Chapter 6

1 These arguments have been developed in greater detail in Vickerman (1974a, 1974d).

2 Recent applications have used a more rigorous statistical procedure to define the classificatory variables which does overcome this problem to some extent; see, for example, Kutter (1973).

3 A sample of 1000 with the 108-cell classification outlined above will result in many cells having too small a sample to yield an unbiased estimate of average trip making.

4 There is a long history of development of these. Wilson (1967, 1969, 1970, 1971) has outlined many of the theoretical developments. Wilson, Hawkins, Hill and Wagon (1969) provide a valuable example of the application of these techniques.

5 It is not necessary to dwell on the choice of best functional form. It has been found that an exponential form gives the best fit to data, viz. $\exp(-\beta_i C_{ij})$. The reader is referred to Wilson (1970, pp. 19, 34–5; 1974, Chapter 12) for further discussion of this issue.

6 For detailed discussions of calibration procedures, see Batty and Mackie (1972) and Wilson (1974), Chapter 12.

7 For a critical assessment of modal split in this context, see Collings (1974).

8 See Wilson (1973); and for a practical example in the case of the Third London Airport, see Flowerdew (1972) for a summary.

9 This assumption of perfect substitutability has been demonstrated by McGillivray (1972).

10 See the studies in the collection edited by Quandt (1970).

11 A more detailed exposition of the development of the indices discussed here has been presented elsewhere; see Vickerman (1974d).

12 See Huff (1963), Lakshmanan and Hansen (1965) and Rhodes and Whitaker (1967).

13 Evidence of this can be found in the *Census of Distribution and Other Services*, carried out by the Board of Trade at intervals.

14 A recent example concerning recreation trips is that by Gordon and Edwards (1973).

15 See, for example, the work of Echenique *et al.* (1969) and Ingram (1971).

16 This has been noted by several writers, for example, Quarmby (1967).

Chapter 7

1 A description of the sample and the nature of the data is given in Appendix B.

2 The Directorate of Statistics at the Department of the Environment provided

a greal deal of assistance in making the data available, and considerable thanks are due. The use made of this data is entirely the author's responsibility, however, no implication of criticism or any indication of the Department's views can be attached to this presentation.

3 A journey is defined as a *one-way* course of travel with a single *main* purpose, which may be comprised of one or more stages. A separate stage is identified by a change of mode, or the need to purchase a separate ticket.

4 Including express and private bus, taxi, bicycle, motor cycle and large commercial vehicles.

5 Complete details of estimated equations for all regions and modes are given in Vickerman (1972b), Chapter 4 and Appendix E.

6 These are the more specific categories used by the Registrar-General based on both types of work and employment status; four groups were specifically identified, Professional and Managerial (S.E.G. 1–4), Non-manual Workers (S.E.G. 5–6), Supervisory and Skilled Manual Workers (S.E.G. 8–9), Unoccupied (all not in an occupation group, mainly housewives, retired persons and students).

7 Ownership is defined in a loose sense relating to the availability of the car to a member of the household, whether owned legally, hired, borrowed or owned by an employer, for the period of the survey.

8 See Goldberger (1964), pp. 248–55. This problem is equivalent to that discussed in Chapter 5.

9 See, for example, the method used by Cicchetti, Seneca and Davidson (1969), Chapter 4.

10 See Vickerman (1974a), for a more detailed exposition of this argument; and for definitions of the terms, Chapter 6.

11 The tabulations are based on those produced by the Department of the Environment from the complete edited data from the Survey. I am grateful to the Department for allowing access to these although it is stressed that the author bears full responsibility for the use and interpretation of the data in this study.

12 See also Beesley and Kain (1964).

13 White (1974).

14 This point has been made strongly by J. M. Thomson in recent evidence to the House of Commons Expenditure Committee (1973).

Chapter 8

1 This was taken from the 1966 Oxford Transportation Study by courtesy of the City Engineer and Surveyor of the City of Oxford. No implication attaches to the use of the data made here.

2 For a good general introduction, the reader is referred to Hoover (1971) or Richardson (1969). A discussion specific to the urban context is contained in Goodall (1972). An excellent short statement of the theoretical aspects is given in Beckmann (1968).

3 The concept was introduced by Alonso (1964). A useful summary is contained in Evans (1973), Chapter 6.

4 This enables the basic principles to be established easily and does not have a material effect on the conclusions; see for example, Evans (1973), pp. 19–20.

5 Quoted in Patmore (1971), p. 80.
6 See Cowling and Rayner (1970), for a discussion of some of the issues in quality competition.
7 Field checks of this method have shown it to be more than 90 per cent accurate.
8 Only two were identified in this study area.
9 We may note in passing that grid pattern studies have been carried out in the United States where urban areas tend to conform to a more regular grid pattern than in Britain; in these cases such studies may be no more free of bias than the procedure adopted here.
10 This appears a rather heterogeneous group but the precise definition of clubs may vary considerably and many clubs may fulfil two or all three roles; for this reason it was felt safer to consider the single category.
11 See Lindgren (1968), pp. 161–5, for a full discussion.
12 Others being Neyman's Type A and the double Poisson.
13 Lindgren (1968), pp. 151–2.
14 An example here is of restaurants and professional services which presumably cluster for business rather than leisure complementarities.
15 This exercise has been presented in Vickerman (1974d) to which the reader is referred for the details of the analysis.
16 For a basic guide to the technique, the interested reader is referred to Harman (1963). An admirable short introduction to the methods used in this analysis is to be found in Lawley and Maxwell (1971, especially Chapters 1 and 4); and see also Jöreskog (1967).
17 Interesting applications can be found in the studies by Wong (1969) and Robson (1969), pp. 58–72.

Chapter 9
1 Price exclusion is strictly always possible in these cases but may present severe practical difficulties such as the need to erect expensive fencing, police the perimeter and collect the fees. In some cases it may, of course, be possible to effect charging through car-park charges.
2 See Forbes (1974), Chapters 2 and 10.
3 Evans, in Forbes (1974, p. 252), provides an interesting illustrative example of the timetabling problems which would be presented when 200 people try to use a 6-acre site!
4 See Weisbrod (1964).
5 Lindsay (1969).
6 Cicchetti and Freeman (1971).
7 This case is argued in detail by Fisher, Krutilla and Cicchetti (1972a and 1972b).
8 A convenient review of concepts of city structure is given in Robson (1969); and see also Richardson (1969), pp. 145–55.
9 Some evidence of socio-economic determined differences in the degree of bias obtained in a short-term comparison of expressed intentions with revealed action has been identified by Elson (1974) in a study of day trippers in Sussex.
10 Although an option demand can exist without the option ever having been

taken up, options must be much less well defined if it has not been possible to include the option within the range of choices available.

11 This concept was introduced with respect to recreation by Mack and Myers (1965).

12 An interesting parallel could be drawn with electricity supply where a sytems approach to investment has become the norm; see Webb (1973), Chapter 5. A basic text on the problem in relation to the electricity industry is that by Turvey (1968).

13 Fisher and Krutilla (1972).

14 This is the case first outlined by Samuelson (1954).

15 See the case of entertainment services investigated by Bohm (1972) and the use of wilderness areas for recreation reported by Fisher and Krutilla (1972).

16 Compare once again the contrasting case of electricity supply.

17 See Arrow (1968 and 1970). The issue with regard to conservation *v.* development which may be important in determining specific recreational uses was first noted by Krutilla (1967); more technical treatments have been given by Fisher, Krutilla and Cicchetti (1972) and by Arrow and Fisher (1974).

18 The literature on this subject is large. Useful summaries are contained in Millward (1971, Chapters 7–8) and Webb (1973, Chapter 7–8); see also Bohm (1974).

19 Lipsey and Lancaster (1956).

20 It should be remembered that we have already allowed for the social benefits of recreation in the resource cost function.

21 On this see Farrell (1968); and the excellent and practical summary in Turvey (1971), Chapter 3.

22 If more than one complementary good is involved then the correction will be determined by a weighted average of the price to marginal-cost deviations.

23 The 'exclusiveness' of many private recreational clubs, and their long waiting lists for membership is indicative of this.

24 A basic reference on urban services is Vickrey (1962). A useful survey of the transport case is that by Beesley (1972), reprinted as Chapter 10 of Beesley (1973).

25 For the parallel case in the transport context of relative levels of subsidy to competing modes, see Fitch *et al.* (1964) and Beesley's critique (1972).

26 On the discrepancy between accounting and economic measures in this context, see Harcourt (1965).

27 Some estimates of the relative sizes of income multipliers for different categories of tourist have been given by Archer and Owen (1971). They conclude that campers may have a larger regional multiplier effect because of the lower level of leakages from such expenditure. This may form a useful policy for future tourist growth but does not allow for the real costs of transferring existing visitors.

Chapter 10

1 The classic case here is that of the Roskill Commission of Inquiry into the Third London Airport. The Commission prepared a short list of four sites from over a hundred in the first instance, but their terms of reference prevented

consideration of alternative types of development and the no-change alternative.

2 The article by Neuberger (1971a) clearly illustrates the problems relating to user benefit.

References

Abrams, M. (1959), *The Teenage Consumer* (London: London Press Exchange).

Adams, B. N. and Butler, J. E. (1966–7), 'Occupational status and husband–wife social participation', *Social Forces*, 45, 501–7.

Alden, J. (1971), 'Double job holding: a regional analysis of Scotland', *Scottish Journal of Political Economy*, 18, 99–112.

Alonso, W. (1964), *Location and Land Use: Towards a General Theory of Rent*, (Cambridge, Mass.: Harvard University Press).

Archer, B. H. (1973), *The Impact of Domestic Tourism*, Bangor Occasional Papers in Economics No. 2 (Cardiff: University of Wales Press).

Archer, B. H. and Owen, C. (1971), 'Towards a tourist regional multiplier', *Regional Studies*, 5, 289–94.

Arrow, K. J. (1963), *Social Choice and Individual Values*, 2nd ed. (New Haven: Yale University Press).

Arrow, K. J. (1968), 'Optimal capital policy with irreversible investment', in *Value, Capital and Growth*, ed. J. N. Wolfe (Edinburgh University Press).

Arrow, K. J. and Fisher, A. C. (1974), 'Environmental preservation, uncertainty and irreversibility', *Quarterly Journal of Economics*, 88, 312–19.

Arrow, K. J. and Kurz, M. (1970), 'Optimal growth with irreversible investment in a Ramsey model', *Econometrica*, 38, 331–44.

Artle, R. (1965), *The Structure of the Stockholm Economy*, American ed. (Ithaca, N.Y.: Cornell University Press).

Batty, M. and Mackie, S. (1972), 'The calibration of gravity, entropy and related models of spatial interaction', *Environment and Planning*, 4, 205–33.

Bayliss, B. T. and Hebden, J. J. (1970), 'The theory and application of index numbers in the transport sector', Working Paper W/TRANS/WP6/262, U.N. Economic Commission for Europe, Geneva.

Becker, G. S. (1965), 'A theory of the allocation of time', *Economic Journal*, 75, 493–517.

Beckmann, M. (1968), *Location Theory* (New York: Random House).

Beesley, M. E. (1965), 'The value of time spent in travelling: some new evidence', *Economica*, 32, 174–85.

Beesley, M. E. (1972), 'Economica criteria for the maintenance, modification or creation of public transport services which may not necessarily be profitable: urban and suburban transport', in *Fourth International Symposium on Theory and Practice in Transport Economics*, European Conference of Ministers of Transport, Paris.

215

Beesley, M. E. (1973), *Urban Transport: Studies in Economic Policy* (London: Butterworth).

Beesley, M. E. and Kain, J. F. (1964), 'Urban form, car ownership and public policy: an appraisal of "Traffic in Towns"', *Urban Studies*, 1, 174–203.

Bergson, A. (1938), 'A reformulation of certain aspects of welfare economics', *Quarterly Journal of Economics*, 52, 310–34.

Bogan, F. A. and Hamel, H. R. (1964), 'Multiple job holders in May 1963', *Monthly Labor Review*, 87, 249–57.

Bohm, P. (1972), 'Estimating demand for public goods: an experiment', *European Economic Review*, 3, 111–30.

Bohm, P. (1974), *Social Efficiency* (London: Macmillan).

British Broadcasting Corporation (1965), *The People's Activities*, Audience Research Department, B.B.C. London.

British Travel Association–University of Keele (1967), *The Pilot National Recreation Survey*, Report No. 1 (London: B.T.A.).

Buchanan, J. M. and Stubblebine, W. C. (1962), 'Externality', *Economica*, 29, 371–84.

Bukharin, N. (1919), *The Economic Theory of the Leisure Class* (London: Lawrence).

Burton, T. L. (1971), *Experiments in Recreation Research* (London: Allen and Unwin).

Campbell, W. J. and Chisholm, M. (1970), 'Local variations in retail grocery prices', *Urban Studies*, 7, 76–81.

Chiswick, B. R. (1967), 'The economic value of time and the wage rate: comment', *Western Economic Journal*, 5, 294–5.

Cicchetti, C. J., Seneca, J. J. and Davidson, P. (1969), *The Demand and Supply of Outdoor Recreation: an econometric analysis* (New Brunswick, N.J.: Rutgers, the State University, Bureau of Economic Research).

Cicchetti, C. J. and Freeman, A. M., III (1971), 'Option demand and consumer surplus: further comment', *Quarterly Journal of Economics*, 85, 528–39.

Clark, C. (1966), 'Industrial location and economic potential', *Lloyds Bank Review*, October.

Clarke, A. C. (1956), 'The use of leisure and its relation to levels of occupational prestige', *American Sociological Review*, 21, 301–7.

Clawson, M. (1959), *Methods of Measuring the Demand for and the Value of Outdoor Recreation*, Reprint No. 10 (Washington, D.C.; Resources for the Future).

Clawson, M. and Knetsch, J. C. (1966), *The Economics of Outdoor Recreation* (Washington, D.C.: Resources for the Future).

Collings, J. J. (1974), 'The application of behavioural mode choice models to leisure travel', *Environment and Planning A*, 6, 169–83.

Commission on the Third London Airport (1970), *Papers and Proceedings*, Vol. VII (London: H.M.S.O.).

Commission on the Third London Airport (1971), *Report* (London: H.M.S.O.).

Common, M. S. (1973), 'A note on the use of the Clawson Method for the evaluation of recreational site benefits', *Regional Studies*, 7, 401–6.

Countryside Commission (1971), *Fourth Annual Report 1970–71* (London: H.M.S.O.).

Countryside Commission (1972), *Fifth Annual Report 1971–72* (London: H.M.S.O.).

Countryside Commission (1974), *Sixth Annual Report 1972–73* (London: H.M.S.O.).

Cowling, K. and Rayner, A. J. (1970), 'Price, quality and market share', *Journal of Political Economy*, 78, 1292–309.

Cox, D. R. (1970), *Analysis of Binary Data* (London: Methuen).

Cullingworth, J. B. (1970), *Town and Country Planning in England and Wales*, 3rd ed. (London: Allen and Unwin).

Dasgupta, A. K. and Pearce, D. W. (1972), *Cost Benefit Analysis: Theory and Practice* (London: Macmillan).

Deakin, B. M. and Seward, T. (1969), *Productivity in Transport*, University of Cambridge, Department of Applied Economics, Occasional Paper No. 17 (Cambridge University Press).

De Donnea, F. X. (1972), 'Consumer behaviour, transport mode choice and the value of time: some microeconomic models', *Regional and Urban Economics*, 1, 355–82.

De Donnea, F. X. (1973), 'Rejoinder', *Regional and Urban Economics*, 2, 411–2.

Department of Employment (Annual), *Family Expenditure Survey* (London: H.M.S.O.).

De Serpa, A. C. (1971), 'A theory of the economics of time', *Economic Journal*, 81, 828–46.

De Serpa, A. C. (1973), 'Microeconomic theory and the valuation of travel time: some clarification', *Regional and Urban Economics*, 2, 401–10.

Dobb, M. H. (1969), *Welfare Economics and the Economics of Socialism* (Cambridge University Press).

Domencich, T. A., Kraft, G. and Valette, J-P. (1968), 'Estimation of urban passenger travel behaviour: an economic demand model', *Highway Research Record*, No. 238.

Dower, M. (1965), *The Challenge of Leisure* (London: Civic Trust).

Echenique, M., Crowther, D. and Lindsay, W. (1969), 'A spatial model of urban stock and activity', *Regional Studies*, 3, 281–312.

Elson, M. J. (1974), 'Recreation preference structures', *Planning Outlook*, Summer, 73–87.

Evans, A. W. (1972), 'On the theory of the valuation and allocation of time', *Scottish Journal of Political Economy*, 19, 1–18.

Evans, A. W. (1973), *The Economics of Residential Location* (London: Macmillan).

Expenditure Committee (1973), Second Report from the Expenditure Committee (Environment and Home Office Sub-Committee), H.C. 57, Session 1972–3, *Urban Transport Planning* (London: H.M.S.O.).

Farrell, M. J. (1968), 'In defence of public utility price theory', in *Public Enterprise*, ed. R. Turvey (London: Penguin Books).

Fines, K. (1968), 'Landscape evaluation, a research project in East Sussex', *Regional Studies*, 2, 41–55.

Fisher, A. C. and Krutilla, J. V. (1972), 'Determination of optimal capacity of resource-based recreation facilities', in Krutilla (1972).

Fisher, A. C., Krutilla, J. V. and Cicchetti, C. J. (1972a), 'Alternative uses of natural environments: the economics of environmental modification', in Krutilla (1972).

Fisher, A. C., Krutilla, J. V. and Cicchetti, C. J. (1972b), 'The economics of environmental preservation: a theoretical and empirical analysis', *American Economic Review*, 62, 605–19.

Fitch, L. C. *et al.* (1964), *Urban Transport and Public Policy* (New York: Chandler).

Flowerdew, A. D. J. (1972), 'Choosing a site for the Third London Airport: the Roskill Commission's approach', in *Cost–Benefit Analysis*, ed. R. Layard (London: Penguin Books).

Forbes, J. (ed.) (1974), *Studies in Social Science and Planning* (Edinburgh: Scottish Academic Press).

Foster, C. D. and Neuberger, H. (1974), 'The ambiguity of the consumer's surplus measure of welfare change', *Oxford Economic Papers*, 26, 66–77.

Frankenberg, R. (1966), *Communities in Britain* (London: Penguin Books).

Gavron, H. (1966), *The Captive Wife* (London: Routledge and Kegan Paul).

Gerstl, J. E. (1961), 'Leisure, taste and occupational milieu', *Social Problems*, 9, 56–68.

Goldberger, A. S. (1964), *Econometric Theory* (New York: John Wiley).

Goldthorpe, J. H., Lockwood, D., Bechhofer, F. and Platt, J. (1969), *The Affluent Worker in the Class Structure* (Cambridge University Press).

Goodall, B. (1972), *The Economics of Urban Areas* (Oxford: Pergamon Press).

Gordon, I. R. and Edwards, S. L. (1973), 'Holiday trip generation', *Journal of Transport Economics and Policy*, 7, 153–68.

Gray, P. G. (1969), *Private Motoring in England and Wales*, Government Social Survey, Report SS 329 (London: H.M.S.O.).

Greater London Council (1966), *London Traffic Survey*, Vol. 2 (London: G.L.C.).

Greater London Council (1968), *Surveys of the Use of Open Spaces*, Vol. 1 (London: G.L.C.).

Greater London Council (1969), *Greater London Development Plan: Report of Studies* (London: G.L.C.).

Gronau, R. (1970), *The Value of Time in Passenger Transportation: The Demand for Air Travel*, National Bureau of Economic Research, Occasional Paper 109 (New York: N.B.E.R.).

Haggett, P. and Chorley, R. J. (1969), *Network Analysis in Geography* (London: Edward Arnold).

Handy, L. J. (1968), 'Absenteeism and attendance in the British coal mining industry: an examination of post-war trends', *British Journal of Industrial Relations*, 6, 27–50.

Hansen, W. G. (1959), 'How accessibility shapes land use', *Journal of the American Institute of Planners*, 25, 73–6.

Harcourt, G. C. (1965), 'The accountant in a golden age', *Oxford Economic Papers*, 17, 66–80.

Harman, H. H. (1967), *Modern Factor Analysis*, 2nd ed. (University of Chicago Press).

Harris, C. D. (1954), 'The market as a factor in the localisation of industry in the United States', *Annals of the Association of American Geographers*, 44, 315–48.

Harrison, A. J. and Quarmby, D. A. (1969), 'The Value of Time in Transport Planning – A Review', 6th Round Table of Economic Research Centre, European Conference of Ministers of Transport, Paris.

Hay, A. M. (1973), *Transport for the Space Economy* (London: Macmillan).

Henderson, A. M. (1940–1), 'Consumer's surplus and the compensating variation', *Review of Economic Studies*, 8, 117–21.

Henderson, J. M. and Quandt, R. E. (1958), *Microeconomic Theory* (New York: McGraw-Hill).

Hicks, J. R. (1943–4), 'The four consumer's surpluses', *Review of Economic Studies*, 11, 31–41.

Hoinville, G. (1971), 'Evaluating community preferences', *Environment and Planning*, 3, 33–50.

Hoover, E. M. (1971), *An Introduction to Regional Economics* (New York: Alfred Knopf).

Hotelling, H. (1929), 'Stability in competition', *Economic Journal*, 39, 41–57.

Huff, D. L. (1963), 'A probabilistic analysis of shopping centre trade areas', *Land Economics*, 39, 81–90.

Hunt, A. (1968), *A Survey of Women's Employment*, Government Social Survey, Report SS379 (London: H.M.S.O.).

Ingram, D. R. (1971), 'The concept of accessibility: a search for an operational form', *Regional Studies*, 6, 101–7.

Jefferys, M. (1952), 'Married women in the Civil Service', *British Journal of Sociology*, 3, 361–4.

Johnson, M. B. (1966), 'Travel time and the price of leisure', *Western Economic Journal*, 4, 135–45.

Jöreskog, K. G. (1967), 'Some contributions to maximum likelihood factor analysis', *Psychometrika*, 32, 443–82.

Kansky, K. J. (1963), *Structure of Transportation Networks*, University of Chicago, Department of Geography, Research Paper No. 84 (University of Chicago Press).

Kraft, G. and Wohl, M. (1967), 'New directions for passenger demand analysis and forecasting', *Transportation Research*, 1, 205–30.

Krutilla, J. V. (1967), 'Conservation reconsidered', *American Economic Review*, 57, 777–86.

Krutilla, J. V. (ed.) (1972), *Natural Environments* (Baltimore: John Hopkins Press, for Resources for the Future).

Kutter, E. (1973), 'A model for individual travel behaviour', *Urban Studies*, 10, 235–58.

Lakshmanan, T. R. and Hansen, W. G. (1965), 'A retail market potential model', *Journal of the American Institute of Planners*, 31, 134–43.

220   *The Economics of Leisure and Recreation*

Lancaster, K. J. (1966), 'A new approach to consumer theory', *Journal of Political Economy*, 74, 132–57.
Lassiere, A. and Bowers, P. (1972), 'Studies of the Social Costs of Urban Road Transport: Noise and Pollution', 18th Round Table of Economic Research Centre, European Conference of Ministers of Transport, Paris.
Lawley, D. N. and Maxwell, A. E. (1971), *Factor Analysis as a Statistical Method*, 2nd ed. (London: Methuen).
꙰ Lewis, R. C. and Whitby, M. C. (1972), *Recreation Benefits from a Reservoir*, University of Newcastle-upon-Tyne, Agricultural Adjustment Unit, Research Monograph 2.
Linder, S. B. (1970), *The Harried Leisure Class* (New York: Columbia University Press).
Lindgren, B. W. (1968), *Statistical Theory*, 2nd ed. (London: Collier-Macmillan).
Lindsay, C. M. (1969), 'Option demand and consumer surplus', *Quarterly Journal of Economics*, 83, 344–6.
Lipsey, R. G. and Lancaster, K. J. (1956), 'The general theory of second best', *Review of Economic Studies*, 26, 11–32.

McGillivray, R. G. (1972), 'Mode split and the value of travel time', *Transportation Research*, 6, 309–16.
꙰ Mack, R. P. and Myers, S. (1965), 'Outdoor recreation', in *Measuring the Benefits of Government Investments*, ed. R. Dorfman (Washington, D.C.: Brookings Institution).
Mansfield, N. W. (1969), 'Recreational trip generation: a cross section analysis of weekend pleasure trips to the Lake District', *Journal of Transport Economics and Policy*, 3, 152–64.
Mansfield, N. W. (ed.) (1971a), *Papers and Proceedings of a Conference on Research into the Value of Time*, Department of the Environment, Time Research Note 16 (London: D.O.E.).
Mansfield, N. W. (1971b), 'The estimation of benefits from recreation sites and the provision of a new recreation facility', *Regional Studies*, 5, 55–69.
Mansfield, N. W. and Watson, P. L. (1971), 'Behavioural models and economic theory: Annex', in Mansfield (1971a).
Marshall, A. (1920), *Principles of Economics*, 8th ed. (London: Macmillan).
Miles, J. C. (1972), *The Goyt Valley Traffic Experiment 1970–1*, Countryside Commission and Peak Park Planning Board, Report CCP 55.
Millward, R. (1971), *Public Expenditure Economics* (London: McGraw-Hill).
Mincer, J. (1962), 'Labour force participation of married women: a study of labour supply', in *Aspects of Labour Economics*, Universities – National Bureau Committee for Economic Research (Princeton University Press, for N.B.E.R.).
Mincer, J. (1963), 'Market prices, opportunity costs and income effects', in *Measurement in Economics*, ed. C. Christ (Stanford University Press).
Ministry of Housing and Local Government (1956), *Open Spaces*, Technical Memorandum No. 6, M.H.L.G. (London: H.M.S.O.).
Mishan, E. J. (1967), *The Costs of Economic Growth* (London: Staples Press).

Mishan, E. J. (1970), 'What is wrong with Roskill?', *Journal of Transport Economics and Policy*, 4, 221–34.

Mishan, E. J. (1971a), 'The post-war literature on externalities', *Journal of Economic Literature*, 9, 1–28.

Mishan, E. J. (1971b), *Cost–Benefit Analysis* (London: Allen and Unwin).

Molyneux, D. D. (1968), 'Working for recreation', *Journal of the Town Planning Institute*, 54, 149–56.

Moses, L. N. and Williamson, H. F. Jnr (1963), 'Value of time, choice of mode and the subsidy issue in urban transportation', *Journal of Political Economy*, 71, 247–64.

Musgrave, R. A. (1969), 'Cost–benefit analysis and the theory of public finance', *Journal of Economic Literature*, 7, 797–806.

Myrdal, A. and Klein, V. (1956), *Women's Two Roles: Home and Work* (London: Routledge and Kegan Paul).

National Board for Prices and Incomes (1969), *Proposals by the London Transport Board for Fares Increases*, Report No. 112, Cmnd. 4036 (London: H.M.S.O.).

Neuberger, H. (1971a), 'User benefit: transport and land use plans', *Journal of Transport Economics and Policy*, 5, 52–75.

Neuberger, H. (1971b), 'Perceived costs', *Environment and Planning*, 3, 369–76.

Nwaneri, V. C. (1970), 'Equity in cost–benefit analysis', *Journal of Transport Economics and Policy*, 4, 235–54.

O'Farrell, P. N. and Poole, M. A. (1972), 'Retail grocery price variations in Northern Ireland', *Regional Studies*, 6, 83–92.

Oort, C. J. (1969), 'Evaluation of travelling time', *Journal of Transport Economics and Policy*, 3, 279–86.

Owen, J. D. (1969a), 'The value of commuter speed', *Western Economic Journal*, 7, 164–72.

Owen, J. D. (1969b), *The Price of Leisure* (Rotterdam University Press).

Owen, J. D. (1971), 'The demand for leisure', *Journal of Political Economy*, 79, 56–76.

Parker, S. R. (1965), 'Work and non-work in three occupations', *Sociological Review*, 13, 65–75.

Parker, S. R. (1971), *The Future of Work and Leisure* (London: MacGibbon and Kee).

Patmore, J. A. (1970), *Land and Leisure* (London: David and Charles).

Paul, M. E. (1971), 'Can aircraft noise nuisance be measured in money', *Oxford Economic Papers*, 23, 297–322.

Peston, M. (1972), *Public Goods and the Public Sector* (London: Macmillan).

Quandt, R. E. (ed.) (1970), *The Demand for Travel: Theory and Measurement* (Lexington, Mass.: D. C. Heath).

Quandt, R. E. and Baumol, W. J. (1966), 'The demand for abstract modes', *Journal of Regional Science*, 6, 13–26.

Quarmby, D. A. (1967), 'Choice of travel mode for the journey to work. Some findings', *Journal of Transport Economics and Policy*, 1, 273–314.

Quarmby, D. A. (1969), 'Transport planning in a multi-resource context, the Morecambe Bay Barrage', Mathematical Advisory Unit, Ministry of Transport, Note 141 (London: M.O.T.).

Rhodes, T. and Whitaker, R. (1967), 'Forecasting shopping demand', *Journal of the Town Planning Institute*, 53, 188–92.
Richardson, H. W. (1969), *Regional Economics: Location Theory, Urban Structure and Regional Change* (London: Weidenfeld and Nicolson).
Robbins, L. (1930), 'On the elasticity of demand for income in terms of effort', *Economica*, 10, 123–9.
Robbins, L. (1971), 'Unsettled questions in the political economy of the Arts', *Three Banks Review*, September.
Robinson, R. V. F., Hebden, J. J. and Vickerman, R. W. (1974), 'Methodological problems in the study of shopping travel', *Proceedings, Retailing and Local Planning Seminar* (London: Planning and Transport Research and Computation Co.).
Robson, B. T. (1969), *Urban Analysis: A Study of City Structure* (Cambridge University Press).
Rogers, A. (1965), 'A stochastic analysis of the spatial clustering of retail establishments', *Journal of the American Statistical Association*, 60, 1094–103.
Rubinstein, D. and Speakman, C. (1969), *Leisure, Transport and the Countryside*, Fabian Research Series, 277 (London: Fabian Society).
Russell, B. (1960), *In Praise of Idleness* (London: Allen and Unwin).

Sadler, P. G. *et al.* (1973), *Regional Income Multipliers* (Cardiff: University of Wales Press).
Samuelson, P. A. (1954), 'The pure theory of public expenditures', *Review of Economics and Statistics*, 36, 387–9.
Shimbel, A. (1953), 'Structural parameters of communication networks', *Bulletin of Mathematical Biophysics*, 15, 501–7.
Sillitoe, K. K. (1969), *Planning for Leisure*, Government Social Survey, Report SS 388 (London: H.M.S.O.).
Smith, M.A., Parker, S. and Smith, C. S. (eds.) (1973), *Leisure and Society in Britain* (London: Allen Lane).
Smith, R. J. (1971), 'The evaluation of recreation benefits: the Clawson Method in practice', *Urban Studies*, 8, 89–102.
Smith, R. J. and Kavanagh, N. J. (1969), 'The measurements of the benefits of trout fishing: preliminary results of a study at Grafham Water, Great Ouse Water Authority, Huntingdonshire', *Journal of Leisure Research*, 1, 316–32.
Sports Council (1968), *Planning for Sport* (London: Central Council for Physical Recreation).
Stone, P. A. (1959), 'The economics of housing and urban development', *Journal of the Royal Statistical Society*, Series A, 122, 417–83.
Szalai, A. (ed.) (1972), *The Use of Time: Daily Activities of Urban and Suburban Populations in Twelve Countries* The Hague: Mouton).

Tipping, D. G. (1968), 'Time savings in transport studies', *Economic Journal*, 78, 843–54.

Townsend, P. (1961), *The Family Life of Old People: An Inquiry in East London* (London: Routledge and Kegan Paul).

Tunstall, J. (1966), *Old and Alone: A Sociological Study of Old People* (London: Routledge and Kegan Paul).

Turvey, R. (1968), *Optimal Pricing and Investment in Electricity Supply* (London: Allen and Unwin).

Turvey, R. (1971), *Economic Analysis and Public Enterprise* (London: Allen and Unwin).

University of Manchester, (1966), *Regional Shopping Centres in North-west England*, Department of Town and Country Planning, University of Manchester.

Veblen, T. (1899), *The Theory of the Leisure Class* (New York: Viking Press).

Vickerman, R. W. (1972b), *The Demand for Shopping and Leisure Travel*, Economics and Policy, 6, 176–210.

Vickerman, R. W. (1972b), *The Demand for Shopping and Leisure Tranvel*, unpublished D.Phil thesis, University of Sussex, Brighton.

Vickerman, R. W. (1974a), 'A demand model for leisure travel', *Environment and Planning A*, 6, 65–77.

Vickerman, R. W. (1974b), 'Consumer demand for recreation and project appraisal', *Proceedings, Planning for Leisure Seminar* (London: Planning and Transport Research and Computation Co.).

Vickerman, R. W. (1974c), 'The evaluation of benefits from recreational projects', *Urban Studies*, 11, 277–88.

Vickerman, R. W. (1974d), 'Accessibility, attraction and potential: a review of some concepts and their use in determining mobility', *Environment and Planning A*, 6, 675–91.

Vickerman, R. W. and Collings, J. J. (1974), 'An alternative approach to forecasting the demand for leisure travel', in *Proceedings of the First International Conference on Transportation Research* (Chicago: Transportation Research Forum).

Vickrey, W. (1962), 'General and specific financing of urban services', in *Public Expenditure Decisions in the Urban Community*, ed. H. G. Schaller (Washington, D.C.: Resources for the Future).

Victor, P. A. (1972), *Pollution: Economics and Environment* (London: Allen and Unwin).

Walters, A. A. (1968), *The Economics of Road User Charges*, World Bank Staff Occasional Papers No. 5 (Baltimore: John Hopkins Press).

Watson, J. (1974), 'The changing economics of the cinema', *Three Banks Review*, June.

Watson, P. L. (1971), 'Behavioural models and economic theory', in Mansfield (1971a).

Webb, M. G. (1973), *The Economics of Nationalised Industries* (London: Nelson).

Weisbrod, B. A. (1964), 'Collective–consumption services of individual consumption goods', *Quarterly Journal of Economics*, 78, 471–7.

Weisbrod, B. A. (1968), 'Income redistribution effects and benefit–cost analysis', in *Problems in Public Expenditure Analysis*, ed. S. B. Chase (Washington, D.C.: Brookings Institution).

White, P. R. (1974), 'Use of public transport in towns and cities of Britain and Ireland', *Journal of Transport Economics and Policy*, 8, 26–39.

Wilensky, H. L. (1960), 'Work, careers and social integration', *International Social Science Journal*, 12, 543–60.

Wilensky, H. L. (1961), 'The uneven distribution of leisure: the impact of economic growth on free time', *Social Problems*, 9, 32–56.

Willmot, P. (1966), *Adolescent Boys of East London* (London:Routledge and Kegan Paul).

Wilson, A. G. (1967), 'A statistical theory of spatial distribution models', *Transportation Research*, 1, 253–69.

Wilson, A. G. (1969), 'Entropy maximising models in the theory of trip distribution, mode split and route split', *Journal of Transport Economics and Policy*, 3, 108–26.

Wilson, A. G. (1970), *Entropy in Urban and Regional Modelling* (London: Pion).

Wilson, A. G. (1971), 'A family of spatial interaction models', *Environment and Planning*, 3, 1–32.

Wilson, A. G. (1973), 'Further developments of entropy maximising transport models', *Transportation Planning and Technology*, 1, 183–93.

Wilson, A. G. (1974), *Urban and Regional Models in Geography and Planning* (London: John Wiley).

Wilson, A. G. and Kirwan, R. (1969), 'Measures of benefits in the evaluation of urban transport improvements', Centre for Environmental Studies, Working Paper 43 (London: C.E.S.).

Wilson, A. G., Hawkins, A. F., Hill, G. J. and Wagon, D. J. (1969), 'Calibration and testing of the SELNEC transport model', *Regional Studies*, 3, 337–50.

Wingo, L. Jnr. (1961), *Transportation and Urban Land* (Washington, D.C.: Resources for the Future).

Winterbottom, D. M. (1967), 'How much urban open space do we need?', *Journal of the Town Planning Institute*, 53, 144–7.

Wong, S. T. (1969), 'A multi-variate analysis of urban travel behaviour in Chicago', *Transportation Research*, 3, 345–63.

Wootton, H. J. and Pick, G. W. (1967), 'A model for trips generated by households', *Journal of Transport Economics and Policy*, 1, 137–53.

Index